Native Acts

Native

Indian Performance, 1603–1832

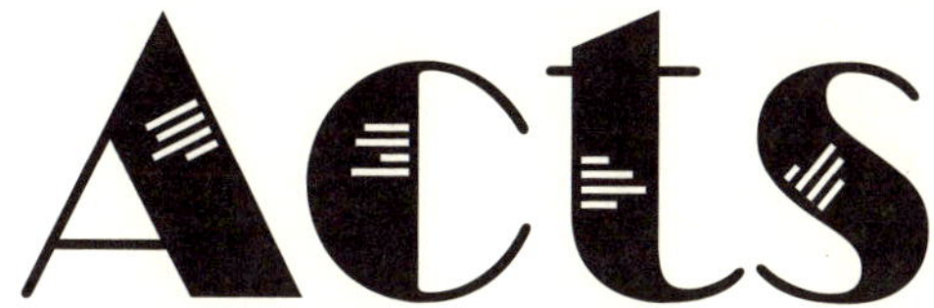

Edited by **Joshua David Bellin** and **Laura L. Mielke**

Afterword by Philip J. Deloria

University of Nebraska Press

Lincoln and London

Library of Congress Cataloging-in-Publication Data

Native acts: Indian performance, 1603–1832 / edited by Joshua David Bellin and Laura L. Mielke; afterword by Philip J. Deloria.
p. cm.
Includes bibliographical references and index.
ISBN 978-0-8032-2632-6 (pbk.: alk. paper)
1. Indians of North America—Public opinion. 2. Indians in popular culture. 3. Indians of North America—History. 4. Indians in literature. 5. American literature—Indian authors. 6. American literature—White authors. 7. Public opinion—North America. I. Bellin, Joshua David. II. Mielke, Laura L.
E98.P99N377 2011
305.897009'03—dc23
2011027370

Set in Sabon.
Designed by Mikah Tacha.

To Roger D. Abrahams

Contents

Native Acts

Introduction

Laura L. Mielke

Forcefully captured by Powhatan Indians while on a mission to locate the source of the Chickahominy River, Captain John Smith was held prisoner for a little over three weeks by the Jamestown colony's Native neighbors. The turning point in his captivity occurred after a three-day ceremony in which a priest, attended by dancers in paint, skins, and feathers, carefully placed meal, grains of corn, and sticks in circles around a fire and delivered a series of orations in order to disclose the captive's intentions toward his people. Smith was then finally brought before their "Emperor" (whom he called Powhatan after the tribe's name) and a group of men and women gathered in the "great house." Smith, referring to himself in the third person, wrote in his 1624 account of the event that, after feasting and cleaning his hands,

> a long consultation was held, but the conclusion was, two great stones were brought before Powhatan: then as many as could layd hands on [Smith], dragged him to them, and thereon laid his head, and being ready with their clubs, to beate out his braines, Pocahontas the Kings dearest daughter, when no intreaty could prevaile, got his head in her armes, and laid her owne upon his to save him from death: whereat the Emperour was contented he should live to make him hatchets, and her bells, beads, and copper; for they thought him as well of all occupations as themselves.[1]

Two days following his daughter's apparent intervention in Smith's execution, Powhatan formalized a friendship with Smith and allowed the captain to return to Jamestown.

Reading Smith's account of the event today, one confronts, among other things, the "unique epistemological challenge" of extracting Indian actions and intentions from texts penned by European colonizers.[2] One wonders what Pocahontas, an eleven-year-old girl whose actual name was Matoaka (Pocahontas being a child's nickname), intended by her actions and what she accomplished in reality. One might very well ask: what did this young woman perform before her leader and father, his captive, and the audience gathered in the great house at Werowocomoco?

And to ask this question about Native performance is to reflect on the complexity of the scene Smith reports and the variety of scholarly interpretations it has received in recent decades. To *perform*, of course, means to present something (like dance, drama, or music) on stage or to an audience. It also means, in the transitive sense, to carry out something promised or commanded or, more broadly, to carry out a particular action or function. Finally, it can denote the formal or solemn execution of a public function, ceremony, or ritual.[3] For those historians who consider Smith's report to be truthful and accurate and his interpretation of events valid, the bold young Pocahontas acted impulsively and sincerely, challenging the authority of her father and of Powhatan custom in order to preserve the life of the fascinating visitor. For others, Smith misinterpreted a Powhatan adoption ceremony—a ritual purification and staging of near death followed by incorporation—wherein Pocahontas played a sacred role. If Smith willfully misrepresented the scene, it is likely that he did so to create a text promoting Virginia colonization and his invaluable connections and expertise. Still other historians, emphasizing the purpose of Smith's Virginia accounts, have charged the shape-shifting captain with fabrication and described the scene as an instance of Smith taking up the theatrical role of colonial hero. In this respect, the passage and the events it describes turn on the complex and perhaps indistinguishable interaction of diverse performances: by Pocahontas, by her father and people, by Smith himself, and by his transatlantic readers.[4]

The Pocahontas story and the controversial nature of Smith's account elucidate the central undertaking of this book: the elusive but necessary recovery of Native people's role in the intercultural performative contexts of the colonial Americas, often (and necessarily) through texts that are themselves complex performances from within intercultural contexts.[5] Traditionally, Smith's account of the Powhatan girl's actions has been read in ways that minimize Indians' participation in these contexts; the tale of a noble young Indian woman driven by love to save the European and embrace the Christian civilization he represents has provided an allegory for providential European ascendance that incorporates and thereby erases the history of peaceful as well as violent Indian-white negotiations in colonial North America. (Ironically, those obscured negotiations were themselves dependent on the kind of performances Smith participated in during captivity.) Yet the exploits of Pocahontas in the great house at Werowocomoco as reported by Smith have not only produced colonialist narratives and dramas; they have periodically served as a resource for American Indians who, in response to the trope of the Indian convert or Noble Savage submitting body and soul to the European colonizer, have enacted an alternate identity and performed public protests against cultural and territorial imperialism and social neglect. Put another way, the Pocahontas legend has become part of what Laura Peers terms "a tradition of cultural performance in which the performance serves as a vehicle for Native agendas and creates an intercultural space which can be controlled by Native performers." Rereading Smith's account today, we thus find an opportunity to challenge the essentialist myths it spawned and to acknowledge a centuries-long process whereby the public actions of Indians—individual, familial, communal, ceremonial, theatrical, political, literary—have countered, informed, and shaped the public actions of European colonizers.[6]

The study of *Indian performance*, by which we mean performance by Indians and the performance of *Indianness* by Indians and non-Indians alike, uniquely clarifies how the struggle for survival as well as supremacy in early North America was constitutive of cultures and, more specifically, of common intercultural practice.[7] Recognizing traditions of performative exchange on North American soil and strategic performative adaptations by American Indians does not, of course, preclude a consideration of the power inequities between Indians and non-Indians. In his insightful overview of American Indian performative traditions, L. G. Moses appropriately insists that "we look at the performance not only for its window into cultural change and persistence, but also for the ways it reveals the working of power, domination, and resistance in Indian-American relations." Certainly Indian performance, physical as well as literary, has in recent years been important to critics' promotion of American Indian literary nationalism. Jace Weaver, Craig S. Womack, and Robert Warrior attribute inspiration in particular to Simon J. Ortiz's account in "Towards a National Indian Literature" of the Acqumeh use of Catholic saints' days ritual to recall the 1598 razing of Acqu by Spanish soldiers. Ortiz identifies such performances as key to understanding American Indian literature's "authenticity" as based not in a lack of reference to colonizing practices but in its clear "struggle against colonialism."[8] In this collection, essays likewise move from performances to texts and back again, offering us stories that recover the cultural, social, political, and artistic agency of Indians in the intercultural contexts of early North America through renewed attention to tactical, often defiant enactments of Indianness. Such work requires not only that contributors carefully contextualize and analyze the thorny records produced in the colonial context but also that they exercise empathy and imagination, humility and nerve, in doing so.

When we refer to *Indianness* in this volume, we mean the acknowledged attribute of direct association with American Indian peoples and cultures; *who* identifies American Indian attributes determines the substance of Indianness at specific moments.[9] In early North America, Europeans' conceptions of Indianness were inextricable from the moral, religious, teleological, political, and economic justifications for their presence. Indigenous bodies, material culture, beliefs, and actions registered for Europeans, among other things, the health of the land, the potential for evangelism, the promise of hospitality, the threat of violence, the echo of Europeans' own past, and the legitimacy of their occupation. When Europeans applied such meanings of the Indian in the activities of trade, mission work, marriage and procreation, political negotiations, and entertainment, they enacted the basis for the colonial project. In response, Indians actively performed Indianness that often directly challenged the scriptural, scientific, legal, and aesthetic narratives animating European colonialism. And when they resisted, revised, or forcefully rejected the category of Indian, they challenged a binary (European versus Native) essential to colonizers' quest for domination on North American soil. The result of these entwined performances of Indianness was a developing, transformative sense of what it meant to live in and be of North America.

Since the emergence of Performance Studies in the late 1980s, a number of works on the history and culture of North America in the eighteenth and early nineteenth centuries, as well as works on the colonial Americas more broadly, have established what my co-editor, Joshua David Bellin, identifies as a *performative paradigm*; they explore the ways in which intentional public acts of entertainment, ritual, and suasion do not simply reflect or represent cultures but, in the words of Rosemarie K. Bank, "constitute cultures."[10] Such an account of culture as performed and the related rendering of the close relationship between textual and oral forms are highly relevant to the study of Indian performance in early North America. Indeed, it should come as no surprise that many of the works falling under the performative paradigm—including ones by Bank, Jay Fliegelman, Joseph Roach, David Waldstreicher, Sandra M. Gustafson, and Carolyn Eastman, to name a few—have addressed to some degree the vital role of American Indian performance in the development of national cultures.[11]

Many of these works have also shown how performance in Early America, and in particular what we might call playacting, was used to reinforce European ideologies of racial-ethnic essentialism and ascendant nationalism. As Laura Browder observes, "The success of ethnic impersonators depends in large part on their manipulation of others' essentialist beliefs about race and ethnicity." In his influential *Playing Indian*, Philip J. Deloria examines the phenomenon of white residents of the thirteen colonies and then the United States engaging in acts of Indian mimicry and imposture. He identifies in particular two paradigmatic moments for such performances, the Revolution and the early twentieth century, when whites took up the Indian role first in the interest of national formation and subsequently in flight from industrialism and other perceived evils of modernity. As purveyors of the civilized attracted by the siren appeal of the wild, whites romantically appropriated the Indian in the context of violent conquest, establishing "a 'have-the-cake-and-eat-it-too' dialectic of simultaneous desire and repulsion." Key to "redface" performance were the reference to essentialist notions of Indianness and an ironic denial of culture-as-performed, for the often ceremonial and always entertaining public display actively naturalized national identity and the civilized/savage binary. At the same time, argues Theresa Strouth Gaul, "marking American Indians as performative" through the plethora of Indian plays in the early nineteenth century "became a way of marking them as potentially more duplicitous than whites."[12] Playing Indian cut two ways, as whites garnered the power of the "authentic" Indian for nationalist purposes and additionally denied American Indians that same empowering authenticity.

While the scholarly texts mentioned pay homage to Indian performance as one aspect of colonial and (more commonly) early national culture, each simultaneously demonstrates the limitations of prevailing historical and theoretical paradigms for understanding such performance. On the one hand, while it is vitally important to reconstruct the suppression and dispossession of Indians by those whites who adopted Indian "play," the scholarly emphasis on these processes has unfortunately underrated or erased the impact of Indian performances on white performances of Indianness, and vice versa.[13] On the other hand, if these representative studies dramatize the cross-fertilization of white and Indian performative traditions in the Revolutionary and Early National periods, they also indicate the extent to which a scholarly focus on the national period has largely eclipsed the contemporary relevance of earlier forms of Indian performance. Whites alone did not set the tone and the terms of these exchanges; rather, these performative occasions arose from the creative, adaptive, and iterative energies of

Indian and white peoples alike from the very earliest encounters. Furthermore, these performative occasions were not distinguished principally by their generation of such abstractions as "identity," "culture," "race," or "nation." Instead, the forms of performance in North American sites of encounter were unique and emergent, rooted in various peoples' distinctive material, linguistic, religious, economic, and artistic practices. Finally, not only is it erroneous to describe these early Indian performances as headed toward an apotheosis in the birth of the United States; it is wrongheaded to assume Indian performances were confined to the English-speaking world or even to North America. Performers crossed regions and continents, nations and languages, revealing the extent to which a continental and transatlantic colonial world was reliant on the dynamics of Indian performance.

By bringing together Native Studies methodology and the performative paradigm of Early American Studies, the essays in *Native Acts* speak specifically to the ways in which the cultures of contact in colonial North America were performed through trade negotiations, legal proceedings, religious rituals, and political ceremonies—and subsequent accounts of such, whether written, oral, or gestural.[14] This approach accomplishes a number of things. Most obviously, the essays of *Native Acts* show how the historical and literary record yields complex and diverse examples of performative exchange in the years prior to 1776, including local forms of material and linguistic negotiation, ceremonial cross-fertilization, and intercultural and intertribal contestation and compromise.

Moreover, these essays call attention to the highly contested nature of colonial cultures in ways not articulated by traditional histories that emphasize military conflict, imperial expansion, and Indian cultural loss. In this respect they take a cue from Richard White, who in his groundbreaking study of the convergence of Algonquian, French, and British in the Great Lakes region (*pays d'en haut*) from the seventeenth through the early nineteenth centuries identifies a geographic and cultural *middle ground*, the site of "alliance through rituals and ceremonials based on cultural parallels and congruences, inexact and artificial as they originally may have been." Yet our contributors keep in mind the limitations of White's thesis, especially the insistence that the (cultural or political) middle ground relied on the mutual dependence of parties and thus disappeared as soon as Euro-American dominance was attainable.[15] The history of Native acts as recorded in documents often implicated in the European colonial project, but also sustained in the performative practices not accounted for in those documents, suggests that mutual accommodation and, more specifically, intercultural performances persisted (and *persist*) long after the establishment in North America of Euro-American nations.

Finally, the essays of *Native Acts* contextualize questions of cultural authenticity and racial purity in the interest of documenting not just oppression but opposition, creativity, and vitality and in the interest of linking performances of Indianness across time. If one begins with the premise that in colonial North America Indians and Europeans performed mutually recognized cultures for and with one another, then one must recognize the influence of both on subsequent national cultures. At the same time, identity and nation become products of ongoing strategic performances rather than markers of static cultures and individuals. Indians and non-Indians alike perform for public consumption to religious, economic, political, familial, and pleasurable ends. Looking back to the Praying Indians of seventeenth-century New England, for example, we see that conversion meant not a simple swapping of an Indian for a European culture but the creation of an Indian Christianity that had implications for adherents' positions within the developing colonial society. Neither did the acquisition of literacy in European languages and related access to scripture and the Western historical record negate Indianness. Rather, it provided another means of performing culture. Many of the texts authored by American Indians and Euro-Americans in the colonial period record the intercultural performances—including the meaning-laden acts of reading and writing—that illustrate so well intercultural evolution and the persistent, continuing resistance of American Indians to white ascendancy through the body, speech, and a wide range of texts.

In sum, the essays of *Native Acts* represent a critical intervention in the scholarship treating the performance of Indianness because they restore Indian peoples to the intercultural matrix from which such performances arose. The contributors to this volume share a commitment to an expansive definition of Indian performance that bridges past and present and reaches across national boundaries, questions conventional designations of "real" and "fake" Indianness or "authentic" and "compromised" American Indian cultures, approaches texts as performances and non-alphabetic Indian communications as texts, and heralds the performative paradigm as an indispensable tool for comprehending the complex production and evolution of postcontact cultures on North American soil. For all these reasons we adopt the term *Native acts* (rather than *Indian play*) as shorthand for American Indian participation and agency in a tradition of Indian performance. *To act*, like its synonym *to perform*, means to carry out a particular action or function, to execute a public ceremony, or to present for others an entertainment, including the representation of another. At the same time, it does not preclude the less positive connotation of simulation or counterfeit.[16] The Native acts chronicled here include instances of American Indian ceremonial participation as recorded by literate observers; American Indian peoples' creative and often pragmatic appropriation of others' cultural practices, including writing and publication; American Indians' strategic expropriation of others' cultural practices for the assertion of political authority or rights; American Indians' dishonesty (as perceived by non-Indians) in such public acts as conversion testimony and treaty negotiations or, more commonly, in their representation of Indian culture for non-Indian audiences; and American Indians' appraisal of other performers' reliability and skill, including their performance as Indians.

To return to our opening figure in light of this redefinition, it appears likely that Pocahontas well understood the variety of Native acts required of and even thrust upon her in the context of the Jamestown colony's founding and the ongoing negotiation between her father and the English leaders who sought to curb his territorial power. The principal documents on Pocahontas and her public frolics as a girl, her (possibly) sacred role as a preteen, and the rituals of the Powhatan great house are Smith's narratives and letters; like so many American Indians, she did not leave a record in her own hand. Her captivity, subsequent marriage to John Rolfe, and conversion to Christianity initiated a peace between Jamestown colonists and the Powhatans. It also provided Pocahontas the means to represent the Powhatans in the London court and potentially to gather invaluable information on the English, whose continued migration threatened the physical well-being of her father's people. If closely observed by Londoners as a representative noble Indian and civilized convert, Pocahontas likely, in turn, directed her own gaze on the court and even on Smith, as when she rebuked him for having led the Powhatans to believe he had died when he returned to London in 1608.[17] One need only read with Native acts in mind to view Pocahontas as a skilled performer who assumed a range of roles, from ethnographic subject to royal ambassador, and demonstrated a keen understanding of the political function of such public presentations as she moved between the worlds of her father and her husband, building a new world between them.

Events essential to the Pocahontas story, captivity and conversion, are two of the most studied occasions for Native acts and associated intercultural negotiation in early North America and as such deserve special mention here. American Indians regularly incorporated white captives socially, especially women, through ceremonial performances that quite literally produced new people and new families. For Indians held "captive" by Euro-American societies, conversion to Christianity, particularly as seen in public displays of religious zeal, became a precondition to social incorporation; however, Indians' public expressions of faith were subject to the scrutiny of many convinced of the savage's innate deviousness. Within the context of these constraints, American Indians' conversion to Christianity, as recorded in missionary tracts and in the first American Indian autoethnographies and autobiographies, was in many ways less an attempt to "fool" whites than a pragmatic action in the interest of physical and cultural survival.[18] American Indian converts practiced an evolving and intercultural faith that provided opportunities publicly to criticize the physical and political hardships brought upon them by their Christian "redeemers." Thus when viewed from an *Indian* perspective, as James Axtell concludes, the success of early Christian missions should be measured by the extent to which Indian Christians were able to incorporate into their faith lives elements of their ethnic identity.[19] Certainly the Praying Indians of seventeenth-century New England were neither feeble accommodationists nor desperate victims but residents of a rapidly changing environment who found in Christian practice and alliances a means of challenging Euro-American authority by reviving and revising traditions of political and religious authority. American Indians who adapted a European faith for Indian life spurred the distrust of those colonists who believed that they were simply putting on an act, remaining unreconstructed savages behind Christian masks.[20]

American Indians' adoption and adaptation of Christianity in early North America produced a wealth of texts making manifest innumerable Native acts. Thus written expression was yet another way in which Indian engagement with Christianity facilitated the performative pursuit of cultural survival. For example, as Craig White documents, John Eliot's transcriptions of seventeenth-century New England Praying Indians' questions, conversion narratives, and dying speeches, while compiled in the interest of Puritan missionary work, serve as unique records of early Massachusett oral traditions and of American Indian interrogations and adaptations of Christian theology and practice. While American Indians have long utilized indigenous literacies, as Kristina Bross and Hilary E. Wyss emphasize with reference to Algonquian communicative practices, literacy in a European language was for many American Indians a promising and malleable technology accessible through Christian education. Viewed in this light, conversion constituted a means of cultural negotiation and assertion rather than of abnegation, and the related texts are themselves performances of such. Wyss and Joanna Brooks chronicle how Native-written texts from the seventeenth through the early nineteenth centuries served as politicized Native acts, communicating American Indians' grievances and demonstrating that Indianness and Christian literacy were not mutually exclusive, and Lisa Brooks traces such political work of Native writing to the present day. "Acts of conversion were acts of self-determination," concludes Joanna Brooks, and committing one's narrative to the page (directly or through an amanuensis) was, finally, a performance of autonomy for the present and the future. Undoubtedly the words and actions of American Indians subject to Christian mission work had a lasting impact on European missions.[21] Thus to reconsider religious conversion as a Native act is to reject racial-ethnic essentialism and to recognize the ways in which American Indians enacted new religious, political, and intellectual traditions that could and do sustain Native communities.[22]

We have organized this collection to reflect patterns and divergences in Native acts as they constituted such emergent traditions. *Native Acts* begins with essays considering the performances that simultaneously illustrated and shattered European colonists' preconceptions of Indian behavior. Approaching a seventeenth-century "problematics" of performance through a mixture of Native Studies, ethnohistory, and performance theory, Matt Cohen draws connections between English records of Algonquian strategic deception in the 1630s and the contemporary controversy in New England over who is "truly" Indian. Zeroing in on the fate of Indian converts during the pan-tribal resistance in New England that came to be known as King Philip's War, Nan Goodman unpacks a cruel irony in the history of Native acts: the Praying Indians' banishment to Deer Island in Boston Harbor and voluntary military service brought about what prior acts of conversion could not—legal status under English common law. Of course neither entrance into English law nor physical displacement extinguished Indianness. Performance as a category, as Cohen concludes his essay, moves us beyond the elusive search for the "authentic" to the recognition that the relational and evolving nature of American Indian cultures does nothing to diminish the reality of Native identity and sovereignty.

John Pollack and Olivia Bloechl shift the geographic focus to seventeenth-century New France but likewise trace European expectations for Indianness and Indians' performative responses. Pollack takes up the construction of indigenous authority via performance, arguing that Samuel de Champlain's *Des Sauvages* (1603) registers the ritual practices, including storytelling, through which French and Innu leaders vied for supremacy in diplomatic, economic, and religious alliances. Bloechl follows the Jesuit missionaries of midcentury who, by comparing Wendat ritual and the Carnival of the French peasantry, at once articulated their fears of sinister and socially destabilizing communal song traditions and inadvertently confirmed the value of such traditions in the indigenous struggle to resist the imposition of external religious and political authority.

Like Pollack, Stephanie Fitzgerald and Caroline Wigginton trace how individual American Indians—in this case, powerful women—established a peculiarly Native authority within and through their relationships with representative European colonists.[23] Fitzgerald recovers the history of Wunnatuckquannum, a seventeenth-century queen sachem on Martha's Vineyard who negotiated tribal and colonial legal systems in order to retain her people's allegiance and to secure their land base. The deeds Wunnatuckquannum left behind record her evolving position among her people and within colonial New England, while serving in the present as vital resources for the Wampanoag's Wôpanâak Language Reclamation Project. Similarly, but in a southerly clime, Wigginton argues that Creek leader, diplomat, and translator Coosaponakeesa insisted on the sovereignty of her people through coded dress and the language of Creek kinship. Identifying a "genealogy of sovereignty," a temporal continuity of performances in the interest of Native peoples,

Wigginton, like others in the collection, documents how Indians in early North America asserted territorial, political, and cultural authority through discursive and embodied Native acts, securing crucial legacies in the process.

Just as Indian representatives performed versions of Indianness to establish political, economic, and cultural authority, they also sought to capitalize on Europeans' expectations for indigeneity by staging notions of "authenticity." Jenny Hale Pulsipher's essay considers John Wompas, a Nipmuc Christian in seventeenth-century Massachusetts known by the English name John White, who attempted to reconcile his participation in colonial trade with his credibility in Nipmuc society. As the seventeenth century progressed—and as King Philip's War forever altered the place of Christian Indians in New England colonial society—Wompas found himself increasingly defined by racial rather than cultural definitions of the individual. In his essay Timothy J. Shannon focuses on the intersection of political and commercial interests for American Indians who traveled to Britain in the wake of the Seven Years' War; the performance of these "Indian kings" in the arenas of diplomacy and popular entertainment at once rested on claims of Indianness and undermined in the public's eye their claims of genuineness. Pulsipher and Shannon remind us that Indians, like whites, were both judges and subjects of performances of ethnicity—and ethnic imposture—in the colonial context, cultivating new performances responsive to the multiple actors and audiences of European imperialism.

The collection concludes with two essays that track the permutations of Indian performance into the more familiar period of the U.S. Early Republic. However, these essays—Phillip H. Round on Indian interventions into and inventions of the public sphere in the late eighteenth century and Theresa Strouth Gaul on Elias Boudinot's performative editing of the

Cherokee Phoenix—offer original readings of this period and gain new resonance and relevance in light of the prominence accorded to Indian performers in the earlier period. Thus the final essays bridge the colonial period and the Removal era, providing a more detailed, nuanced historical map for the shifting construction and reception of Indianness as enacted by American Indians. The volume concludes with Deloria's reflection on his formulation of "playing Indian" and the need to consider Native agency in the history of performances of Indianness.

The essays of *Native Acts* enrich our understanding of how American Indians of early colonial North America complicated and concretized, claimed and reclaimed, the meaning of Indianness through performance, a process that continues to this day. They employ the performative paradigm of Early American Studies, with its focus on the enactment of culture and its challenge to the stale historical narratives of overpowering cultural imperialism or romantic multiculturalism, and they affirm the Native Studies emphasis on establishing "an alternative historiography of nonwhiteness."[24] In the process, the contributions to this volume demonstrate the ways in which writings about Native acts from the colonial period are not simply incomplete, unreliable, or dead records of actions long lost. They are themselves performances, linked to well-established, living traditions of which they are unique manifestations, and they deserve to be read carefully, creatively, and respectfully.

Ultimately, the essays in this volume help us understand the ongoing relevance of Native acts from the seventeenth through the early nineteenth centuries as American Indians continue to contest racism and political and social inequality through performative resistance, innovation, and transformation. Peers reports in her illuminating study of American Indians' roles in contemporary living history sites that the American Indian interpreters she interviewed time and again declared they were "playing themselves," "expressing their contemporary identity as persons rooted in their heritage."[25] The essays in this volume return to a neglected time in American Indian performance in order to recover traditions of American Indian agency. Native acts were not and are not "just play" but an assertion of a persistent and vibrant American Indian presence on North American soil.

Notes

I am deeply indebted to my co-editor, Joshua David Bellin, for his steady guidance and careful editing as this introduction evolved. I am also grateful to Roger Abrahams, attendees of my presentation to the University of Kansas American Studies Department, and the reviewers for University of Nebraska Press for helpful responses to various drafts.

1. Smith, *Captain John Smith*, 64–65.
2. Cohen, *Networked Wilderness*, 9.
3. "perform, v.," OED *Online*.
4. Examples of each of these interpretations may be seen in the most recent books on the history of Powhatan Indians and the Jamestown colony. In *Love and Hate in Jamestown*, Price accepts as true Smith's account of Pocahontas's intervention, building on Lemay's book-length defense, *Did Pocahontas Save Captain John Smith?* (Price, *Love and Hate*, 243–45). In *The Jamestown Project*, Kupperman asserts that Smith underwent an adoption ceremony, citing Gleach's *Powhatan's World and Colonial Virginia* (Kupperman, *Jamestown Project*, 228)—an interpretation also embraced by Allen (*Pocahontas*, 52–56). Notably, ethnohistorian Rountree, in *Pocahontas, Powhatan, Opechancanough*, asserts that the Powhatans had no such ceremony, that Pocahontas was too young and unimportant to attend any official gathering in the great house, and thus that Smith's account is false (76–82). No matter what the analysis, few would disagree with Richards's description of Smith as having "a theatrical vision that . . . makes him the central actor in a land free of playhouses and an enervating obsession with social performance" (*Theater Enough*, 85). Horn concludes: "What we can say with some certainty is that the ritual did not happen as [Smith] described it" (*A Land as God Made It*, 68).

5. That is, this book is concerned with what Bellin calls "the complex, conflictual, cross-cultural acts that lie at the heart of American life and literature" (*Medicine Bundle*, 4). In this way, *Native Acts* draws on two prominent strains in Performance Studies: an interest in discursive performances, or language that "does work," as initiated by Austin, and an attention to embodied performances, as highlighted in the work of Taylor (who calls instances of nondiscursive performance "performatics" to distinguish them from Austin's "performatives"). For a cogent treatment of these divergent strains in Performance Studies see Taylor, *The Archive and the Repertoire*, 4–6.
6. Peers, *Playing Ourselves*, 61. American Indians staging themselves, intervening in the tradition of white Indian performance, is also a stated concern of Bank in "Staging the 'Native.'" On the ideological use of the Pocahontas legend in American culture, see especially Tilton, *Pocahontas*. Regarding Indian adaptations or expropriations of the Pocahontas figure, I am thinking in particular of such nineteenth- and early twentieth-century activist-authors as Gertrude Bonnin (Zitkala-Ša), Sarah Winnemucca Hopkins, and Emily Pauline Johnson, each of whom used public performances in Indian dress of music or oratory to advocate for the rights of North American Indians.
7. My co-editor, Bellin, first defined Indian performance in these terms in "John Eliot's Playing Indian," 3. See also Bellin, *Medicine Bundle*, 3.
8. Weaver, Womack, and Warrior, *American Indian Literary Nationalism*, xix; Ortiz, "Towards a National Indian Literature," 256.
9. For this reason Harmon concludes Indianness to be "a multitude of identities" due to its innumerable and even conflicting sources: individual, tribal, non-Indian, pan-Indian, historical, genetic, and political, to name just a few that she mentions (Harmon, "Wanted," 254).
10. Bank, *Theatre Culture in America*, 9. On the emergence of a performative paradigm in Early American Studies, see Bellin, "The Place of Performance" and *Medicine Bundle*, 12.
11. For example, Roach examines the Mardi Gras Indians of New Orleans as an example of *surrogation*, or a collective performance that attempts to fill the vacancy and loss created by the violence of colonization; those who play Indian draw on the performance of actual American Indians and thus are actually threatened with being replaced "by those whom they imagined into existence as their defini-

tive opposites" (Roach, *Cities of the Dead*, 6). In *In the Midst of Perpetual Fetes*, Waldstreicher presents the case that U.S. nationalism is constituted not by communal assent but by concrete performances of contested, local meanings, including American Indian oratories and texts that challenge the meaning of the American Revolution. Similarly, emphasizing "diverse, interactive, and simultaneous cultural universes" in what she deems the "theatre culture" of antebellum America, Bank traces how performances of Indianness by Indians and non-Indians in political and theatrical settings outside Indian country informed and responded to one another (Bank, *Theatre Culture in America*, 29). Gustafson chronicles how American Indian orators capitalized on the image of "a 'savage' speaker whose oral heritage endowed him or her with a greater authenticity than textbound white orators" and employed writing tactically in text-driven Euro-America to demonstrate intellectual, spiritual, and legal equality (Gustafson, *Eloquence Is Power*, xxii). More recently, Eastman traces the evolving role of Indian oratory (actual and fabricated) in the formation of an elocutionary culture essential to the post-Revolutionary formation of a U.S. public (*A Nation of Speechifiers*, chap. 3).

12. Browder, *Slippery Characters*, 10–11; Deloria, *Playing Indian*, 3; Gaul, "'The Genuine Indian,'" 17. For a fuller description of United States nationalism and the use of the Indian to justify imperialism and to craft an ancient prehistory, see Marienstras, "The Common Man's Indian."

13. That said, a small number of critical studies have traced Native influence on performances during the heyday of white appropriations of Indianness. For example, Kamrath locates in the American Indians' speeches transcribed in eighteenth-century colonial periodicals evidence that Revolutionary rhetoric and public displays of nascent nationalism drew upon Indian performance. Abrahams identifies a 1786 meeting between a Seneca band led by Cornplanter and Philadelphia's "Sons of Tammany" as a moment of mutual Indian play; the latter claimed the role of legendary Indian sachem Tammany as an expression of sovereignty, the former as a means of burying their prior alliance with the British. And in "Staging the 'Native,'" Bank considers the participation of American Indian men, including Sauk leader Black Hawk, in the theatrical performance of Indianness in the 1820s and 1830s, highlighting the exchange of performance traditions but also the very different cultural stakes for Indians and their white contemporaries.

14. In "New England, Nonesuch," Cohen calls for just such a combination of Native Studies and Performance Studies methodology in order to challenge "the idea that textuality is a transhistorical constant" (313).
15. White, *The Middle Ground*, 93. For treatments of how the concept of the middle ground has been misused, see in particular *The Middle Ground Revisited*, a special issue of *William and Mary Quarterly* edited by Sleeper-Smith, and Deloria's afterword to the present volume. In "Romance on the Middle Ground," Herman was one of the first to criticize White's theory as subject to abuse by those longing "for a truly pluralistic, multicultural society" (291).
16. "act, v.," OED *Online*.
17. On Pocahontas's visit to London, see Townsend, *Pocahontas and the Powhatan Dilemma*, 135–58. Of her recorded rebuke of Smith, Townsend observes, "She was clearly expressing profound sadness and anger, not unrequited love. She spoke rather of political matters. Her father had established a kin relationship with this man, implying reciprocity and honesty. Smith had defaulted on both counts" (155). The final chapter of Allen's *Pocahontas* argues most explicitly for Pocahontas's role as political and spiritual ambassador/spy on her London trip (253–302).
18. Here I use American Indian autoethnography to refer to a study of American Indian cultures written by a member of that culture and American Indian autobiography to indicate a first-person life story written or dictated by the subject. On these genres respectively see especially Michaelsen, "Introduction," and Krupat, *Voice in the Margin*, chap. 4.
19. Axtell, "Some Thoughts on the Ethnohistory of Missions." Axtell's claim is reinforced by Burkhart's examination of an indigenous Christianity apparent in sixteenth-century Christian devotional songs composed by Nahua (Aztec) converts in "The Amanuenses Have Appropriated the Text." For a rich description of intercultural faith among seventeenth-century Huron and Montagnais Indians of New France and the Massachusett, Wampanoag, and Nipmuc tribes of southern New England, see Ronda, "'We Are Well as We Are.'"
20. Van Lonkhuyzen, "A Reappraisal of the Praying Indians." On Puritan unease over the Praying Indian's performance of Christianity, see especially Bellin, "John Eliot's Playing Indian."
21. White, "The Praying Indians' Speeches"; Bross and Wyss, "Introduction"; Wyss, *Writing Indians*, 1–16; Joanna Brooks, *American Laza-*

rus, 18; Lisa Brooks, "Digging at the Roots." Three works tracing the Native impact on European missions come to mind. In *Dry Bones and Indian Sermons*, Bross argues that from the 1640s through King Philip's War (1675–76), New England Puritanism was defined by its mission to local American Indians, and the figure of the Praying Indian proved essential to Puritan self-conceptions and authorship. Stevens, in *The Poor Indians*, shows how, in the subsequent century, English missionary tracts on American Indians contributed to the larger culture of sensibility. And Pointer, in *Encounters of the Spirit*, examines the ways in which Spanish, French, and English missionaries from the 1520s through the 1790s were affected by the religious beliefs and practices of indigenous peoples.

22. Relevant here is Warrior's identification of Native nonfiction as constituting an intellectual tradition crucial to "the intellectual health of Native America, its people, and its communities" (*People and the Word*, xiv).

23. Unfortunately such recovery of American Indian *women's* Native acts is a rare accomplishment. As Wyss notes in "Native Women Writing," very little Native women's writing from this period has been found in the archive, and given this lack, Native women's performances must be read between the lines of what we do have.

24. Fitzgerald and Wyss, "Land and Literacy," 273.

25. Peers, *Playing Ourselves*, xxiii, 84. As Wilmer writes, Indian performance is vital "both historically and in the modern world as a means of preserving and reasserting cultural values amid Eurocentric incursions and globalized lifestyles" (Wilmer, "Introduction," 1).

Works Cited

Abrahams, Roger D. "White Indians in Penn's City: The Loyal Sons of Saint Tammany." In *Riot and Revelry in Early America*, ed. William Pencak, Matthew Dennis, and Simon P. Newman, 179–204. University Park: Pennsylvania State University Press, 2002.

"act, v." OED *Online*. November 2010. Oxford University Press. http://www.oed.com/view/Entry/1889 (accessed March 14, 2011).

Allen, Paula Gunn. *Pocahontas: Medicine Woman, Spy, Entrepreneur, Diplomat*. San Francisco: Harper Collins, 2003.

Austin, J. L. *How to Do Things with Words*. Cambridge: Harvard University Press, 1962.

Axtell, James. "Some Thoughts on the Ethnohistory of Missions." In *After*

Columbus: Essays in the Ethnohistory of Colonial North America, 47–57. New York: Oxford University Press, 1988.

Bank, Rosemarie K. "Staging the 'Native': Making History in American Theatre Culture, 1828–1838." *Theatre Journal* 45 (1993): 461–86.

———. *Theatre Culture in America, 1825–1860*. Cambridge: Cambridge University Press, 1997.

Bellin, Joshua David. "John Eliot's Playing Indian." *Early American Literature* 42 (2007): 1–30.

———. *Medicine Bundle: Indian Sacred Performance and American Literature, 1824–1932*. Philadelphia: University of Pennsylvania Press, 2008.

———. "The Place of Performance." *Early American Literature* 42 (2007): 355–62.

Brooks, Joanna. *American Lazarus: Religion and the Rise of African-American and Native American Literatures*. Oxford: Oxford University Press, 2003.

Brooks, Lisa. "Digging at the Roots: Locating an Ethical, Native Criticism." In *Reasoning Together: The Native Critics Collective*, ed. Craig S. Womack, Daniel Heath Justice, and Christopher B. Teuton, 234–64. Norman: University of Oklahoma Press, 2008.

Bross, Kristina. *Dry Bones and Indian Sermons: Praying Indians in Colonial America*. Ithaca: Cornell University Press, 2004.

Bross, Kristina, and Hilary E. Wyss. "Introduction." In *Early Native Literacies in New England: A Documentary and Critical Anthology*, ed. Kristina Bross and Hilary E. Wyss, 1–13. Amherst: University of Massachusetts Press, 2008.

Browder, Laura. *Slippery Characters: Ethnic Impersonators and American Identities*. Chapel Hill: University of North Carolina Press, 2000.

Burkhart, Louise M. "The Amanuenses Have Appropriated the Text: Interpreting a Nahuatl Song of Santiago." In *On the Translation of Native American Literatures*, ed. Brian Swann, 339–55. Washington DC: Smithsonian Institution Press, 1992.

Cohen, Matt. *The Networked Wilderness: Communicating in Early New England*. Minneapolis: University of Minnesota Press, 2010.

———. "New England, Nonesuch." *American Literary History* 22 (2010): 307–19.

Deloria, Philip J. *Playing Indian*. New Haven: Yale University Press, 1998.

Deloria, Philip J., and Neal Salisbury, eds. *A Companion to American Indian History*. Malden MA: Blackwell, 2002.

Eastman, Carolyn. *A Nation of Speechifiers: Making an American Public after the Revolution*. Chicago: University of Chicago Press, 2009.

Fitzgerald, Stephanie, and Hilary E. Wyss. "Land and Literacy: The Textualities of Native Studies." *American Literary History* 22 (2010): 271–79.

Fliegelman, Jay. *Declaring Independence: Jefferson, Natural Language and the Culture of Performance*. Stanford CA: Stanford University Press, 1993.

Gaul, Theresa Strouth. "'The Genuine Indian Who Was Brought upon the Stage': Edwin Forrest's *Metamora* and White Audiences." *Arizona Quarterly* 56, no. 1 (2000): 1–27.

Gleach, Frederic W. *Powhatan's World and Colonial Virginia: A Conflict of Cultures*. Lincoln: University of Nebraska Press, 1997.

Gustafson, Sandra M. *Eloquence Is Power: Oratory and Performance in Early America*. Chapel Hill: University of North Carolina Press, for Omohundro Institute of Early American History and Culture, Williamsburg VA, 2000.

Harmon, Alexandra. "Wanted: More Histories of Indian Identity." In Deloria and Salisbury, *Companion*, 248–65.

Herman, Daniel J. "Romance on the Middle Ground." *Journal of the Early Republic* 19 (1999): 279–91.

Horn, James. *A Land as God Made It: Jamestown and the Birth of America*. New York: Basic Books, 2005.

Kamrath, Mark. "American Indian Oration and Discourses of the Republic in Eighteenth-Century American Periodicals." In *Periodical Literature in Eighteenth-Century America*, ed. Mark Kamrath and Sharon M. Harris, 143–78. Knoxville: University of Tennessee Press, 2005.

Krupat, Arnold. *The Voice in the Margin: Native American Literature and the Canon*. Berkeley: University of California Press, 1989.

Kupperman, Karen Ordahl. *The Jamestown Project*. New York: Harvard–Belknap, 2007.

Lemay, J. A. Leo. *Did Pocahontas Save Captain John Smith?* Athens: University of Georgia Press, 1992.

Marienstras, Elise. "The Common Man's Indian: The Image of the Indian as a Promoter of National Identity in the Early National Era." In *Native Americans and the Early Republic*, ed. Frederick E. Hoxie, Ronald Hoffman, and Peter J. Albert, 261–96. Charlottesville: University Press of Virginia, for the United States Capitol Historical Society, 1999.

Michaelsen, Scott. "Introduction." In *The Limits of Multiculturalism: Interrogating the Origins of American Anthropology*, ix–xxvii. Minneapolis: University of Minnesota Press, 1999.

Moses, L. G. "Performative Traditions in American Indian History." In Deloria and Salisbury, *Companion*, 193–208.

Ortiz, Simon J. "Towards a National Indian Literature: Cultural Authenticity in Nationalism." *MELUS* 8, no. 2 (1981). Rpt. in Weaver, Womack, and Warrior, *American Indian Literary Nationalism*, 253–60.

Peers, Laura. *Playing Ourselves: Interpreting Native Histories at Historic Reconstructions*. Lanham MD: AltaMira Press, 2007.

"perform, v." OED *Online*. November 2010. Oxford University Press. http://www.oed.com/view/Entry/140780 (accessed March 14, 2011).

Pointer, Richard W. *Encounters of the Spirit: Native Americans and European Colonial Religion*. Bloomington: Indiana University Press, 2007.

Price, David A. *Love and Hate in Jamestown: John Smith, Pocahontas, and the Start of a New Nation*. New York: Vintage, 2005.

Richards, Jeffrey H. *Theater Enough: American Culture and the Metaphor of the World Stage, 1607–1789*. Durham: Duke University Press, 1991.

Roach, Joseph. *Cities of the Dead: Circum-Atlantic Performance*. New York: Columbia University Press, 1996.

Ronda, James P. "'We Are Well as We Are': An Indian Critique of Seventeenth-Century Christian Missions." *William and Mary Quarterly* 3rd ser. 34 (1977): 68–82.

Rountree, Helen C. *Pocahontas, Powhatan, Opechancanough: Three Indian Lives Changed by Jamestown*. Charlottesville: University of Virginia Press, 2005.

Sleeper-Smith, Susan, ed. *The Middle Ground Revisited*. Special Issue, *William and Mary Quarterly* 3rd ser. 63 (2006): 1–208.

Smith, John. *Captain John Smith: A Select Edition of His Writings*. Ed. Karen Ordahl Kupperman. Chapel Hill: University of North Carolina Press, for Omohundro Institute of Early American History and Culture, Williamsburg VA, 1988.

Stevens, Laura. *The Poor Indians: British Missionaries, Native Americans, and Colonial Sensibility*. Philadelphia: University of Pennsylvania Press, 2004.

Taylor, Diana. *The Archive and the Repertoire: Performing Cultural Memory in the Americas*. Durham NC: Duke University Press, 2003.

Tilton, Robert S. *Pocahontas: The Evolution of an American Narrative.* Cambridge: Cambridge University Press, 1994.

Townsend, Camilla. *Pocahontas and the Powhatan Dilemma.* New York: Hill and Wang, 2004.

Van Lonkhuyzen, Harold W. "A Reappraisal of the Praying Indians: Acculturation, Conversion, and Identity at Natick, Massachusetts, 1646–1730." *New England Quarterly* 63 (1990): 396–428.

Waldstreicher, David. *In the Midst of Perpetual Fetes: The Making of American Nationalism, 1776–1820.* Chapel Hill: University of North Carolina Press, for Omohundro Institute of Early American History and Culture, Williamsburg VA, 1997.

Warrior, Robert. *The People and the Word: Reading Native Nonfiction.* Minneapolis: University of Minnesota Press, 2005.

Weaver, Jace, Craig S. Womack, and Robert Warrior. *American Indian Literary Nationalism.* Albuquerque: University of New Mexico Press, 2006.

White, Craig. "The Praying Indians' Speeches as Texts of Massachusett Oral Culture." *Early American Literature* 38 (2003): 437–67.

White, Richard. *The Middle Ground: Indians, Empires, and Republics in the Great Lakes Region, 1650–1815.* Cambridge: Cambridge University Press, 1991.

Wilmer, S. E. "Introduction." In *Native American Performance and Representation*, ed. S. E. Wilmer, 1–16. Tucson: University of Arizona Press, 2009.

Wyss, Hilary E. "Native Women Writing: Reading between the Lines." *Tulsa Studies in Women's Literature* 26 (2007): 119–25.

———. *Writing Indians: Literacy, Christianity, and Native Community in Early America.* Amherst: University of Massachusetts Press, 2000.

[1]

Lying Inventions

Native Dissimulation in Early Colonial New England

Matt Cohen

Truth is a Native, naked Beauty; but
Lying Inventions are but Indian Paints,
Dissembling hearts their Beautie's but a Lye,
Truth is the proper Beauty of Gods Saints.
Roger Williams, *A Key into the Language of America* (1643)

"'Indian as performance' is not an idea that has caught on," writes Craig Womack, "unless one is referring to notorious fakers—the likes of Grey Owl and Jamake Highwater."[1] Womack's opposition to the utility of "Indians as performance" opens a host of questions, not only about the many meanings of *performance* or *acting*—to the discussions of which Native America, past and present, has much to contribute—but about the politics of embodied representation. Those questions resonate from disciplinary discussions in the academy to the performance of Indianness in contemporary media and courtrooms. The performative lens seems at once to verify Indianness and to undermine the possibility of identity-based definitions. But Womack's mention of "fakers" also raises the question of simulation or dissimulation: given almost any definition of

"Indian," it may be possible to forge an Indian identity. Such concerns have a long history. Focusing on their manifestation in early colonial New England, I argue that claims of deception are hotspots for thinking about the utility of performance as a category of analysis no less than the historical dynamics of cultural conflict and dispossession.

In his seminal work on the ethnohistory of early colonial eastern woodlands Native societies, James Axtell argued against widespread colonial European claims that Indians were born liars. Axtell maintained that Native speakers could not have deceived in this way, because they lived in an oral culture. While Natives were "notoriously taciturn among Europeans," Axtell writes, nonetheless "as peoples without writing they believed in the inviolability of the spoken word, particularly in public councils and treaties."[2] Apart from the odd technological determinism that underlies such an assertion—that writing makes possible verbal deception—the numerous examples of Native performance discussed in this volume suggest that Axtell overstates his case. Recent work on material forms of representation among indigenous Americans (such as paths, bark inscriptions, and wampum) suggests the extent to which the aural and the inscribed worlds intertwined.[3] Europeans like Roger Williams, in such depictions of Indians as the stanza with which this chapter begins, certainly represented Indians for their own ends, yet here Williams depicts both truth and deception as available to Natives. To examine questions of deception or epistemological uncertainty is vital to an understanding of Indian performance because in order to extend our knowledge of Indian agency in the past, we need to acknowledge that Natives can deceive like other humans.

My analysis of Indian deception, then, riffs on both Williams and Womack. Womack and many other Native critics have emphasized the roles of property and space in the study of indigenous American representation: the question of when or whether Indians dissimulate is inseparable from claims to ownership or use of land. Yet no less important in studying Indian or European performances are the historically specific notions of performance holding sway at a given moment in the past. And finally, today's uses of the term *performance*, uses that fuel Womack's dismissal, might by that same emotional token call on us to locate performance theory that resonates with Native intellectual goals and debates today. My object is not to define *performance* so much as to suggest that its utility lies in how it makes us think about the temporality of analysis. It demands historicization, in this case an understanding of the complexity of seventeenth-century ways of thinking about performance, imitation, and dissimulation. Performance also demands transhistorical thinking, toward which end I read several individual episodes of Indian acting through the lens of both historical circumstance and present-day arguments from performance theory.

If a performance mediates conscience and context through a body, it also mediates the past and the future through the present. The problematics of performance in the seventeenth century continue to shape both the structure and the content of anxieties about Indian performance today. If, as Michael Taussig argues, there is a persistently "elusive pattern of mimesis and alterity underscoring colonialism," New England still exhibits that warp and weft.[4] The tools of Native Studies, ethnohistory, and performance theory highlight those patterns. In this essay I use these tools not to define performance or its meanings once and for all, any more than to say for certain when an Indian or Englishman was "lying" or not, but to show some of the histories of embodied representation and the relations they have evoked.

Given the heated, wide-ranging conversations about truth telling, diplomacy, equivocation, and the dangers of theatrical performance in England during the early colonial era, it would have been surprising to find a unitary notion of acting or of truth standards in English colonial communities. The Puritans' deprecation of Machiavellian diplomacy and personal conduct, rooted in an emphasis on inward purification, gave them a keen eye for and broad definition of performance. Still, such attitudes were not consistently expressed among the various dissenting Protestant groups that settled New England. Nor must we necessarily take the nonconformists' self-definitions with respect to performance as authoritative. As many scholars have argued, the northern colonies were home to plenty of theater, from the gestural and linguistic politics of "plain speech" and "right walking" to the spectacles of trials and punishments and what Anne Kibbey has called the materialism of Puritan iconoclasm.[5]

Daniel Tuvill's diplomacy manual titled *The Dove and the Serpent*, first published in 1614, captures the conflicted pragmatism of an approach to embodied representation that was shaped by both religion and the spectacular politics of the early seventeenth century. Structuring itself on Matthew 10:16, in which Jesus (perhaps quoting an older aphorism) asks his followers to be "wise as serpents, and harmless as doves," *The Dove and the Serpent* encourages its readers to "honour an untainted Merit" but simultaneously to work hard to "discover a dissembling Herod" by a cunning skepticism. The book insists that a person's speech "is the onely Character, by which a man expresseth himself unto the life." Yet much of the text is devoted to protecting the reader from the naïve notion that oratory was a window onto the character of the speaker: "The World," it warns, "affords us almost nothing now, which is not personated and disguised." The most important implication of such an attitude, Tuvill implicitly argues, is that a person must be self-conscious—must perform a role—in conversation, and to a greater extent the more public the occasion. Those who possess virtue "should set some reasonable glosse and flourish upon it," lest they be, at best, ignored.[6]

Even the Quakers, whose theory of speech demanded the channeling of God's voice, struggled with how to avoid becoming the "double and cloven-hearted Parasites" against which *The Dove and the Serpent* warned. "When thou art obliged to speak, be sure to speak the Truth," wrote William Penn, "for Equivocation is *half way* to Lying; as Lying, the *whole way to Hell.*"[7] The spiritual significance of dissimulation was intimately tied to problems of social order and governance. In some Congregationalist communities in New England a confession was required as demonstration that a potential church member had received grace and, by extension, was entitled to civil membership as well. The comparatively generic quality of the confession (which drew on William Perkins's description of the ten stages of Christian conversion) raised questions about how such confessions were to be certified. Such questions grew even more pronounced in the case of the confessions of faith by John Eliot's "praying Indians."[8] In extreme attempts to discern the relation between the interior self and exterior behavior, such as witchcraft trials, the agency of the devil became increasingly important. Cotton Mather, late in the century, expressed concern over the mockery of religious practice in the case of both English witchcraft and Indian ceremonies: "Tis very Remarkable to see what an Impious & Imputent *Imitation* of Divine Things, is Apishly affected by the Devil, in several of those matters, whereof the Confessions of our Witches . . . have informed us."[9]

Such performances were imagined to be rooted in a potentially infectious idolatry to which the New World was particularly subject. English antitheatricalism was an important shaping context for this understanding of performance in the early colonial era. Complex disagreements over the spiritual, political, and social dangers of the theater underlay the prohibition of theater in the northern colonies (and in England between 1642 and 1660). Those disagreements haunt the reports of performances that appear in early colonial literature. The grounds on which Puritans objected to the theater ranged from theological accusations of idolatry to gendered ideologies that saw cross-dressing as a degenerative violation of natural male superiority. Many antitheatrical critics saw pagan religious rituals lying at the root of theatrical performances—an attitude that crucially shaped negative depictions of Native American "anticks" and ceremonies.[10]

In the legal and diplomatic realms, too, controversy raged over questions of honesty, equivocation, dissimulation, and the protocols for establishing truth. Oaths *ex officio* became a particular flashpoint for debate. Such oaths permitted authorities to interrogate individuals in the absence of a formal charge, which could result in self-incrimination. Punishing people for their ideas, not their actions, struck many English people as suspiciously similar to the Spanish Inquisition. Oaths "occupied a liminal position between outward behaviour and inward belief," observes Ethan Shagan, "a point where people were required by law to align their words with their thoughts, potentially giving the courts direct access to their consciences."[11] Defenders of the oath *ex officio* argued that an oath was an act and thus a ritual—and while the monarchy claimed no authority over thoughts, it did claim authority over ceremonies, rituals, and forms. For detractors, opposition to the oath's forced and inexorable transformation of thoughts into words and thence into deeds was part of a broader resistance to the forced clarification of legal and religious boundaries, both in the political structure of the English polity and in its public speech. Roger Williams insisted that the "Holy name of God [is] highly dishonoured by the Legall Oaths of this *Nation*" because the practice presumed that it was a converted believer who was taking an oath, which in "Millions" of cases was not true.[12]

If worries about the theater and oath taking had deep roots in religion, concerns about dissimulation in negotiation drew on classical precedents. The Ciceronian tradition, on one hand, argued that honesty in negotiation was a matter of reputation and hence that public negotiations should prioritize the honor of the state. Some deception was allowed on the part of a person speaking in the state's interest; an honest negotiator was true to the polity, if not always to himself. On the other hand, the Stoic tradition, which harmonized with aspects of the burgeoning Protestant understanding of honesty, emphasized the integrity of individual thought and feeling. A performance of honesty might injure worldly reputation while constituting a godly act.[13] Tuvill's *Dove and the Serpent*, for one, largely sided with the Ciceronians, while strict nonconformists cleaved to demanding personal honesty.

All of these intertwined contexts shaped early settler reactions to American Indian acts. At the same time, such controversies affected the form and content of descriptions of Native actions—descriptions that were, in this respect, themselves performances somewhere between honesty and dissimulation. At the broadest scale, European concerns with the art of imitation and its etiology (was a performance diabolical, natural, or divine?) shaped the politics and literature of colonization. Diversity held sway, however, at the local scale of a single interaction with a Native group or individual or in the case of a particular publication, each of which might be fueled as much by immediate political goals as by pervasive concerns with performance. Moreover, in the New England contact zone, such concerns could be found on the Algonquian side as well.

There is no doubt that New England's Native peoples considered performance an important category of behavior. Yet if performance had different meanings in seventeenth-century England than it does today, it is equally difficult to speak of a unified set of attitudes toward bodily enactment among Algonquians of the same era. Certainly eastern indigenous communities (upon whose actions my examples draw) valued honesty in formal negotiations. Some polities' mnemonic strategies for recording diplomatic interactions, in fact, assured such integrity by distributing memory among a group of people assigned to remember particular elements of an agreement, usually in conjunction with the physical marker of an exchange of wampum. Over the course of the seventeenth and eighteenth centuries, English written instruments were adopted as a part of the attempted enforcement of integrity in negotiations. But this kind of performance neither ensured agreement across cultural/political boundaries nor characterized all Native interactions. Deception in war was valued highly, and there is also ample evidence of deception in peace. In the recorded literary tradition of the Northeast, dissimulators are plentiful. Among Delaware storytellers the culture hero Wehixamukes, the "man who misunderstands," functioned to discipline hearers to speak precisely, because Wehixamukes confuses literal and commonsense meanings of words. Such stories encouraged listeners to think about the historical layers and metaphorical powers of language, about how phrases come to mean something other than what they say.[14] In such stories, no less than in the English religious discourses that underwrote anxieties about dissimulation, supernatural or other-than-human beings surveilled human performances, ready to punish those who were dishonest or who misled for the wrong reasons.

The complexity of overlapping indigenous and European contexts for understanding forms of embodied representation, as Richard White has observed, suggests a dynamic methodological approach to moments of colonial intercultural performance. Rather than looking at Native acts from any single seventeenth-century attitude toward performance, we might consider how these acts functioned as membranes between or among worlds in co-evolution. The following three stories refract the transferences and the misroutings—the divergent paths of interpretation—that could emerge from Native acts. Two stories come from the Pequot War, the first major conflict between Natives and Europeans in New England and one that initiated longstanding suspicion on both sides. As Joyce Chaplin has shown in her path-breaking work on technology and English colonization, American Indian warfare in the East usually involved both an acknowledgment of social boundaries and an awareness that cultural permeability could be a source of strength.[15] Imitation and dissimulation were associated, among English settlers, with notions of outdated or "savage" modes of combat (and were sometimes explicitly compared to Irish practices). At the same time these acts of deception prodded at the core of modern English hermeneutical problems. The final episode discussed is from a time of peace, just before the Pequot War, showing the diplomatic use of deception to strengthen intercultural bonds through ironic, but humorous, critique.

As Captain John Underhill sailed to Block Island in 1636 under a commission to punish the Pequot people for offenses against the English, he no doubt had occasion to reflect on preceding Indian combats. The success of surprise attacks by both sides—such as Myles Standish's assassination of Wituwamat and other Native leaders at Wessagusset, or Opechancanough's massive assault on Virginia settlers in 1622—called the utility of formal European military procedure into doubt. Native warriors were good at deception, and if the reports coming from Lieutenant Lion Gardener at Fort Saybrook were right, they were constantly surveilling English movements. The Pequots were hiding in the woods, waiting for Gardener's ill-disciplined men to wander off hunting, away from the strong-house in the corn fields; they were lurking in the hay meadows in ambush; they were invisibly patrolling the rivers, from which they allowed drowned English bodies to float back down to Saybrook, such as one "with an arrow shot into his eye through his head."[16] Underhill's twenty or so soldiers were comparatively inexperienced when it came to such chilling communiqués from an enemy. Most were in the company for the same reasons he was: a belief in English superiority and a desire for the land or booty that would likely come with successful service. Underhill himself had been granted one hundred acres of land for fighting the Natives near Brookline a few years earlier.[17]

This combat was not likely to be so easy. The Pequots were rumored to be fierce opponents, and on the European side, motives for the attack were mixed. English reactions to the murder of a trader, John Oldham, on Block Island triggered Underhill's mission. Interpretations of the political motivations for the attack vary. The Manissean people of Block Island, key manufacturers of wampum, had been tributaries of the Pequots, and the two groups probably shared relatives.[18] At the time of the murder of Oldham and his crew, however, the Narragansetts and their leader Miantonomi controlled the island's tribute. Miantonomi, seeking alliance with the English against the Pequots, launched a raid on the island in an attempt to demonstrate his control over his tributaries. But he also suggested to the Massachusetts Bay leaders that Oldham's killers had sought refuge with the Pequots. The leaders took advantage of this rumor and resurrected an old complaint against the Pequots. The Massachusetts Bay leaders ordered an attack on Block Island and then demanded that the Pequots deliver up the killers (and tribute) in order to prevent war with the English.

Algonquian dissimulation was on masterful display at Block Island. The stage was set before the raiding party arrived. Perhaps tipped off by the Narragansett raid just before, or by news that the Puritan boats were underway, the Manisseans knew when and where the attackers were going to arrive. "Coming to an anchor before the island," Underhill reports, "we espied an Indian walking by the shore in a desolate manner, as though he had received intelligence of our coming. Which Indian gave just ground to some to conclude that the body of the people had deserted the Island." Offering this affective information, an early example of the stereotype of the melancholy Indian, allows Underhill to stage a heuristic drama. An English interpretive practice ("just ground . . . to conclude") is posited, given a rationale and a piece of evidence (Indian "desolat[ion]"), and then dismissed—and yet this information is spectacularly *included*, despite being inessential to the combat description. "But some knowing them for the generality to be a warlike nation," Underhill tells us, "were not persuaded that they would upon so slender terms forsake the Island, but rather suspected they might lie behind a bank," which, as it turns out, they did indeed, attacking from hiding as soon as the English came ashore. Underhill thus reveals that the lone Native's emotion has its cause in information technology unknown to most Europeans, hidden channels of communication suspected only by experienced men like himself. And, though Underhill does not make the reference specifically, perhaps it is only men who remember the story of a similar trick by Sinon and the Achaeans in their wooden horse who can understand Indian performance.[19]

Underhill and his men escaped the shoreline trap, but they did not manage to take advantage of it. The hidden Manissean bowmen ended up being almost all the Natives the war party saw on Block Island, "the Indians being retired into swamps," Underhill complained, "so as we could not find them." Scorched earth then became the policy of the frustrated English, a targeted destruction of all Native resources and dwellings only interrupted when Underhill feared that "we should make an alarm by setting fire on them" and again risk losing what he suggested they already lacked, the element of surprise. "The Block Islanders," Alfred Cave writes, "were virtually invisible." More precisely, seen from the Manissean point of view, they were camouflaged. What is camouflaged is made to appear as environment; what the English took for trees, reeds, brush, or animals, along with their sounds and smells, included scores of Natives acting, sending out what the English would receive as "noise" across the sensory spectrum. Despite Underhill's estimate of fourteen killed, only one death is confirmed by other sources, and one Block Islander may have been captured.[20]

Underhill's casualty count, in light of his paradoxical report that the Indians could not be found, hides Native agency, even as his description of the melancholy Indian on the shore highlights the Indians' ability to fool Europeans (or at least those untrained in the classics). This rhetorical strategy calls to mind Joseph Roach's concept of "surrogation," or cultural performances designed to fill perceived vacancies, and the way in which colonial performances suppress the cultural dynamics and histories of the indigenous population in the act of justifying their dispossession. Yet as Roach further suggests, such acts of erasure can never be complete, for colonial histories and identities depend on the intercultural contexts they seek to suppress. Insisting that since the seventeenth century, "local cultural productions have been hybridized routinely by the hemispheric circulation of collectively created forms," Roach argues that colonial identities "have endured—and can continue to endure—only as relationships."[21] Such a focus on how new, intercultural relations are forged even as they are forgotten or covered up might be understood to harmonize with some Native American intellectuals' call for an emphasis on relationality over one on play acting or colonial erasure through rituals of displacement. That is to say, Native American performances often exposed colonial mechanisms of forgetting by rehearsing relations, embodying their politics by demanding that new kinds of ties emerge out of a mutual recognition of both the successes and the failures of old ones.

The demand for mutual recognition could take the more direct form of an imitation of Englishness itself. Such imitation could be comforting, as when for some English observers it demonstrated the newfound Christian piety among the Praying Indians. But behind such demonstrations always lurked the possibility of deception. As Homi Bhabha famously notes of colonial emulation, "Mimicry is at once resemblance and menace."[22] Perhaps the most disturbing Native simulation was the wearing of clothes taken from slain English people. After they attacked Wethersfield, for example, the Pequots rigged English clothes as symbolic sails in their canoes, a macabre mockery of English seagoing technology. They then upped the ante, using the clothes as trophies and as an emotional weapon:

> some of their armes they got from them, others put on the English clothes, and came to the Fort jeering of them, and calling, come and fetch your English mens clothes againe; come out and fight

> if you dare: you dare not fight, you are all one like women, we have one amongst us that if he could kill but one of you more, he would be equall with God, and as the *English* mans God is, so would hee be; this blasphemous speech troubled the hearts of the souldiers, but they knew not how to remedy it in respect of their weaknesse.[23]

This is finely honed information warfare. The Pequots—by playing English, as it were—reanimate the English soldiers' dead countrymen, all the while transforming them into "Indians" who mock the soldiers both as live opponents and in the guise of ghostly figures of the dead calling for revenge. Such practices are endemic in the world history of warfare, and they were richly haunting for Puritans. The way this jibe plays on gender ideology, English perceptions of Natives as heathen, and the confessed unpredictability of the Puritan god suggests how closely the Pequots had been observing the settlers.[24]

The Puritans' distaste for idols, Anne Kibbey argues, extended beyond man-made objects into the world of human body movements. Through a trope known as *figura*, which indicated a gestural quality unique to a body or phenomenon, the same evils brought on by the use of imagery, crosses, sculptures of saints, and other material renditions of faith could be engendered by human movement. We might think of *figura* today as that sense that makes it possible to recognize an acquaintance from far away by gait alone. For seventeenth-century Europeans, it could be used to tell when the devil had possessed a person, causing "antick" movements and unholy sounds. In this case the instance of *figura* is complicated by the Pequots' use of English clothes. If the Pequots had noticed the English tendency to understand civility as a function of outward behavior and dress, then might not their mockery indicate a deliberate refusal of such standards, rather than a putatively natural barbaric tendency? Logically, such a gesture suited other important nonconformist tenets, such as the constant appreciation of the fleeting quality of life and the deprecation of such outward matters as sartorial choice (as Roger Williams emphasizes in this essay's epigraph).[25] If there was something devilish about Pequot movements, such gestures made in English garb reflected back questions the Puritans were asking themselves about the justice of their prosecution of the war.

Judith Butler has influentially argued that dressing in drag unsettles the naturalness of gender difference by inducing an awareness in spectators of how such differences are performed.[26] By extension, one might argue that Indian performances of Englishness called attention to the unnaturalness of national identity, reminding the English of members of their own kind who had "gone Indian" (what Axtell terms the "white Indians" of North America) or who were blasphemers, or, alternatively, of the quickness with which Indians could take up English appearances. Yet while such an unsettling of national identity might have occurred for some observers of Indian acts, for others, such as the dissenters and strangers who fought in the Pequot War, "Englishness" might not have been the most stable of identifications in the first place. In this respect, the safer analytical bet is offered by Roach, who proposes an intermediate step in the process by which performance disturbs norms: "the anxiety generated by the process of substitution," he argues, is "a momentary self-consciousness about surrogation that constitutes what might pass for reflexivity." It is not always that a performance proves the unnaturalness of gender, or Indianness, say, but that it shows how a substitution of one gender or culture can destabilize a viewer's understanding of his or her own behavior.[27] The ontological may hold, but the episteme is shaken. Indians might replace Englishmen by becoming Englishmen, both in terms of the occupation of land

and of ostensibly national behavior. A performative tactic like the one the Pequots used might induce enough fear to make a difference in a battle. Alternatively, it might create sufficient self-doubt among the English to force diplomacy.

"From Montaigne to Artaud," writes Roach, "Native American and especially Mesoamerican customs and practices have played the roles of ethnographic provocation and hyperbolic mirror."[28] But it is not just in European or settler accounts that such customs and practices have functioned in this way. William Apess's "Indian's Looking-Glass for the White Man" (1833) famously appropriated the mirror metaphor in the nineteenth century, calling attention to the hypocrisy of racism among whites who called themselves Christians.[29] Much earlier, in the mid-seventeenth century, the powerful Wampanoag sachem known as Massasoit (and also as Ousamaquin) played a practical joke on the colonists at Plymouth that similarly called attention to how performance problematized ethnographic clarity in colonial interactions.

The fulcrum of the trick was Massasoit's good relationship with Plymouth's ambassador Edward Winslow, who had helped cure the sachem of a threatening illness in the early years of English colonization in New England. John Winthrop recorded what he called a "pleasant passage . . . acted by the Indians" in his journal for 1634. As Winslow was returning from a trip to Connecticut territory,

> intendinge to returne by land, he went to Osamekin the Sagamore his olde Allye, who offered to conducte him home to Plim: but before they tooke their iornye Osamekin sent one of his men to Plim: to tell them that mr winslowe was dead, & directed him to shewe how & where he was killed: wherevpon there was muche feare & sorrowe at Plim; the next daye when Osamekin brought him home, they asked him why he sent such worde, &c: he an-

> sweared, that it was their maner to doe so, that they might be more wellcome when they came home.[30]

Reversing the roles of his health crisis eleven years earlier, Massasoit sends deliberate misinformation to the Plymouth colony, asking a messenger to deceive the settlers with realistic details about Winslow being murdered. Receiving responses of mystification instead of relieved laughter when he shows up with the still-living Winslow, Massasoit then augments the misinformation in answer to the naïve question about his motives. Massasoit mocks the English notion of culture itself—a warning that still resonates as we try to read this incident today—by claiming that such deliberate misinformation is a Wampanoag "maner," a trait or ritual. It is a many-edged joke, even leaving aside the amusement the recorder Winthrop clearly enjoys (partly at the expense of his competitors at Plymouth and partly at the verification it seems to offer that God intended some to be leaders and others to be followers). *Where would the colony be without Winslow?* asks Massasoit implicitly, suggesting that Winslow's ambassadorship to Native America (just as Tuvill had warned the shyly virtuous) might be underrated by the otherworldly Plymouth separatists.

The Winslow/Massasoit episode recalls performance theorist Peggy Phelan's argument that performance draws power from its being "unmarked"—unrepeatable, unrecordable in its full sensory complexity, and spectacularly under the control of the performer. Performance is, for Phelan, "representation without reproduction," since every performance features, and makes, a change.[31] In this case unverifiability plays a key role in Massasoit's layering of the lesson that the practical joke offers. The nontextual nature of the Wampanoags' performance, in combination with various textualized versions of it (first Massasoit's "explanation," then Winthrop's description), maintains an undecidability across cultural rhetorical norms. Though presumably Massasoit's jest offers an occasion for reminding his hearers that discerning the truth in messages is a problem shared by everyone, it hints more deeply that uncertainty and ambiguity are conditions of being an audience. It reminds the English that though they have escaped death, they have not yet mastered local information systems, and that a Native audience is aware that its "maner" is being observed.

Jean Baudrillard's influential text *Simulacra and Simulation* suggests both why indigenous American simulations were so disturbing to English viewers then and why they might still be now. "Parody renders submission and transgression equivalent," Baudrillard observes, "and that is the most serious crime, because it *cancels out the difference upon which the law is based.*"[32] For English settlers, the blurring of difference induced fear. Baudrillard's argument suggests that such fear arose not merely because Indians became *figurae* of the devil's minions but because they fundamentally challenged the representational order itself. Law—and thus the legitimacy of interactions with Natives over land, trade, or religion—depended upon differentiating among individuals and peoples. Indian mockery suggested that Natives knew this was the English way but that they did not choose to participate in differential categorization except on their own terms.

Let us return, then, to the question of the temporality of performance—to the apparent gap between Roger Williams's "Indian Paints" and Craig Womack's deprecation of "Indian as performance." Today the question of indigenous fidelity is bound up with the hotly debated issue of "wannabe" Indianness—and once again the Pequots are central to the controversy. Many Native New Englanders do not bear the stereotypical phenotype of Indians or other identifying markers such as a traditional tribal language. Their stories are mosaics, heavily recombined histories designed not to recover a "real thing that happened in the past" but to promote and recount survival in the face of colonial land grabs, cultural identity theft, and racism.[33] For all of New England's indigenous population, successive fragmentations of communities and families by war, displacement, and disease were exacerbated in subsequent centuries by policies that often made it impossible to stay on the reservation, because one could not earn enough to survive there. Such conditions necessitated the development of representational practices that defeat the analyst's dream of access to pure, unadulterated information about a society. They also make it hard to establish the kind of proof of continuity and continuous tribal governance demanded by the U.S. government's recognition process. When the Pequots acquired gaming rights and began to build tribal enrollment, some critics both within and beyond Indian country argued that the tribe was made up of fakers.[34]

The advantage of performance as an analytical rubric is not that it will settle such controversies—will tell us whether Ward Churchill is a "real" Indian or whether Charles Eastman was assimilationist at root.[35] With luck, it will change the questions. The uncomfortable trans-temporality of performance, the way it weaves together past understandings with revisions, becomes ever clearer the more historical rigor goes into illuminating any particular performance. Seventeenth-century Algonquian performances hold a lesson and are a material precedent for what is happening today. Pequots and Wampanoags of the seventeenth century acted in ways that destabilized English ideas about culture or behavior, contesting the alienation of Native land and forms of intercultural relation. Pequots who today are controversially "real" gain authority to turn parts of Connecticut into land held in federal trust and invite foreign capital in to help build a billion-dollar-a-year casino industry.

This income model unhitches profit from private property ownership and appears to pose a threat to the coherence of the state.

"Indian identity is something people do," writes Scott Lyons, "not what they are, so the real question is, what should we do?"[36] This is a hard question, when brought to bear on the juncture of performance and American Indian politics. There are at least two kinds of "property" at stake—land and group identity. Williams's "Indian Paints," Lyons points out of the history of treaty making in North America, were sometimes essential to protecting Native interests, and they demand a deeply historical approach to identity, both of individuals and of groups. Those paints never quite made an *untruth*, Lyons might reply to Williams, under the pressure of colonialism. Yet such a historical approach must be as self-conscious about its own status as a present-day performance as it is about accessing those moments when relations between Indian and colonial groups were rehearsed with a critical edge. If performances are membranes between cultures, they are also membranes among historical moments or periods. Performance analysis itself, then, in the context of Native American Studies at least, must be cautious to capture both the concrete effects of performances and the ways in which those effects never completely define a given Indian performance.

The better to foster dynamic legal protocols that are capable of functioning interculturally, then, we might entertain an emphasis on relationality rather than insisting upon absolute standards for authenticity or truth, sovereignty, or property. Performance articulates motive and reception, enactors and observers of culture, and regimes of politics and embodied identity. Performance as an analytic cannot promise to verify. It can, however, serve as a way of promoting relationality as a basis for legal processes and cultural interactions. Drawing on a past, performance is therefore at least partially conservative in the most basic sense, but it also works actively to create a present. If a status quo is maintained, it is not through inaction or a lack of resistance but through continued performances that suppress or contain alternatives. By the same token, radical performances can threaten and sometimes alter the status quo. This way of studying performance can be helpful in dealing with the complexities of American Indian history after colonization because it is sensitive to the maintenance of boundaries even as, in a long-term or wide-angle view, it regards culture as emergent. "After all," writes Lisa Brooks, "if there are no 'real' Indians left, there are no 'real' Indian land claims."[37]

Notes

I would like to thank Ralph Bauer, Jane Calvert, Christopher Teuton, Christopher Labarthe, Andrew Newman, Edlie Wong, Caroline Wigginton, Ethan Shagan, Jason Powell, and the editors of this volume for their help in shaping this essay.

1. Womack, in Acoose et al., *Reasoning Together*, 23.
2. Axtell, "Babel of Tongues," 18, 49.
3. See Brooks, *Common Pot*, 219–54; and M. Cohen, *Networked Wilderness*, 1–30.
4. Taussig, *Mimesis and Alterity*, 95.
5. See St. George, *Conversing by Signs*, 7, 160, 205–95; Gustafson, *Eloquence Is Power*, 1–39; Brown, *The Pilgrim and the Bee*, 21–67; Kamensky, *Governing the Tongue*, 3–16; and Kibbey, *Interpretation of Material Shapes*, 42–64.
6. Tuvill, *Dove*, A1r, 2, 7, 18.
7. Tuvill, *Dove*, 13; Penn, *Some Fruits*, 139. See also Bauman, *Reputation of Truth*, 65–76, 217–29.
8. On the epistemological crisis of Indian conversion, see Bellin, "John Eliot."
9. Mather, *Seasonable Discourses*, 104. See also Rivett, "Evidence of Grace," discussing the convergence of the evidentiary regimes of a burgeoning scientific attitude and those seeking proof of God's regenerative favor in the seventeenth century.
10. See Abrahams, "Antick Dispositions"; Barish, *Antitheatrical Preju-*

dice; Diehl, *Staging Reform*, 1–25. Antitheatricalism's roots in Christian disagreements about whether performances represented a kind of idolatry were not limited to Reformation and Counter-Reformation differences; see O'Connell, *Idolatrous Eye*, 30–31.

11. Shagan, "English Inquisition," 543.
12. Williams, *Hireling ministry*, 34.
13. See Hampton, *Fictions of Embassy*, 18, 46–49; and Powell, "Thomas Wyatt."
14. See the section on Narragansett councils and terms related to lying in Williams, *Key*, 134; also Bragdon, *Native People*; Richter, *Ordeal of the Longhouse*, 1–49; Salisbury, *Manitou and Providence*, 39–59; White, *Middle Ground*, 50–93; and Newman, "'They had not understood,'" 10–12.
15. Chaplin, *Subject Matter*, 79–115.
16. Gardener, "Lion Gardener," 129.
17. On Underhill see Shelley, *John Underhill*; and Cave, *Pequot War*, 140–67.
18. See Salwen, "Indians of Southern New England"; and Cave, *Pequot War*, 64.
19. Underhill, *Newes*, 51–52.
20. Underhill, *Newes*, 54; Cave, *Pequot War*, 112.
21. Roach, *Cities of the Dead*, xii.
22. Bhabha, *Location of Culture*, 86.
23. Gardener, "Lion Gardener," 16.
24. See also Axtell, *European and the Indian*, 297–311.
25. Kibbey, *Interpretation of Material Shapes*, esp. 44–64.
26. Butler, *Gender Trouble*, 175–93.
27. Roach, *Cities of the Dead*, 6.
28. Roach, *Cities of the Dead*, 131.
29. Apess, *On Our Own Ground*, 95–102.
30. Winthrop, *Journal*, 124–25.
31. Phelan, *Unmarked*, 3.
32. Baudrillard, *Simulacra and Simulation*, 21.
33. See, among many others, Grumet, ed., *Northeastern Indian Lives*, 1–12; Brooks, *Common Pot*, 163–97; Den Ouden, *Beyond Conquest*, 1–38; Hauptman and Wherry, eds., *Pequots*, 117–40; Weinstein, ed., *Enduring Traditions*, xiii–xx; and Peters, *Wampanoags*, 8–53.
34. At least three books have been published by trade presses in the last six years that describe the establishment of gaming enterprises at Pequot. Some suggest that the Pequots are a legal fraud, yet that there is

something admirable about this simulacrum; others are less friendly. See Eisler, *Revenge of the Pequots*; Fromson, *Hitting the Jackpot*; and Benedict, *Without Reservation*. For a negative reaction to the Pequots from within Indian country, see Red Shirt, "These Are Not Indians"; but see also Justice's critique of Red Shirt in Acoose et al., *Reasoning Together*, 156–59.

35. For a synopsis of the Churchill controversy, see Byrd, "'Living My Life Deadly,'"; for a recent summary of the debate about Eastman, see Cooper, "On Autobiography."

36. Lyons, *X-marks*, 40.

37. Brooks, *Common Pot*, xxxvii.

Works Cited

Abrahams, Roger D. "Antick Dispositions and the Perilous Politics of Culture: Costume and Culture in Jacobean England and America." *Journal of American Folklore* 111 (1998): 115–32.

Acoose, Janice, et al. *Reasoning Together: The Native Critics Collective*. Ed. Craig S. Womack, Daniel Heath Justice, and Christopher B. Teuton. Norman: University of Oklahoma Press, 2008.

Apess, William. *On Our Own Ground: The Complete Writings of William Apess, A Pequot*. Ed. Barry O'Connell. Amherst: University of Massachusetts Press, 1992.

Axtell, James. "Babel of Tongues: Communicating with the Indians in Eastern North America." In *The Language Encounter in the Americas, 1492–1800*, ed. Edward G. Gray and Norman Fiering, 15–60. New York: Berghan, 2000.

———. *The European and the Indian: Essays in the Ethnohistory of Colonial North America*. New York: Oxford University Press, 1981.

———. "The White Indians of Colonial America." *William and Mary Quarterly* 3rd ser. 32 (1975): 55–88.

Barish, Jonas A. *The Antitheatrical Prejudice*. Berkeley: University of California Press, 1981.

Baudrillard, Jean. *Simulacra and Simulation*. Trans. Sheila Faria Glaser. Ann Arbor: University of Michigan Press, 1994.

Bauman, Richard. *For the Reputation of Truth: Politics, Religion, and Conflict among the Pennsylvania Quakers*. Baltimore: Johns Hopkins University Press, 1971.

Bellin, Joshua David. "John Eliot's Playing Indian." *Early American Literature* 42 (2007): 1–30.

Benedict, Jeff. *Without Reservation: How a Controversial Indian Tribe*

Rose to Power and Built the World's Largest Casino. New York: Harper, 2001.

Bhabha, Homi K. *The Location of Culture*. London: Routledge, 1994.

Bragdon, Kathleen J. *Native People of Southern New England, 1500–1650*. Norman: University of Oklahoma Press, 1996.

Brooks, Lisa. *The Common Pot: The Recovery of Native Space in the Northeast*. Minneapolis: University of Minnesota Press, 2008.

Brown, Matthew P. *The Pilgrim and the Bee: Reading Rituals and Book Culture in Early New England*. Philadelphia: University of Pennsylvania Press, 2007.

Butler, Judith. *Gender Trouble: Feminism and the Subversion of Identity*. New York: Routledge, 1990.

Byrd, Jodi A. "'Living My Life Deadly': Red Lake, Ward Churchill, and the Discourses of Competing Genocides." *American Indian Quarterly* 31 (Spring 2007): 310–32.

Cave, Alfred A. *The Pequot War*. Amherst: University of Massachusetts Press, 1996.

Chaplin, Joyce E. *Subject Matter: Technology, the Body, and Science on the Anglo-American Frontier, 1500–1676*. Cambridge: Harvard University Press, 2001.

Cohen, Matt. *The Networked Wilderness: Communicating in Early New England*. Minneapolis: University of Minnesota Press, 2009.

Cooper, Tova. "On Autobiography, Boy Scouts and Citizenship: Revisiting Charles Eastman's *Deep Woods*." *Arizona Quarterly* 65, no. 4 (2009): 1–35.

Den Ouden, Amy E. *Beyond Conquest: Native Peoples and the Struggle for History in New England*. Lincoln: University of Nebraska Press, 2005.

Diehl, Huston. *Staging Reform, Reforming the Stage: Protestantism and Popular Theater in Early Modern England*. Ithaca: Cornell University Press, 1997.

Eisler, Kim Isaac. *Revenge of the Pequots: How a Small Native American Tribe Created the World's Most Profitable Casino*. Lincoln: Bison, 2002.

Fromson, Brett Duval. *Hitting the Jackpot: The Inside Story of the Richest Indian Tribe in History*. New York: Grove, 2003.

Gardener, Lion. "Leift Lion Gardener his relation of the Pequot Warres." In *History of the Pequot War: The Contemporary Accounts of Mason, Underhill, Vincent, and Gardener*, ed. Charles Orr, 113–49. New York: AMS, 1981.

Grumet, Robert S., ed. *Northeastern Indian Lives, 1632–1816*. Amherst: University of Massachusetts Press, 1996.

Gustafson, Sandra M. *Eloquence Is Power: Oratory and Performance in Early America*. Chapel Hill: University of North Carolina Press, 2000.

Hampton, Timothy. *Fictions of Embassy: Literature and Diplomacy in Early Modern Europe*. Ithaca: Cornell University Press, 2009.

Hauptman, Laurence M., and James Wherry, eds. *The Pequots in Southern New England: The Fall and Rise of an American Indian Nation*. Norman: University of Oklahoma Press, 1990.

Kamensky, Jane. *Governing the Tongue: The Politics of Speech in Early New England*. New York: Oxford University Press, 1997.

Kibbey, Anne. *The Interpretation of Material Shapes in Puritanism: A Study of Rhetoric, Prejudice, and Violence*. New York: Cambridge University Press, 1986.

Lyons, Scott Richard. *X-marks: Native Signatures of Assent*. Minneapolis: University of Minnesota Press, 2010.

Mather, Cotton. *Seasonable Discourses upon Some Common, but Woful Instances. . . .* London, 1695.

Newman, Andrew. "They had not understood it was to be done that way": Colonial Land Transactions, Interpretation, and Equivocation. Unpublished manuscript.

O'Connell, Michael. *The Idolatrous Eye: Iconoclasm and Theater in Early Modern England*. New York: Oxford University Press, 2000.

Penn, William. *Some Fruits of Solitude, in Reflections and Maxims Relating to the Conduct of Human Life*. London: Thomas Northcott, 1693.

Peters, Russell M. *The Wampanoags of Mashpee: An Indian Perspective on American History*. Somerville MA: Nimrod, 1987.

Phelan, Peggy. *Unmarked: The Politics of Performance*. London: Routledge, 1993.

Powell, Jason. "Sir Thomas Wyatt and Sir Francis Bryan: Plainness and Dissimulation." In *The Oxford Handbook to Tudor Literature, 1485–1603*, ed. Mike Pincombe and Cathy Shrank. New York: Oxford University Press, forthcoming.

Red Shirt, Delphine. "These Are Not Indians." *American Indian Quarterly* 26, no. 4 (2002): 643–44.

Richter, Daniel K. *The Ordeal of the Longhouse: The Peoples of the Iroquois League in the Era of European Colonization*. Chapel Hill: University of North Carolina Press, 1992.

Rivett, Sarah. "Evidence of Grace: The Science of the Soul in Colonial New England." Ph.D. diss. University of Chicago, 2005.

Roach, Joseph. *Cities of the Dead: Circum-Atlantic Performance*. New York: Columbia University Press, 1996.

Salisbury, Neal. *Manitou and Providence: Indians, Europeans, and the Making of New England, 1500–1643*. New York: Oxford University Press, 1982.

Salwen, Bert. "Indians of Southern New England and Long Island: Early Period." In *Handbook of North American Indians*, vol. 15: *Northeast*, ed. Bruce G. Trigger, 160–76. Washington DC: Smithsonian Institution, 1978.

Shagan, Ethan. "The English Inquisition: Constitutional Conflict and Ecclesiastical Law in the 1590s." *Historical Journal* 47 (2004): 541–65.

Shelley, Henry C. *John Underhill: Captain of New England and New Netherland*. New York: D. Appleton, 1932.

St. George, Robert Blair. *Conversing by Signs: Poetics of Implication in Colonial New England Culture*. Chapel Hill: University of North Carolina Press, 1998.

Taussig, Michael. *Mimesis and Alterity: A Particular History of the Senses*. New York: Routledge, 1993.

T[uvill], D[aniel]. *The Dove and the Serpent, in which is conteined a large description of all such points and principles, as tend either to conversation, or, negotiation*. London: 1614.

Underhill, John. "Newes from America." In *History of the Pequot War: The Contemporary Accounts of Mason, Underhill, Vincent, and Gardener*, ed. Charles Orr, 47–92. New York: AMS, 1981.

Weinstein, Laurie, ed. *Enduring Traditions: The Native Peoples of New England*. Westport CT: Bergin, 1994.

White, Richard. *The Middle Ground: Indians, Empires, and Republics in the Great Lakes Region, 1650–1815*. New York: Cambridge University Press, 1991.

Williams, Roger. *The hireling ministry none of Christs, or, A discourse touching the propagating the Gospel of Christ Jesus*. London: 1652.

———. *A Key into the Language of America*. Ed. John J. Teunissen and Evelyn J. Hinz. Detroit: Wayne State University Press, 1973.

Winthrop, John. *The Journal of John Winthrop, 1630–1649*. 2 vols. Ed. Richard S. Dunn, James Savage, and Laetitia Yeandle. Cambridge: Harvard University Press, 1996.

[2]

The Deer Island Indians and Common Law Performance

Nan Goodman

In late October 1675, after the Indians had won a number of strategic battles in King Philip's War, colonial authorities banished roughly five hundred Praying Indians, all noncombatants, to Deer Island, a bleak and barren rock in the Boston harbor. In the idiosyncratic terms of this banishment, which ordered the Indians to "be forwith sent for, & disposed of to Deare Island as the place appointed for their present aboade," we witness not only one of the war's greatest atrocities but also the grounds for a previously unnoticed change in the way Indians came to be represented under English law.[1] Specifically, it was in part as a result of their banishment that the Indians of the Plymouth and Massachusetts Bay colonies moved from a legal status dependent almost exclusively on territorial affiliations—and thus largely without a performative dimension—to one dependent on their actions, and thus partially performative in the legal sense.

The use of performance theory to understand the Praying Indians has gained numerous adherents in recent years, no doubt because many aspects of their dual identities—part Christian, part Indian—were so obviously staged.[2] Yet unlike an earlier generation of scholars who saw in these cultural accommodations a fatal ambiguity that led, in the words of one commentator, to "cultural suicide," current scholars now view the converts' performances in a far more positive light.[3] Joshua David Bellin and Sarah Rivett, for example, have found in the conversion narratives evidence not of capitulation to Puritan forms of expression but of a newly dynamic form of religious expression all their own, while James Ronda, Jenny Hale Pulsipher, and Daniel Mandell, among others, have enabled us to see the newly mixed identities of the Indians as a way of maintaining their place in a range of practices, from farming to politics.[4]

One area of Praying Indian performance, however, has slipped through the cracks: legal performance. To be sure, since Ann Marie Plane observed in 1998 that "even the best analyses of early American law have failed to mention the fate of indigenous legal systems," much work has been done to uncover what legal performance might have meant in Native terms.[5] As useful as such work on indigenous legal autonomy and sovereignty has been, however, it fails to address how the Indians "performed" within the terms of law familiar to the Puritans: the legal system known to the English as the common law. Traditionally understood as the body of judge-made law determined on a case by case basis, the common law was said to come from "the ancient constitution," an unwritten body of laws that emerged as doctrine in the fifteenth century but did not achieve widespread acceptance until the early seventeenth, when it was defined, as J. G. A. Pocock puts it, as "common custom, originating in the usages of the people and declared, interpreted and applied in the courts."[6] At the heart of this definition lay the belief that the law was based on traditions for which a person's actions were the source. And in turn, this belief underlay the peculiarly intimate relationship between the common law and the idea of performance.

Unlike other forms of law, the common law derived from, even as it addressed itself to, the actions of the people, which made seventeenth-century conceptions of legal persons markedly different from those that came before or followed. As Richard White explains, while seventeenth-century legal persons were still subjects in name and not yet citizens, they might nonetheless best be seen as "centers of personal agency" whose relationship to the law was reciprocal.[7] Premised on the common law's understanding of custom as the actions that, though unwritten, passed directly into law by virtue of the universality of their practice, such reciprocal agency meant that performance according to the common law was less about legal ritual or specific declarations of authority (the traditional ways in which scholars have viewed legal performance) than it was about the apparently transparent way people's everyday actions—as opposed to their aspirations, assumptions, or beliefs—helped make the law.[8] Such a legal sense of performance comes closest to a model offered by performance theorist Marvin Carlson that is neither ritualistic nor linguistic but based on a measure of comparison: when we speak of a child's performance in school or a car's performance on the road, Carlson explains, "the emphasis . . . is on the general success of the activity in light of some standard of achievement that may not itself be precisely articulated."[9]

Needless to say, under such a system—where even the most commonplace manifestations of human agency were potentially constitutive of the law—the Indians, as humans with customs of their own, might have posed a considerable threat to Puritan legal norms. But the agency at the heart of the common law was not, conveniently, open to all, for as the common lawyers insisted, only the English could make English law.[10] "The Englishman, who saw his realm as a fabric of custom," explains Pocock, "saw proprietor, litigant, judge, counselor, and prince as engaged in a constant activity, one of preserving, refining, and transmitting the usages and customs that made him and England what they were."[11] Indeed, the story of the Praying Indians before Deer Island is in large part the story of their mostly failed attempts to achieve recognition under the common law by adopting English habits of dress, language, and prayer; try as they might, as non-English, they could neither claim legal standing under the common law nor participate in the customs that produced it.

Deer Island changed all this. It was only after the Indians had been banished to Deer Island and the categories of Indian territorial sovereignty and autonomy had been disabled that the Indians finally achieved what had not been possible before: they emerged as agents under the common law. Far from being only one more in a long line of territorial hardships that began with European conquest and ended with the system of Indian reservations, Deer Island represents a radical departure from the history of the gradual dwindling of the Indians' sovereignty.[12] In sending the Indians to a place *within* the Puritan jurisdiction instead of outside it, the Puritans effected a banishment that was unlike any other, including their own banishment from England: previously defined by colonial law through their geographical coordinates, the Indians suffered an identificatory rupture in their banishment that altered the categories by which they knew themselves and by which they were known to the English—that is, the categories of cultural and legal contact.[13]

The result of this rupture was deterritorialization. Put another way, after their banishment to Deer Island, it was no longer possible to think of the Praying Indians in terms of the old territorially based legal categories that offered them a protected place not within but alongside the Puritan legal order.[14] Of course if through the operation of deterritoralization the Deer Island banishment made it possible to rethink the legal status of the Indians for the first time since the colonial encounter, it did not by itself create the opportunities for legal action into which the newly deterritorialized Indians might fit. Rather these were provided on the one hand by preexisting identities—like that of the Christian Indian—and on the other hand by newer identities—like that of the Indian soldier fighting on the English side. As we shall see, it was in their roles as soldiers for the English that the banished Indians were finally able to insert themselves as actors into the common law, in part because their military actions were so conspicuously agential that they could not be ignored and in part because the military (in the form of the militia) served the colony as a peripheral social system, the regulations of which differed from but ultimately filtered back into the larger social sphere.

In the discussion that follows I trace the emergence of this new common law identity for the Indians in some of the literature from the period immediately before, during, and after the Deer Island banishment, literature that includes records by John Eliot of Indian conversions, histories of King Philip's War by Benjamin Church and William Hubbard, the official report on the Praying Indians by Daniel Gookin, and the certificates and petitions filed after the war by the Indians and by the English on their behalf, many of which Gookin reprints in his history. What these records share is a concern with Indian performance—with Indians engaged in Indian, English, or quasi-Indian/quasi-English acts—and what they reveal is a gradual coming to terms with the way in which these acts did or did not measure up to the expectations enshrined in custom and the law. More specifically, we can see in the texts' manipulation of certain verbs—that part of speech traditionally reserved for the representation of action—the extent to which the Puritans struggled with Indian acts and ultimately, although by no means unanimously, came to identify their military accomplishments with common law agency. In the conversion narratives, where Indian performance is equated with Christian acts of piety, Indian action takes the form of a wish or aspiration and is expressed in an optative modality; in the histories, where Indian performance is associated with early but ultimately unsuccessful military contributions, Indian acts take the form of the hypothetical and are expressed in the subjunctive; and in the certificates, where Indian performance is finally regarded as militarily significant, Indian acts are presented as statements of fact and are expressed in the indicative mood. In these previously neglected certificates, in other words, the identities that had been lost through the Indians' banishment and then gained through their military service are for the first time juxtaposed, and the shift in the Natives' legal status becomes visible.

In beginning this decidedly alternative legal history with an examination of the status of the Indian within the conversion narratives translated and collected by John Eliot, I want to stress a connection between the Puritans' religious and legal narratives that compels us to go beyond the strictly legal documents—the court and probate records—that legal historians have mined in the past. Other than acknowledging that the Puritan commonwealth was indeed a church-state, not enough has been done to link legal and religious forms of discourse in early New England. And yet of all the subject positions occupied by the Indians before their banishment to Deer Island, the one that came closest to posing a challenge to the exclusivity of their territorial legal identities was that of the Christian or Praying Indian.[15] In adopting Christianity the Indians were also adopting a quasi-legal identity that was formed at the point where legal and religious discourse intersected. This intersection is evident both in the description of the Indian subjects in Eliot's reports and in the dualistic structure of those reports, written as they were not only for the Society for the Propagation of the Gospel, a religious body that facilitated conversion by disbursing funds for missionary purposes, but also for Parliament, a legal body that helped determine who among those not born in England might still be counted as English. It is not surprising that, divided between these two audiences, the rhetoric of the conversion narratives shows the Indians occupying an ambiguous place between two discourses—the legal and the religious—from which they emerge as agents yearning for the English God but never quite ready to receive him.

An example of such ambiguity can be found in Eliot's *Tears of Repentance* (1653) and in his *Late and Further Manifestation of the Progress of the Gospel amongst the Indians in New England* (1655), where the Indians often cast themselves as first sinning and then repenting in rapid succession.[16] One of the most dizzying of such confessions is Monequassun's in *Tears of Repentance*:

> When I first heard instruction, I believed not, but laughed at it, and scorned praying to God; afterward . . . I still hated praying, and I did think of running away . . . but after that I thought I would pray rightly to God, and cast away my sins; then I saw my hypocrisy, because I did ask some questions, but did not do that which I knew. . . . Then again a little my heart was turned after God . . . [and] then I thought that as yet, I do not repent, and believe in Christ; . . . and then I prayed to God . . . [and] after that again, I did a little break the Word of Christ.[17]

More circuitous than most, the "one step forward, two steps back" movement represented in this passage was nevertheless characteristic of a general trend in which the Indians' agency toward conversion is constructed as aspirational or preparative. Indeed, in his preface to *Tears of Repentance*, Richard Mather writes that "since the Word of God hath been taught and preached among them, the Spirit of the Lord hath been working thereby in the hearts of many of them such Illumination, such Conviction, & c. as may justly be looked at (*if not as a full and through Conversion, yet*) as an hopeful beginning and preparation thereto."[18] Intending to praise the Indians' progress toward conversion, Mather nevertheless draws our attention to their status as novices in that regard by distinguishing between the "full and through [*sic*] conversion" which is not yet theirs and "an hopeful beginning."

The Indians' special relationship to and affinity for prayer, above all other forms of religious instruction or practice, seems also to have contributed to their characterization by Mather and others as perpetual aspirants toward conversion and yet never in possession of it. "Their frequent phrase," Eliot writes, "of Praying to God, is not to be understood of that Ordinance and Duty of Prayer only, but of all Religion, and comprehendeth the same meaning, with them, as the word [Religion] doth with us."[19] Much has been written on what prayer might have meant to the Indians—Robert James Naeher speculates, for example, that the Indians made it the cornerstone of their Christianity because "it met, in a meaningful and emotionally satisfying way, deep human needs"—but there can be little doubt that while the Puritans prized prayer, they did not view it as sufficient for conversion.[20] In particular, learning how to read and to restate the lessons of the Bible correctly by listening to lengthy sermons on Bible passages was also key, but in this skill there is little evidence that the Indians excelled. In fact, the Indians' apparent inability to articulate the wisdom they had gleaned from prayer—even though that ability would itself have been insufficient—was almost certainly, from the

Puritan point of view, an additional stumbling block in their progress toward conversion. Of course while Eliot's efforts to record their confessions suggests that he, perhaps alone, had confidence in their ability to express themselves, he also reveals the limits of that confidence by asking them to restate their conversion experiences over and over again—a process that devalued their narratives as both literary and legal documents. For the English, the narrative structure of the conversion account spoke for itself: the English convert wrote or related personal experience in front of gathered church authorities and on that occasion the narrative was deemed sufficient or insufficient to the task of bearing witness to the individual's sanctification. The Indian convert, by contrast, who also spoke before church authorities, typically spoke on more than one occasion, largely because of being called back to repeat, clarify, or amend earlier statements. One subject heading in Eliot's *Tears* is representative of this syndrome: "The next," he writes, "are the Confessions of Nishohkou; who twice made preparitory Confessions."[21]

Though perhaps intended to display the Praying Indians in the best possible light, the frequent amendments of their conversion accounts not only contravened Puritan church policy but also violated the principles of Anglo-American law, whereby speech presented as testimony under oath was restricted to a single iteration. The existence of multiple confessions not only created uncertainty about the authenticity of any single statement but also reinforced the optative nature of the Indians' expression overall. Each confession in this light could only figure as an effort toward or wish for conversion rather than as conclusive evidence of it and thus made the possibility of thinking of the Indians as potential converts and potential common law actors even more remote. It remains only to be said that in urging the Indians to cut their hair, learn the English language, wear English clothes, and fence in their property, Eliot not only helped them prepare for conversion but also invited them into a cultural protocol that laid the groundwork for common law performance. There was, however, no chance that while being readied for conversion, the Indians' performance of Englishness, in the absence of religious conversion, would qualify them for common law membership, and thus they remained in a marginal place with respect to the English common law.

If the Praying Indian was introduced to but ultimately denied the status of common law agent, the same could not be said of the Praying-Indian-turned-soldier—the Shooting Indian, as it were. From their perch on Deer Island, Praying Indians were released individually or in small groups to serve as spies, scouts, guides, and soldiers and thus exercised their agency on behalf of the English in a central and highly visible manner.[22] To be sure, this was not the first time the English had turned to Indians in time of war: the Mohegans had joined forces with Connecticut to defeat the Pequots in 1637, and the use of Indians as guides in battle was not unknown. Yet in these cases the Indians were seen not as legal agents but as military allies who were judged according to the law of sovereign nations, not the common law. This point bears repeating, for it was to their status as sovereign nations that the Indians returned after their brief emergence into the common law during the Deer Island episode, proving only, as the history of their subsequent sequestration shows, that despite its name, this sovereign status was more easily manipulated by English and American common law actors.

For that brief Deer Island period, however, with their sovereign and territorial identities no longer intact, a number of new options for interpreting Indian actions presented themselves, and their status as common law actors was for the first time seen as a possibility. Among other things, in the absence of a dominant sovereign identity, the Praying Indians on Deer Island were given the freedom not only to take on the role of soldier, as the English understood it, but to pursue actions to their own desired ends. So consequential were the actions of the Indian soldiers for the war's outcome that they were recorded not in a quasi-legal form like that of the conversion narrative, but in the legally proximate form of history. A record of fact and of physical evidence prized by the law in general, historical narrative was especially privileged by the common law because history—the story of ancient customs—was, as Edward Coke and many other common lawyers conceived it, the foundation for the law. Even more to the point, the common law embodied the very logic of history in its procedural reliance on precedent: the adjudication of the facts of a case in the present based on a comparison with those of a case in the past.

That said, the histories ultimately proved even more resistant than the conversion narratives to the representation of the Indians as agents. With the exception of Gookin's *Doings and Sufferings*, they either skirt the issue of the Praying Indians' participation in the war—Nathaniel Saltonstall's "The Present State of New-England with Respect to the Indian War" (1675) and Increase Mather's *A Brief History of the Warr with the Indians in New-England* (1677) fall into this category—or acknowledge their presence only grudgingly—here William Hubbard's *Narrative of the Indian Wars in New England* (1677) and Benjamin Church's *Diary of King Philip's War, 1675–1676* (written some years after the war and first published in 1716) are exemplary. But in their grudging recognition these histories reveal their struggle to contain and delimit the representation of actions that were at the same time receiving a more favorable construction elsewhere, as we shall see. The effect of this struggle, though not exactly like the subjunctive Gookin deploys, raises questions about what might have happened under different circumstances or how the story might have been written if the events had been viewed through different eyes.

For both Church and Hubbard, the primary strategy for containing the importance of the Indians' actions revolves around distinguishing them from those of their English counterparts. For Hubbard, the actions of the English soldiers are nothing if not heroic; on one occasion they are described as offering "a resolute and valiant repulse," on another "a stout resistance." The Indian soldiers, by contrast, are typically described as "faithful"—a trait taken for granted among the English troops.[23] That Hubbard chooses faithfulness as a measure of the Indians' military service reinforces his sense that, while significant, their actions are not of the history-making kind. As such, even when he occasionally details the movements of the more noteworthy Indians, he does so in a way that emphasizes their native sagacity over their physical prowess: the Indians are depicted as engaged in "politic stratagems," including hiding behind trees, wearing moccasins instead of noisy boots, and blacking their faces to look more like the enemy. These acts lend the appearance not of courage—the word used to describe the English—but of cleverness, or what Hubbard in a phrase that damns with faint praise calls their "subtle service."[24]

Church follows Hubbard's lead in representing the Indians by recording their presence while devaluing their service, especially when compared to that of the English soldiers. The English, famously, had pursued Philip on their own for months, only to lose more men in ambushes than ever before, and it was only when they engaged Church, a captain of the forces of the United Colonies, and allowed him to put together a mixed company of Indians and Englishmen, that they began to make real progress. But while Church's military strategy suggests his high opinion of the Indians as soldiers, his narrative proves more a tribute to his own genius in deploying them than a celebration of their military skills. He begins his description of their service by dwelling at length on the controversy caused by his suggestion to use the Indians in the first place. "As for sending out Indians," he reports, "they thought it no ways advisable and, in short, none of his [Church's] advice practicable." Not long afterward, however, he notes that he was given power "to commission a company of 200 where the English do not exceed the number of 60."[25] To be sure, subsequent descriptions occasionally mention Indian military actions, but so fixed is Church on congratulating himself that he reduces the Indians under his command to mere products of his leadership. Indeed, Church appears by his own reckoning such a magnetic leader that unlike Hubbard, he attributes no particular ingenuity or subtlety to the Indians but praises them solely for doing his bidding.

In the central role it accords the Praying Indians as soldiers and agents, the history written by Daniel Gookin stands alone and, if only for its focus on the Indians as opposed to the English, signals that its treatment of the Indians' place in history will be more generous and capacious. Gookin writes: "Sundry persons have taken pains to write and publish historical narratives of the war, between the English and Indians in New England, but very little hath been hitherto declared (that I have seen) concerning the Christian Indians, who, in reality, may be judged to have no small share in the effects and consequences of his war."[26] The key phrase in this passage is "effects and consequences," for it suggests that Gookin, in stark contrast to his peers, intends not only to catalogue heroic feats performed by the Indians but to consider those feats as precedent setting. Gookin, who served as a Bay Colony magistrate from 1652 to 1676 and was superintendent of the Indians from 1661 to

1687—an official and legally recognized colonial post—not surprisingly writes of the Indians with a heightened appreciation for the legal ramifications of their "doings," as he dubs their actions during the war. In his emphasis on the precedent-setting nature of the Indians' actions, for example, Gookin often turns his attention to their outcome, stressing the specific ways in which these actions altered events. On one occasion he tells the story of how he secured the temporary release of two Praying Indians from Deer Island to "gain intelligence of the state of the enemy": "The two spies," he explains, not only "acquitted themselves in the service prudently" but provided vital information to the English: "the enemy purposed, within three weeks, to fall upon Lancaster . . . as this man declared."[27]

If Gookin displays a keen awareness of what it might have meant to acknowledge Indian soldiers as agents and to give them appropriate reward for their agency, however, the fact that he tells a story in which colonial prejudice against Indians still looms large dictated that his legal witness would remain a preliminary one. Giving voice to his frustration with the constraints imposed on the Indian soldiers, Gookin effects a substantive and stylistic shift roughly halfway through his history, substituting for a detailed inventory of the actions the Indians *actually* undertook a description of how much their actions *could have* meant had they been given a wider scope. On the general subject, for example, of keeping the Praying Indians in their own towns and using them as a kind of front line for the English, Gookin writes: "And *had* the suggestions and importunate solicitations of some persons, who had knowledge and experience of the fidelity and integrity of the praying Indians *been attended and practiced* in the beginning of the war, many and great mischiefs *might have been* according to reason prevented."[28] Gookin adopts the same subjunctive formulation in more specific circumstances as well. Speaking of the initial plan to keep the Indians in the field instead of disbanding them, he writes: "and *had their counsel been practised*, as I was credibly informed by some upon the place, he [king Philip] *had probably been taken*, and his distressed company at that time." On yet another occasion, he observes, "so that if the counsel of our Christian Indians *had been put in practice*, according to rational probability they had taken or slain Philip, and so retarded his motion that the rest *might have come up* with him and destroyed his party."[29]

Replete with these and similar expressions, the second half of *The Doings and Sufferings of the Christian Indians* reads like an extended exercise in the hypothetical, a fantasy of what would have happened had the circumstances of the war played out otherwise. In this sense, the second half of Gookin's history reinforces the injustice of English actions documented in the first half, not by continuing to attribute blame for them to the English but by imagining the outcome of the war's various moments differently. In constructing a hypothetical history, moreover, Gookin does not depart from a common law paradigm but works within it by attending to the importance of historical precedent and yet altering it just enough to reinsert acts that were in the past unfairly excluded from it. Certainly in adopting the subjunctive mode to tell his story, Gookin provides a way of working around the historically based language of the common law that would gain wide acceptance within a later race-based jurisprudence explicitly devoted to rectifying centuries of past wrongs. "The principle of rectification [for past wrongs]," explains Robert Nozick, "will make use of its best estimate of subjunctive information about what would have occurred . . . if the injustice had not taken place."[30]

Still, if through his use of the subjunctive Gookin opened up a rhetorical space for talking about the Indians as if they were history-making agents in King Philip's War, he, like his fellow historians, could not fully bring about the translation of that rhetoric into a common law context. Like the cases that finally overturned unjust precedents in the context of racial prejudice, that achievement would be left to the legal documents themselves, in particular the certificates he appends to his text, which move beyond the para-legal writing of history to encompass legal fact. Unlike his subjunctive narrative, these documents shift into the indicative mode not only to prove the Indians' bravery but to serve as passports to a widening sphere of agency for the Indians.

Though largely composed of language we might call boilerplate, the certificates can be classed into three types, revealing a range of common law commitment to Indian agency. The first type makes the weakest and most general claim on the Indians' behalf: that they were of good character and proved courageous and loyal in the war. An example can be found in the certificate by Major Thomas Savage:

> These do certify that I, Thomas Savage, of Boston, being commander of the English forces at Mount Hope, in the beginning of the war between the English and Indians, about July 1675, and afterward in March, 1676, at Menumesse and Hadley. In both which expeditions, some of the Christian Indians belonging to Natick, &c., were in the army; as at Mount Hope, were about forty men, and at Menumesse six men. I do testify, on their behalf, that they carried themselves well, and approved themselves courageous soldiers, and faithful to the English interest.
>
> Dated at Boston, the 20th day of December, 1677[31]

The generality of Savage's language is evident in his reference to the Indians as groups: "about forty men, and at Menumesse six men." Yet even here one notes important signs of the kinds of agential individuation on which the common law relied. In contrast to the histories, the groups formed by the Indians appear small and selective; they are placed at the scene of specific battles, and they are considered part of the "army," a measure of their acceptance by the English never seen before.

The individuation that begins to emerge in Savage's certificate grows more prominent in the second type of certificate, which ascribes to the Indians an even more visible agency. This type of certificate is exemplified by "Captain Samuel Hunting's Certificate about the Christian Indian Solider":

> These are to certify, that I, Samuel Hunting, of Charlestown, in New England being, by authority of the Governor and Council, appointed commander of the praying Indians living in the Massachusetts colony, in New England, in the war against the barbarous Indians. . . . The said company, with myself, served the country, in several expeditions, for about one year's time. In all which service, the said Indians behaved themselves courageously and faithfully to the English interest; and I conceive that the said company did kill and take prisoners above two hundred of the enemy, and lost but one man of ours; besides about one hundred persons they killed and took prisoners at other times, when I was not with them, and they went out volunteers. And, in testimony of the truth hereof, I have hereunto set my hand, this 13th day of December, 1677.[32]

Several features of Hunting's certificate are noteworthy. He refers to the Indians not only as being in the army but as constituting a company of soldiers unto themselves, and he ascribes to them certain memorable feats, including the taking of prisoners. He also notes that unlike the English soldiers who were paid for their military service, the Indians served as volunteers, which underscored the need to compensate them after the war. Finally, Hunting remarks that the Indians acted on their own; though he commanded them, there were times, he notes, when they acted "when I was not with them."

The third type of certificate is perhaps the most interesting in that it acknowledges the transition of the Praying Indians from banished Indians to soldiers, offering direct evidence that during the war and in the postwar period the Indians assumed an entirely new legal identity. "Captain Daniel Henchman's Certificate concerning the Praying Indian Soldiers" is of this type:

> These may certify, that I, Daniel Henchman, of Boston, being appointed and authorized by the Governor and Council of Massachusetts, not only to look unto and order the praying Indians, for some part of the time that they were confined to Deer Island; but, likewise, to have the command of several of them as soldiers, both at Mount Hope, in the beginning of the war, 1675; and also in another expedition, May and June, 1676, when I had the command of the English forces at Weshakum, Mendon, and Hadley; in all which time I had experience of the sobriety, courage, and fidelity of the generality of those Indians. And this I do testify, under my hand, and could say much more on their behalf, if time and opportunity permitted. Dated at Boston, this 29th of November, 1677.[33]

Here Henchman indicates that he had two different relationships with the Indians. In the first, before their release from Deer Island, they appeared to be little different from children under his supervision. In the second, however, they transformed themselves into soldiers under his command, capable of performing new actions and, in the process, of taking on new agential roles. By including both types of relationships, Henchman at once signals and certifies the emergence of the Indians' new legal identity.

Although each of these three types of certificates suggests a slightly different and still tentative approach to the Indians' entrance into the common law, together they represent a clear effort to elevate the Indians' actions during the war into a basis for legal compensation, the ultimate sign of incorporation by the common law. When carried by the Indians outside their towns, these certificates guaranteed the "life and liberty" that had previously been promised to the Praying Indians but rarely realized. Of course, there were still instances in which the certificates were ignored by English authorities, but for the most part they were honored. More significantly, these certificates paved the way for the Praying Indians to assert a legal voice of their own: emboldened by these English authored documents, the Indians commenced a petition-writing campaign to request leniency for kin still being held as prisoners by enemy Indians.[34] Worth noting, moreover, is that in these Indian-authored petitions the Indian veterans did not beg for mercy, which was then as now an extralegal measure with little to no value as precedent, but rather asked that the precedent for recognizing and rewarding military service set by the common law be followed in their case as it was in the case of the English.[35] Here again we see the importance of the pairing of the Indians' banishment with their military roles in facilitating their transition to common law status.

Finally, and perhaps most significantly, both Indian- and English-authored certificates changed the status of the Indian within English common law by enabling the Indians to participate in the judicial system in ways that embraced issues beyond those of personal liberty and that extended beyond the immediate postwar period. Jean O'Brien, for example, makes the point that many Indians who had served the English as soldiers were able to parlay their military service into protection against fraudulent land deals. "Having approved our selves faithfull to ye English interest," reads one such petition, "In ye Late Warr, and joined them most of us As Souldiers . . . we Doe hereby Declare to the hond [*sic*] Court yt wee or pdeceser had & have a Naturall Right to Most of the Lands

Lying in the Nipmuck Country . . . for which we Desire the Country & Genll Court will give us a Compensation."[36] For years after King Philip's War, through King William's War and Queen Anne's War, Indians were frequently employed as soldiers and were recognized legally for that service by means of monetary payments, titles to land, job opportunities, and greater freedoms. Traditionally a refuge for the rootless, the military had proved once again to be a fertile place for identity transformation.

Still, it must be noted that while their military involvement afforded them a new legal status under the common law, it also led to devastating losses. Several reports from the eighteenth century that document the drastic reduction in Indian populations in the colonies specifically point to the Indians' service in the century's wars as the principal culprit.[37] If the movement of the Indians into the category of common law performance was an achievement in one sense, it was a failure in others, as it led not only to loss of life but to mounting prejudice against them. For just as the deterioration of their territorial and sovereign identities had prompted colonial authorities to acknowledge the Indians in terms of a new identity, this new identity—of common law performer—figured in the creation of a still newer, racial designation that, as history has shown, worked to diminish Indian stature and rights. As Pulsipher notes, "by the beginning of the eighteenth century, popular animus against the Indians was finally matched by legislation that codified divisions between English and Indians along race lines."[38] If the common law designation of Indian acts and identities became possible only in the absence of earlier designations based on territory and sovereignty, in other words, it may be that these racial designations became possible only in the presence of the common law categories as the legal authorities searched for yet another way of making the Indian "other" again.

Because it was in the performance of their racial identities that questions about Indian authenticity typically arose, this racialized identity has dominated Performance Studies, including legal Performance Studies, of the Indians since the eighteenth century. In turn, such a focus has led scholars to emphasize the appropriation of Indian identity by the colonists and the new nation. But as the Deer Island banishment and its textual ramifications show, in the period leading up to and immediately following King Philip's War, before the law had carved out a racialized place for the Indian, the question was not whether whites were playing Indian but whether the Indians were playing—or players—at all. The question, in short, was the far more basic one of whether Indian acts, like those of their English counterparts, could be seen as customary and thus be written into law, not by way of the quasi-legal optative or subjunctive moods but in the indicative of a shared Indian and English legal reality.

Notes

1. Shurtleff, *Records*, 5:57. On the Deer Island banishment see Drake, *King Philip's War*, 87–88; Kawashima, *Igniting King Philip's War*, 146; Lepore, *Name of War*, 138–45; O'Brien, *Dispossession by Degrees*, 61–62, 67–68; and Pulsipher, *Subjects*, 143–47.
2. See, for example, Axtell, "Some Thoughts on the Ethnohistory of Missions"; Bross, *Dry Bones and Indian Sermons*, 21–28; White, "The Praying Indians' Speeches as Texts of Massachusetts Oral Culture"; and Wyss, *Writing Indians*, 19–21.
3. Ronda, "'We Are Well,'" 67.
4. See Bellin, "John Eliot"; Rivett, "Empirical Desire"; Ronda, "'We Are Well'"; Mandell, "'Christian English Neighbors'"; Pulsipher, *Subjects*, 136–37.
5. Plane, "Legitimacies," 56–57. On the Indians' highly developed legal and political systems, see Bragdon, *Native People*, 14–155; and O'Brien, *Dispossession by Degrees*, 19–21. On Indian status in colonial law as landowners, see Leavenworth, "'Best Title'"; Springer, "Indians and the Law"; and Banner, *How the Indians Lost*

Their Land, 10–48. Additional studies include Kawashima, "Legal Origins," which examines the legal basis of the reservation system; and Bragdon, "Crime and Punishment," which discusses the Indians' status in criminal law cases.

6. Pocock, *Politics*, 209.
7. White, "'Although I am dead,'" 410.
8. In the common law, "custom" embraced a vast range of everyday practices, including but not limited to the way people tended their crops, grazed their cattle, passed estates through families, or sold their wares. The common law thus presented itself as an impregnable, never-ending feedback loop at the center of which was a vision of the law as an historical constant, where the acts of persons in the past were binding on and yet subject to alteration by people in the present. "The act of a public society of men done five hundred years since," wrote Richard Hooker, one of the fathers of the common law, "standeth as theirs who presently are of the same societies, because corporations are immortal; we were then alive in our predecessors, and they in their successors do live" (*Laws*, 93). See Karsten, *Between Law and Custom*, and Kelley, *Human Measure*, 168–74, for illuminating discussions of custom in culture and law. See also Peters, "Legal Performance," for a working definition of performativity in the law.
9. Carlson, *Performance*, 5.
10. Using Englishness as a basis for denying the Indians status as common law agents may come as a surprise to those who recall the European debates about whether the Indians could be considered human in the first place. But this question had for the most part been decided in the Indians' favor, so the authorities who sought to exclude them from the legal arena had to look elsewhere, at which point nationality presented itself.
11. Pocock, *Machiavellian Moment*, 341.
12. For previous scholarly references to the Deer Island banishment, see the texts cited in endnote 1 as well as Banner, *How the Indians Lost Their Land*, 191.
13. The singularity of the Deer Island banishment is reinforced by the history of the events that immediately preceded it. These included numerous failed efforts to dispose of the Indians from the praying towns in response to outbreaks of extraordinary hostility on the part of English soldiers and inhabitants of towns nearby. Most of these initial efforts failed because the accommodations that were chosen to

sequester the Indians, usually townhouses or private homes, were too small or too vulnerable to mob violence and authorities feared the Indians would be killed. Deer Island was unique in being both large enough and sufficiently remote to contain all the Christian Indians from Natick as well as many from the other praying towns. See Bodge, *Soldiers in King Philip's War*, 397.

14. Needless to say the hostile Indians, who included all the Indians fighting against the English in King Philip's War, were not implicated in this deterritorialization. They thus remained associated with their land but in a way that provoked their ultimate annihilation.
15. The Praying Indians of Natick were examined three times from 1652 to 1659; only in 1660 did the Puritan elders finally sanction full communion, and then only for eight confessors. Nor did these eight ever achieve the status English Christians enjoyed. See O'Brien, *Dispossession by Degrees*, 51.
16. Rivett accounts differently for such hesitation, reading it as evidence of the effort on the part of Eliot and others to bring out the atavistic or primitive nature of the Indians' conversion. But even in her account, these repeat performances suggest the insufficiency of the Indians' conversion. See Rivett, "Empirical Desire," 41.
17. Eliot, *Tears of Repentance*, 13.
18. Eliot, *Tears of Repentance*, C, my emphasis.
19. Eliot, *Tears of Repentance*, B2.
20. Naeher, "Dialogue in the Wilderness," 367.
21. Eliot, *Tears of Repentance*, 33.
22. The historical status of the military also facilitated the transition of the Indian into common law agency. At the heart of the common law but simultaneously an alternative to it, the military was often a place for the rootless to establish themselves. At the same time, the early colonial militia—the body of civilian volunteers from which the fighting army was gathered—represented a strangely democratic institution in a society where democracy did not reign. On the colonial militia, see Ansell, "Legal and Historical Aspects"; L. Breen, "Religious Radicalism"; T. Breen, "English Origins"; Shy, "New Look"; and Zelner, "Essex County." For a theory of the democratic militia, see especially Sharp, "Leadership and Democracy."
23. Hubbard, *Narrative*, 117, 170, 185.
24. These stories can be found in Hubbard, *Narrative*, 152–54. Very occasionally Hubbard mixes praise for the Indians' faithfulness with brief mention of their courage. For example, he writes, "It is worth

the noting what faithfulness and courage some of the Christian Indians, with the said Captain Pierce shewed in the fight" (152). At such moments, however, he is careful to qualify the Indians' courage: "many of them have proved not only faithful, but very serviceable and helpful to the English; they usually proving good seconds, though they have not ordinarily confidence enough to make the first onset" (155).

25. Church, *Diary*, 128.
26. Gookin, *Historical Account*, 55.
27. Gookin, *Historical Account*, 486, 488.
28. Gookin, *Historical Account*, 436, my emphasis. Though several witnesses perceived the injustice of sending the Indians to Deer Island, Gookin alone complained about the continued injustice of sending those who had performed valiantly in battle back to their prison after they returned from the field.
29. Gookin, *Historical Account*, 445, 447, my emphasis.
30. See Nozick, *Anarchy*, 152–53. See also Best, *The Fugitive's Properties*, 221–24, for how this kind of language plays out in the context of landmark Supreme Court race cases of the twentieth century.
31. Gookin, *Historical Account*, 524.
32. Gookin, *Historical Account*, 525.
33. Gookin, *Historical Account*, 524.
34. This is not to say that these petitions were always successful. Several of the Indians who fought in the war on the side of the English petitioned to save loved ones, but the council often rejected those pleas. See Gookin, *Historical Account*, 528.
35. See the records at the end of Bodge, *Soldiers in King Philip's War*, 484–86, for English soldiers invoking such precedents well into the eighteenth century.
36. Quoted in O'Brien, *Dispossession by Degrees*, 66.
37. Mandell presents the devastating tally of dead, wounded, and diseased Indians as a result of their military service in "'Christian English Neighbors.'"
38. Pulsipher, "'Our Sages,'" 441.

Works Cited

Ansell, S. T. "Legal and Historical Aspects of the Militia." *Yale Law Journal* 26 (1917): 471–80.

Axtell, James. "Some Thoughts on the Ethnohistory of Missions." *Ethnohistory* 29 (1982): 35–41.

Banner, Stuart. *How the Indians Lost Their Land*. Cambridge: Harvard University Press, 2007.

Bellin, Joshua David. "John Eliot's Playing Indian." *Early American Literature* 42 (2007): 1–30.

Best, Stephen. *The Fugitive's Properties*. Chicago: University of Chicago Press, 2004.

Bodge, George Madison. *Soldiers in King Philip's War*. Baltimore: Genealogical Publishing, 1976.

Bragdon, Kathleen. "Crime and Punishment among the Indians of Massachusetts." *Ethnohistory* 28 (1981): 23–32.

———. *Native People of Southern New England*. Norman: University of Oklahoma Press, 1999.

Breen, Louise. "Religious Radicalism in the Puritan Officer Corps: Heterodoxy, the Artillery Company, and Cultural Integration in Seventeenth-Century Boston." *New England Quarterly* 68 (1995): 3–43.

Breen, T. H. "English Origins and New World Development: The Case of the Covenanted Militia in Seventeenth-Century Massachusetts." *Past and Present* 57 (1972): 74–96.

Bross, Kristina. *Dry Bones and Indian Sermons: Praying Indians in Colonial America*. Ithaca: Cornell University Press, 2004.

Carlson, Marvin. *Performance: A Critical Introduction*. London: Routledge, 1996.

Church, Benjamin. *Diary of King Philip's War, 1675–76*. 1716. Chester CT: Pequot, 1975.

Drake, James D. *King Philip's War: Civil War in New England, 1675–1676*. Amherst: University of Massachusetts Press, 1999.

Eliot, John. *Tears of Repentance or a Further Narrative of the Progress of the Gospel amongst the Indians in New England*. 1653; Whitefish MT: Kessinger Reprint, 2003.

Gookin, Daniel. *Historical Account of the Doings and Sufferings of the Christian Indians* in *New England in the Years 1675–1677*. 1836; Whitefish MT: Kessinger Reprint, 2003.

Hooker, Richard. *Of the Laws of Ecclesiastical Polity*. Cambridge: Cambridge University Press, 1989.

Hubbard, William. *A Narrative of the Indian Wars in New England 1814*. 1814; Whitefish MT: Kessinger Reprint, 2005.

Jennings, Francis. *The Invasion of America*. New York: Norton, 1976.

Karsten, Peter. *Between Law and Custom*. Cambridge: Cambridge University Press, 2008.

Kawashima, Yasuhide. *Igniting King Philip's War: The John Sassamon Murder Trial*. Lawrence: University Press of Kansas, 2001.

———. "Legal Origins of the Indian Reservation in Colonial Massachusetts." *American Journal of Legal History* 13 (1969): 42–56.
———. *Puritan Justice and the Indian*. Middletown CT: Wesleyan University Press, 1986.
Kelley, Donald. *The Human Measure*. Cambridge: Harvard University Press, 1990.
Leavenworth, Peter S. "'The Best Title that Indians Can Claime.'" *New England Quarterly* 72 (1999): 275–300.
Lepore, Jill. *The Name of War: King Philip's War and the Origins of American Identity*. New York: Knopf, 1998.
Mandell, Daniel. "'To Live More Like My Christian English Neighbors.'" *William and Mary Quarterly* 3rd ser. 48 (1991): 552–79.
Mather, Increase. *A Brief History of the War with the Indians in New-England*. Reprinted in *So Dreadfull a Judgment: Puritan Responses to King Philip's War, 1676–1677*, ed. Richard Slotkin and James K. Folsom. Middletown CT: Wesleyan University Press, 1978.
Naeher, Robert James. "Dialogue in the Wilderness: John Eliot and the Indian Exploration of Puritanism as a Source of Meaning, Comfort, and Ethnic Survival." *New England Quarterly* 62 (1989): 346–68.
Nozick, Robert. *Anarchy, State, and Utopia*. New York: Basic, 1974.
O'Brien, Jean. *Dispossession by Degrees: Indian Land and Identity in Natick, Massachusetts, 1650–1790*. Cambridge: Cambridge University Press, 1997.
Peters, Julie Stone. "Legal Performance Good and Bad." *Law, Culture and the Humanities* 4 (2008): 179–200.
Plane, Ann Marie. "Legitimacies, Indian Identities, and the Law: The Politics of Sex and the Creation of History in Colonial New England." *Law and Social Inquiry* 23 (1998): 55–77.
Pocock, J. G. A. *The Machiavellian Moment*. Princeton: Princeton University Press, 2003.
———. *Politics, Language, and Time: Essays on Political Thought and History*. Chicago: University of Chicago Press, 1989.
Pulsipher, Jenny Hale. "'Our Sages are Sageles'": A Letter on Massachusetts Indian Policy after King Philip's War." *William and Mary Quarterly* 3rd ser. 58 (2001): 431–48.
———. *Subjects unto the Same King: Indians, English, and the Contest for Authority in Colonial New England*. Philadelphia: University of Pennsylvania Press, 2005.
Rivett, Sarah. "Empirical Desire: Conversion, Ethnography, and the New Science of the Praying Indian." *Early American Studies* (2006): 16–45.

Ronda, James. "'We Are Well as We Are': An Indian Critique of Seventeenth-Century Christian Missions." *William and Mary Quarterly* 3rd ser. 34 (1977): 66–82.

Saltonstall, Nathaniel. "The Present State of New-England with Respect to the Indian War." In *Narratives of the Indian Wars, 1675–1699*, ed. Charles H. Lincoln, 24–50. New York: Barnes and Noble, 1914.

Sharp, Morrison. "Leadership and Democracy in the Early New England System of Defense." *American Historical Review* 50 (1945): 244–60.

Shurtleff, Nathaniel B., ed. *Records of the Governor and Company of the Massachusetts Bay in New England, 1674–1686*. 5 vols. Boston: William White, 1854.

Shy, John W. "A New Look at Colonial Militia." *William and Mary Quarterly* 3rd ser. 20 (1963): 175–85.

Slotkin, Richard. *Regeneration through Violence: The Mythology of the American Frontier, 1600–1860*. Norman: University of Oklahoma Press, 2000.

Springer, James. "American Indians and the Law of Real Property in Colonial New England." *American Journal of Legal History* 30 (1986): 25–40.

White, Craig. "The Praying Indians' Speeches as Texts of Massachusett Oral Culture." *Early American Literature* 38 (2003): 437–67.

White, Richard. "'Although I am dead, I am not entirely dead. I have left a second of myself': Constructing Self and Persons on the Middle Ground of Early America." In *Through a Glass Darkly: Reflections on Personal Identity in Early America*, ed. Ronald Hoffman, Mechal Sobel, and Fredrika Teute, 404–18. Chapel Hill: University of North Carolina Press, 1997.

Wyss, Hilary E. *Writing Indians: Literacy, Christianity, and Native Community in Early America*. Amherst: University of Massachusetts Press, 2000.

Zelner, Kyle. "Essex County's Two Militias." *New England Quarterly* 72 (1999): 577–93.

[3]

Native Performances of Diplomacy and Religion in Early New France

John H. Pollack

When François Gravé Du Pont came ashore near Tadoussac on May 27, 1603, accompanied by Samuel de Champlain, a small group of sailors, and two Innu men returning to their homeland after a year in France, they found themselves invited to a party that had already started.[1] Assembled on the banks of the St. Lawrence River were perhaps one thousand people from three Native groups: Innu (Montagnais), Algonquin (Anishinabek), and Maliseet (Etchemin).[2] This meeting has been interpreted in many ways: as feast, victory celebration, cultural encounter, political alliance, and as an origin point for "New France." It has a central place in most narratives of early Canada, although only traces of the episode remain in the written record.

In this essay I focus on the major documentary source describing the event, *Des Sauvages, ou, Voyage de Samuel Champlain*, first printed in Paris in late 1603.[3] A significant portion of *Des Sauvages*, a brief (72-page) text, centers upon Champlain's description of a *tabagie*, a complex political, diplomatic, and religious ritual held at Tadoussac by the allied tribes. A number of historians have argued that French attendance at the *tabagie* had vital implications for French colonial ambitions, in that it marked the beginnings of an Innu-Franco entente or alliance that allowed the French access to the fur trade at Tadoussac. The Native performances that make up the *tabagie*, I argue, construct the alliance itself. In turn, modern readings of these performances, and of Champlain's interpretation of them, shape our understandings of their political significance (or insignificance); these readings even have implications for contemporary legal claims to Native sovereignty.

Des Sauvages also makes clear that agreements between French and Native groups for trade, or for military cooperation against mutual enemies, were forged through a process of cultural and religious dialogue and debate, involving speeches and exchanges of stories. In the third chapter Champlain presents a religious discussion he has held with one Native leader, perhaps the Innu sagamore Anadabijou, in which the sagamore explains his people's beliefs through a series of vivid stories, while the Frenchman responds with Christian tales. The extended storytelling, unusual in the literature of colonial North America, represents a public performance, as much for the French as for any Native audience, which helps to shape a colonial alliance.

Stable Innu-French relations may have depended upon these Native performances and the French willingness to be spectators at them. To be sure, the stories presented in *Des Sauvages* may have been misheard, mistranslated, or even fabricated to make Native inhabitants appear as willing partners or even as potential Christian converts. Yet manipulated or not, these narratives do reveal a crucial aspect of early Euro-Native relations in the St. Lawrence Valley: the vital importance for the French of listening to the Native populations whose cooperation their colonial projects required. This essay contends that the work of treaty and alliance formation and the work of performative storytelling cannot be separated. Our interpretive challenge is to try to resituate these stories, not only within larger Native traditions of oral performance but also as focused, precisely directed, historically specific events.

The stories Champlain and Anadabijou shared also found their way into other European texts: in varied form they were told and retold, suggesting the cultural value of storytelling for peoples on both sides of the Atlantic. Native performances, that is, shaped political alliances and left crucial traces in French texts. I suggest that we can grasp some of the impact of this storytelling performance by seeing the stories reemerge, albeit in altered forms, in later French accounts. These performances and exchanges of stories were central to early New France as the French, the Innus, the Algonquins, the Maliseets, and other Native groups created it, just as our readings of them are central to the stories we ourselves tell about Canada's colonial history.

After a brief first chapter describing the French ships' voyage from Honfleur to the mouth of the St. Lawrence, Champlain turns in the second chapter of *Des Sauvages* to the "good reception" given the French by the "grand Sagamore of the Savages of Canada" after they landed near Tadoussac.[4] The Innus, within whose territory Tadoussac lay, were central figures in a large and growing fur trade, with the summer gathering site at Tadoussac their most important trading point, and it is possible that the "one thousand" Natives Champlain observes had gathered precisely because they knew French traders would be arriving to meet them.[5]

Proceeding to the "lodge of their grand Sagamore, named Anadabijou," the French and the two Innus with them found between "80 and 100" Innus "making *Tabagie* (that is to say, a feast)."[6] Little is known about Anadabijou, the leader on whom Champlain focuses his attention at this moment, but he seems to have occupied an important place in the region before his death in 1611.[7] Champlain provides details of the Innus' tabagie, describing the meats they cook and the accompanying dances, and he writes that the event celebrates a victorious attack upon the Iroquois, during which members of "three Nations," the allied Innus, Algonquins, and Maliseets, had surprised, killed, and taken the scalps of about one hundred Iroquois.[8]

The French arrival turns the Innu victory tabagie from a tribal celebration into an intercultural diplomatic meeting, one that offers tantalizing, if frustratingly limited, insights into the French colonial project and the Innus' views of it. As Camil Girard and Edith Gagné have pointed out, historians seeking to determine what occurred during the tabagie have offered a range of interpretations, based mainly on a brief passage in the second chapter of the text.[9] In the lodge of Anadabijou the two returning Innus recount the good treatment they received in France and the desire of King Henry IV to people their land and support them in their battles against Iroquois enemies.[10] According to Champlain, the "grand Sagamore" [*grand Sagamo*], having listened carefully, then shares tobacco with Gravé Du Pont, Champlain, and "certain other Sagamores," likely the Algonquins and Maliseets:

> After smoking some time, he began to address the whole gathering, speaking with gravity, pausing sometimes a little, and then resuming his speech, saying to them, that in truth they ought to be very glad to have His Majesty for their great friend. They all answered with one voice, *Ho, ho, ho,* which is to say, *yes, yes.* Continuing his speech, he said that he was well content that His said Majesty should people their country, and make war on their enemies, and that there was no nation in the world to which they

> wished more good than to the French. Finally, he gave them all to understand the advantage and profit they might receive from His said Majesty.[11]

Readers familiar with European writings on early colonial America may evaluate this passage with a certain suspicion. Champlain neatly transcribes Anadabijou's pronouncements—although what the sagamore actually said must have been mediated by one or more translators, whose words were then in turn modified and summarized by Champlain. The moment represents what Eric Cheyfitz has labeled a "fiction of translation," in which language barriers and cultural differences seem almost to disappear in the service of apparent cross-cultural comprehension.[12]

Here, though, I would like to stress the performative nature of the scene. While we should acknowledge that Champlain and others involved in producing the printed text *Des Sauvages*—scribes, readers, editors, printers—modified and altered Native words and speeches, we may also see in this passage a representation, albeit an imperfect one, of Native performances that occurred along the St. Lawrence in the year 1603, witnessed by the French. Anadabijou's words, addressed to the Innus, the other Native leaders present, and the French, are clearly a kind of ritualized public speech, which proceeds deliberately, with careful pauses for the assent of listeners. The Innus and other northeastern groups, according to numerous sources, had developed what James Axtell has called "intensely oral cultures," in which Native leaders were obliged to persuade rather than coerce other tribal members, using their rhetorical skills, in order to obtain their consent for collective actions.[13] In order to be comprehensible, performances like Anadabijou's also required an audience's interpretation. For the Innus and other Natives present, presumably, moments like this were familiar, if nonetheless significant, occurrences, whereas for a French arrival like Champlain, what was happening in front of him would have been entirely new. Yet Anadabijou's performance must remain joined with Champlain's interpretation of it—that is, we cannot really *hear* Anadabijou without *reading* Champlain.

Most modern historians of New France have paid a good deal of attention to the episode: indeed, stories of the early years of the colony have depended to a great extent upon readings of Champlain's words here, and hence upon interpretations of Anadabijou's performance. But stories differ, sometimes radically. Some historians have argued that at this moment the Native groups present reached an accord among themselves, allowing the French to explore the interior and to establish commercial relationships in support of the fur trade.[14] Bruce Trigger, for example, sees in this encounter an Innu attempt to leverage French support in order to broaden their anti-Iroquois alliance and solidify their control of the fur trade.[15]

For others, this scene is of greater transatlantic significance and marks an agreement or treaty establishing an alliance between the French and these Native groups. Olive Patricia Dickason concludes that the Innus granted the French permission to establish trade relations in Innu-controlled territories and engaged their assistance against Innu enemies in exchange for trading privileges: she labels the agreement "a pact of friendship . . . which allowed the French to establish on Montagnais territory but which did not involve land title."[16] Dickason notes, too, the centrality of rhetorical acts for the alliance's formation: Champlain, she writes, was "entering into an alliance according to Amerindian ritual—by which, in effect, the council was the treaty."[17]

Dickason's word *treaty* suggests an accord fully understood by and binding on both parties, although this was clearly no written treaty in Western terms. Following Dickason, other historians have been even more expansive in their readings of the episode's significance. Alain Beaulieu calls the 1603 encounter a "fundamental moment" in which was concluded an alliance "decisive in the history of New France." According to Beaulieu, "it is likely that both parties saw it as a way to strengthen their ties": "it is obvious," he writes, "that Chief Anadabijou accepted Henry IV's proposal for an alliance, that he gave the French permission to populate the country, and that he hoped to see benefits—no doubt on the trade and military fronts—from their settlement in the region."[18] David Hackett Fisher argues that the tone of the discussions between Native and French leaders was marked by "dignity, forbearance, and respect." He recreates the scene in vivid (if not fully documented) detail—"billowing clouds of white smoke rising above the lodges, a swirl of color and movement in the camp, crowds of young braves and beautifully dressed Indian maidens," and Iroquois captives, bound and tortured. He also follows Beaulieu in seeing the meeting as "the beginning of an alliance between the founders of New France and three Indian nations," one that offered the Natives "a potential ally against their mortal enemies" and the French "support for settlement, exploration, and trade." The discussions between Champlain and Anadabijou marked "the beginning of a relationship that was unique in the long history of European colonization in America," and their cooperation epitomizes a "spirit" that needs to be recalled and even rebuilt.[19]

To assert that Anadabijou's performance creates an alliance with the French that would develop into a long-term partnership is to suggest that these Native peoples not only tolerated but even solicited French colonization. Girard and Gagné note that arguments over the 1603 meeting and the existence of this "first intercultural alliance," and thus over

Anadabijou's performance, have had important ramifications for contemporary legal and political debates over indigenous rights: at stake are whether Native communities gave permission to European arrivals for use and settlement of territory and the status accorded by the French in the early colonial period to First Nations who are still attempting to prove claims to sovereignty.[20]

Although many Western-trained historians have interpreted the Innu performance as a grant of favorable conditions to the French arrivals, it is possible to tell an entirely different story about the May 1603 meeting. Anthropologist Sylvie Vincent has attempted to look at Innu versions of the event, focusing not on Anadabijou's words or the Innu ceremonies but upon modern Innus' own accounts of what transpired.[21] Not surprisingly, Innu versions differ sharply from those I have just summarized: in these, no territory was offered to the French after their arrival, except perhaps a small area of land near Québec, and even that was ceded only reluctantly, in exchange for French economic, not military, assistance.[22]

To Vincent, the existence of differing interpretations of this event suggests that history-telling itself is radically divergent from Native and European points of view: "the fact that Innu history and Western history do not share the same concerns or instruments entails that they create different universes." Attempting to synthesize the various accounts would thus result in the loss of the most essential characteristics of the Native version, "depriving it of its contradictions, its luxuriance, its apparent uncertainties, the questions it provides answers to, its modes of explanation, its symbols—in short, its very nature and, with this, its meaning."[23] Writing of another early encounter, that between Crees and English on Hudson's Bay in 1611, Toby Morantz comes to a similar conclusion: to attempt a synthetic history, one that combines "rich archival documentation" with an "even more extensive and richer oral tradition," she argues, "distort[s] and destroy[s] the depiction of the relationships, the symbolism, the patterning, and the integrity" of the oral tradition."[24] To Vincent and Morantz, European and Native stories must remain separate lest the former, whether in histories, textbooks, or legal decisions, completely subsume the latter.

If, however, Vincent and Morantz remind us that we must be extremely careful when telling stories about moments like 1603, we ought not to take their warnings as an excuse to ignore Natives' words altogether, even if we "hear" them only when reading a European printed book or manuscript. One reason that we must not ignore Native words and performances here is that Champlain and the French themselves could not afford to do so. Historian Patricia Seed has suggested that moments like these were "theatrical rituals of French political possession," but it might be better to say that during this episode, it is Anadabijou and the Innu, not the French, who dramatize their power and influence.[25] The few French sailors under Gravé Du Pont were at best junior partners in the victory celebration at Tadoussac, visitors eager to negotiate but in no position to dictate any terms. I would suggest, therefore, that Champlain's inclusion of Anadabijou's words shows how vital it was for the French to listen to the Native populations of eastern North America upon whom their colonial ambitions depended. Any apparent cultural openness in Champlain's text results not from some innate French sympathy for Native cultures but instead from the French recognition that they *must* heed Native discourse, and attend to Native performances, if they are to maintain their place in Canada.

My argument here is in part similar to the one Myra Jehlen deploys in her important essay on John Smith and Powhatan.

Jehlen reasons that Smith writes from a position of "uncertainty" as to the eventual outcome of Anglo-Indian encounters in Virginia. Smith's text is as much "report" as "interpretation" and may even include materials that contradict English views, such as Powhatan's critiques of the English colonizers.[26] Champlain, like Smith, writes from a position of colonial "uncertainty": in 1603 it was entirely unclear whether the exploration, settlement, and trade advocated in *Des Sauvages* would receive support from the French Crown. Equally in doubt was whether any of these activities would be tolerated by the Native peoples who controlled access to the inner St. Lawrence Valley.

The next scene of *Des Sauvages* reveals that within this context of collaboration and competition, wariness and uncertainty, space may be open for an exchange of stories—narratives shared by two groups, or exchanged between a Native leader and a French explorer, each listening to the other with a mix of interest, eagerness, puzzlement, and incomprehension. Champlain reports that on May 28, 1603, the Innus moved their camp to be nearer their other allies and the French at Tadoussac, and the third chapter of *Des Sauvages* begins on June 9, when the tabagie resumes. After describing a dance in which Algonquin women move around a collection of enemy heads, Champlain quotes the Algonquin sagamore he calls Besouat, usually called Tessouat by historians, who tells his Innu and Maliseet allies that this is the manner in which his people celebrate a war victory.[27] The Innus and Maliseets perform their own dances in return, and the allies exchange knives, kettles, meat, and other items.

Champlain's narrative then takes a brief general turn, akin to accounts of New World manners and customs common in earlier, if usually far more substantial, European texts. He writes of the "very cheerful disposition" of the Natives and of elders' deliberate rhetorical skill, marked by careful pauses, when speaking during formal ceremonies. He also describes the intense privation that nomadic existence can bring on during particularly cold winters. The Innus, he writes, could "learn very well" how to till the land since many of them have sound judgment.[28] Yet they are, on the whole, a people "without law," Champlain says, "as far as I could see and learn from the said grand Sagamore."[29] The "law" to which Champlain refers is not civil ordinance but Christian revelation, the "law of grace." The comment suggests that Champlain may be seeking traces of such "law," signs that the Innus would be receptive to the Christian message. What follows is a remarkable discussion between himself and the sagamore, an exchange of questions and stories concerning the creation of the world and the beliefs of Native peoples and European Christians. There are three Native tales included in this chapter, to which Champlain responds with Christian accounts. Each merits quotation in full.

The discussion begins with Champlain's statement that these Natives do believe in "a God, who has made all things." This provokes his opening question to the sagamore: since they believe in one and only one God, how, Champlain asks, did this God create the world?

> He answered me, that after God had made all things, He took a number of arrows, and stuck them in the ground, whence He drew men and women, which have multiplied in the world up to the present, and had their origin in this fashion. I replied to him, that what he said was false; but that in truth there was but one God, who had created all things on earth, and in the heavens. Seeing all these things so perfect, without anybody to govern this world beneath, He took the slime out of the earth, and of it created Adam, our first father. While Adam slept, God took a rib of the said Adam, and out of it formed Eve, whom He gave him

for his companion; and that it was the truth that they and we had our origin after this manner, and not from arrows as was their belief. He replied nothing, save that he approved rather what I said, than that which he told me.[30]

Champlain's words seem to dominate this section of the text, his summary of biblical creation taking up far more space than the sagamore's version. The sagamore responds with a mixture of silence and some kind of acceptance, which Champlain is ready to read as acquiescence to the truth of his own story. After noting the sagamore's silence, Champlain returns to his apparent concern over possible Native polytheism, again asking the sagamore "whether he did not believe there was more than one God."[31] The sagamore responds with a description of Native divinities reassuringly similar to, yet at the same time oddly discordant with, the Christian Trinity: "one God, one Son, one Mother, and the Sun, which were four; yet that God was above them all; but that the Son and the Sun were good . . . but that the Mother was of no value, and ate them up, and that the Father was not very good."[32]

Champlain argues that this view is erroneous, too, and the sagamore shows "some slight belief" in his response. The Frenchman's next question concerns the manifestation of God on earth:

I asked him whether they had not seen, or heard their ancestors tell that God had come into the world. He told me that he had not seen Him; but that in the old time there were five men who went toward the setting sun and met God, who asked them, "Whither go ye?" They said, "We go in search of a living." God answered them, "You shall find it here." They went on without regard to what God had said to them: who took a stone, and touched two of them with it, and they were turned into stones. And He said again to the other three, "Whither go ye?" And they answered as

> the first: and God said to them again, "Go no further, you shall find it here." And seeing that nothing came to them, they went on: and God took two sticks, and touched the two with them, and they were turned into sticks; and the fifth halted and would go no further. And God asked him again, "Whither goest thou?" "I go in search of my living." "Stay, and thou shalt find it." He stayed without going any further, and God gave him meat, and he ate it; after he had made good cheer, he returned among the other savages, and told them all the above story.[33]

Champlain in this case provides no Christian parallel to the sagamore's tale, although the story itself would surely have struck French readers as similar both to Old Testament narratives and to Christ's parables in its implicit lesson about heeding God's words, and thus about the need for faith. At the same time, it is tempting to read the story as a Native warning to Champlain and the French not to proceed any further in their own travels but instead to stay close to Tadoussac, where there is meat aplenty, where they may celebrate together, and where they may find their "living" through trade.

In the final story the sagamore makes his longest speech, which in turn elicits Champlain's longest response:

> He told me also, that once upon a time there was a man who had a good supply of tobacco (which is a herb, of which they take the smoke), and that God came to this man, and asked him where was his tobacco-pipe. The man took his tobacco-pipe and gave it to God, who smoked tobacco a great while: after He had smoked enough, God broke the said pipe into many pieces: and the man asked Him, "Why hast Thou broken my pipe? Surely Thou seest that I have no other." And God took one of His own, and gave it to him, saying to him: "Here is one that I gave thee, carry it to thy grand Sagamore; charge him to keep it, and if he keep it well, he shall never want for anything whatever, nor any

> of his companions." The man took the pipe, and gave it to his grand Sagamore, and as long as he kept it the savages wanted for nothing in the world; but afterwards the said Sagamore lost this pipe, and this is the reason of the great famine which sometimes comes among them. I asked him whether he believed all this; and he said yes, and that it was true. Now I believe this is the reason why they say that God is not very good. But I replied and told him, that God was wholly good; and that without doubt it was the Devil who had appeared to those men . . . that we believe in this great God, who of His goodness had sent us His dear Son, who, being conceived by the Holy Ghost, became human flesh in the virginal womb of the Virgin Mary, lived thirty-three years on earth, working infinite miracles . . . shed His blood, and suffered death and passion for us and for our sins, and redeemed mankind. . . . I told him this was the belief of all Christians, who believe in the Father, the Son, and the Holy Ghost, which nevertheless are not three Gods, but one same and one sole God, and a Trinity.[34]

This story describes another pact between God and his people, ratified by the ritual of smoking and embodied by the sacred pipe itself, a pact which is then broken when the sagamore loses the pipe, resulting in the sporadic return of "great famine." While the account seems to echo the biblical fall from grace rather neatly, Champlain interprets the sagamore's story as a diabolical vision and summarizes for him Christian truths—the life of Christ and the Trinity.

Unlike Anadabijou's performance in the second chapter, these exchanges have received scant attention from modern commentators. I propose that the stories here relate very closely to the tabagie and apparent alliance formation of the previous chapter and indeed form part of the same set of strategic performances. Yet the stories pose even greater interpretive challenges than Anadabijou's speeches concerning the French presence on the St. Lawrence. To begin: who, exactly, is speaking here? The Native leader referred to in the text just before this moment is the Algonquin Besouat, or Tessouat, and some readers have assumed that the religious discussion occurs between him and Champlain.[35] However, others conclude that when Champlain says he will recount what he could "see and learn from the said grand Sagamore" [*grand Sagamo*], the "*grand Sagamo*" is not Tessouat but instead Anadabijou, to whom Champlain has previously assigned this title. Beaulieu argues that Champlain seems to have taken Anadabijou as a leader who had influence over the other Native leaders present, mistaking what was a cooperative intertribal alliance for a hierarchical one.[36] Then again, if the *grand Sagamo* had the authority Champlain ascribes to him, why would he have deigned to speak with Champlain, a junior member of the expedition, instead of the French leader, Gravé Du Pont? As we will see, this confusion over who is actually participating in the debate has a long history, with some early seventeenth-century readers just as puzzled as their modern counterparts have been.

For some readers, knowing which Native leader is talking is of little importance: according to Dominique Deslandres, the discussion is simply between Champlain and "the Aboriginals of the St. Lawrence."[37] Deciding which Native leader is conversing with the French does matter, though, if we wish to know *whose* stories these are. Are they Innu, Algonquin, or Maliseet tales, or should we say that they are in some more general sense "Algonquian" or "Aboriginal"? Are they simply Champlain's words, imposed upon Native speakers, or not his at all? As a number of critics of Native American literature have pointed out, the identity of speakers matters in part because speakers, and the groups to which they belong, "own" the stories they tell.[38]

If these stories do belong to one of these Native groups, they would presumably be retold at other times and in other places. However, another interpretive conundrum posed by these tales is their apparent lack of connection with stories collected by modern anthropologists (most notably Frank Speck) from tribes including those present at the 1603 tabagie. Speck worked extensively among the Innu (Montagnais-Naskapi) bands in and near the Labrador Peninsula from the early 1900s through the 1930s, collecting stories and attempting to characterize the "mythology" of these peoples. Many of the tales he collected focus upon the trickster-transformer Tseqa'bec, who killed monsters and cannibals and whom Speck labeled a kind of "national character hero."[39] None of the stories collected by Speck or alluded to in other sources, however, features the tobacco pipe, which is of such central importance in the third story Champlain hears.[40] Nor, if we believe that Champlain heard the stories from the Algonquin Besouat, can I locate similar stories in later Algonquin tales—nor in those of the Penobscots or other northeastern groups.[41] The narratives bear some resemblance to Jesuit missionary Paul Le Jeune's 1634 account of Innu beliefs, which describe how a god named "Messou" repaired the world after a flood using arrows: "as to the Messou, they hold that he restored the world, which was destroyed in the flood; whence it appears that they have some tradition of that great universal deluge which happened in the time of Noë. . . . He shot arrows into the trunks of trees, which made themselves into branches; he performed a thousand other wonders."[42] However, little else in the narrative recorded by Le Jeune, whose texts are often cited by historians and anthropologists, echoes that in *Des Sauvages*.[43]

The few critics who have focused on the exchange of stories have not only overlooked these interpretive problems but also accorded the debate itself little significance. According to Marcel Trudel, the young Champlain is essentially an observer here, and a rather pretentious one at that, who, after watching the victory celebration, bores Native leaders with a religious lecture and writes with naïveté about his hopes of turning their people into Christianized sedentary farmers. Champlain, himself possibly a recent convert to Catholicism, may have written a particularly orthodox Catholic version of the creation in order to satisfy any doubters among his own French audience.[44] Thus for Trudel, Native beliefs serve only as a kind of foil against which Champlain might define his own orthodoxy.

Following Trudel, other critics focus on Champlain's words rather than the sagamore's. For Deslandres, Champlain attained a "quite superficial" idea of Native cosmology at Tadoussac, being content to claim the sagamore's silence in response to his own stories as "a rhetorical victory."[45] To Alain Beaulieu and Réal Ouellet, these passages expose the "antithetical, irreconcilable" values of French and Native peoples, with the French asserting themselves as the sole bearers of truth.[46] Even if this exchange resembles a dialogue, and prefigures others to follow in seventeenth-century texts, for them it is in no way "dialogic," according to the formulation of Mikhail Bakhtin: that is, the text does not truly register the presence of an "other" voice.[47] Following this line of reasoning, even if Champlain *did* hear Native stories, we might argue that the text of *Des Sauvages* distorts them in translation or misquotes them altogether, in a process of falsification whereby Champlain tells Native tales mirroring Christian versions, while dismissing other elements in their creation stories as "bestial." These passages, that is, may represent another instance of Cheyfitz's "fictions of translation."[48] Other critics, including Stephen Greenblatt and Walter Mignolo, have underscored the ways in which Europeans often subtly, but nevertheless violently, enforced their own cultural visions in early American texts, dismissing Native cultures or translating them out of existence.[49] Greenblatt, writing of an English near-contemporary of Champlain, Thomas Hariot, notes that Hariot's account of Virginia includes a "momentary" record of other voices but that ultimately the moment of inclusion is "part of the process whereby Indian culture is constituted as a culture and thus brought into the light for study, discipline, correction, transformation."[50]

Notwithstanding the stories' numerous historical and interpretive uncertainties, I am not convinced that we must accept this Eurocentric vision of *Des Sauvages*, in which Native ideas appear only in manipulated, mistranslated forms, or only as a sign to readers of what will soon be eliminated. I would return instead to the performative context of the exchange: a small group of French sailors and soldiers, eager to forge some kind of diplomatic relations with three Native groups who vastly outnumber them, and requiring, within this context, some recognition of (and participation in) indigenous performative protocols. Lacking, at least in 1603, the power of colonizers, the French had little choice but to listen to their allies' words, and just as Champlain must have learned much from the Innus and Algonquins about trade routes and canoe technology, it is possible to imagine him attempting to comprehend Anadabijou's narratives. Hence it seems more appropriate to propose a "dialogic" reading of *Des Sauvages*, in which Native concepts and European ones coexist within the larger performative context, each retaining its own voice, with neither side dominant.[51]

Without doubt, Champlain attempts to contain the Innu stories by surrounding them with his Christian responses, and insisting, far more than Anadabijou, upon the truth of his own narrative. He may have recorded a particularly distorted version of these narratives, and most likely did, given his own unfamiliarity with Native stories and the apparent lack of trained interpreters and go-betweens (we do not know if the two Innus who traveled with the French took on any such roles). He may well have reshaped the Native accounts or selected elements that would strike readers as pre- or proto-Christian, an encouragement to those French who hoped for Native conversions. Nevertheless, the very presence of those stories in *Des Sauvages* suggests a recognition that both sides' stories must form part of the work of building intercultural cooperation. Champlain and the French would have to *listen to*, if not fully *accept*, different points of view. For the Innus, the acts of talking and listening, of exchanging speeches and stories, were precisely what forged cooperative relationships with the French—and Champlain, by including those acts in *Des Sauvages*, implicitly recognizes their importance.

And if this performative context was indeed as significant to the diplomatic exchange as I am suggesting, it follows that we must consider not only the Native "point of view" but the various and shifting meanings these performances might have had within both Native and Euro-American tellings (and retellings). Thus, for example, if we consider the encounter from another angle—trying to "face east," as Daniel Richter suggests—then the stories the French were hearing, if not necessarily comprehending, appear in a considerably different light.[52] They were, first of all, summer stories, narratives featuring human beings with links to the present, and not sacred creation myths, stories "of the ancient times when the Earth was being created and the animals were in the form of people," which were reserved for retelling during the winter.[53] This may help explain why we do not see them either in Le Jeune's account of his winter voyage or in the writings of modern anthropologists, most of whom searched for creation stories and foundational "myths," overlooking other kinds of tales. One aspect of the stories here that is in keeping with those recorded later is the way in which, in them, humans interact matter-of-factly with supernatural beings: for the Innus, according to Eleanor Leacock, "Gods and other supernatural beings were not held in awe."[54]

Moreover, if these stories were told with Native auditors in mind, they may simultaneously have been tailored by their Native speaker to suit a French audience. As Julie Cruikshank has suggested in her investigations of storytelling among Yukon elders, Native stories, while providing "social memory, however adequate or inadequate," may also, directly or indirectly, challenge other stories, including Euro-American tales.[55] Cruikshank points out that stories and oral traditions are not "natural" or unchanging artifacts: "They have social histories, and they acquire meanings in the situations in which they emerge, in situations where they are used, and in interactions between narrators and listeners."[56] Let us consider Anadabijou, then, giving stories that he knew his French listeners would understand, while listening and agreeing politely to theirs. As a means of building a trading and diplomatic relationship, this gesture would have made sense: Anadabijou could thereby link his people to the French by sharing connected stories, nodding assent to theirs, and emphasizing common ground rather than provoking cultural clashes.

Although the later paths of these stories within Native cultures may be uncertain, we can turn in another, perhaps surprising, direction to follow the stories—their subsequent reemergence in French printed texts. From examining these it appears that Anadabijou was partly successful in creating a shared medium of intercultural exchange. The stories he traded with Champlain did not end with the publication of *Des Sauvages*; quite the contrary, they circulated widely for at least three decades. French readers could have encountered them in newslike chronicles, in historical writing, or in missionary accounts, all of which reached a larger readership than Champlain's 1603 pamphlet. At the same time, Innu tales took on new shapes in French retellings, and French versions altered their context, import, and even their origins. I conclude this essay with a brief look at some of these French retellings.

One of Champlain's early readers was the chronicler and scholar Pierre-Victor Palma-Cayet, whose *Chronologie septenaire de l'histoire de la paix* [Septenary Chronicle of the History of the Peace], a chronological summary of important events between 1598 and 1604, went through at least five editions in 1605, 1606, 1607, 1609, and 1611.[57] As its title suggests, Cayet's *Chronologie* sets out to mark the reign of Henry IV as an era of "peace," and the text marshals diplomatic, military, and economic events, both foreign and domestic, to demonstrate a harmonious re-nationalization of the French state. In that context the *Chronologie*'s abridgement of *Des Sauvages* is striking for what Cayet chooses to include and exclude. The episode begins with Gravé Du Pont's presentation to the king of the two Innus he took with him to France the previous year and his decision, based on their information about the St. Lawrence, to return for a sustained exploration of the interior.[58] On that return voyage, Cayet notes, Du Pont is accompanied by "several other sea captains"—the text does not name Champlain at all.[59] Thus the character around whom modern discussions of this text center disappears entirely, leaving the French leader Du Pont and the Native peoples as the central protagonists.

In the *Chronologie* a friendly alliance between Du Pont's French and the Innus, Algonquins, and Maliseets fits neatly into the larger story of peacemaking. Cayet's narrative excludes the contents of the first chapter of *Des Sauvages*, which detail the geographical specifics of the voyage to Canada, and moves immediately to the meeting of Du Pont and his crew with Anadabijou. After noting (using Champlain's words) the excellent reception provided the French, Cayet cites the "harangue" or speech given by one of the two returning Innus, praising the good treatment they had received in France. He also includes Anadabijou's response, welcoming the French as his "great friend," praising the king, and, as in *Des Sauvages*, suggesting his happiness with the French willingness to people "their land" and send aid in the fight against their enemies. Cayet's summary includes all of Champlain's details concerning the Natives' encampment, but it excludes the geographical notes at the end of Champlain's second chapter as well as the entire opening of the third, which describes Besouat and the Algonquin victory ceremonies.

Discussion of contentious religious matters, on the other hand, would likely have seemed out of place in a text committed to bridging Catholic-Protestant tensions within France—and thus, while the *Chronologie* does not eliminate all references to the religious debate between Champlain and Anadabijou, it does condense and reshape them. Compare the text of *Des Sauvages* with that extracted in the *Chronologie*:

> They are for the most part a people that have no law, as far as I could see and learn from the said grand Sagamore, who told me that in truth they believe there is a God, who has made all things. Then I said to him, "Since they believe in one God only, how had He brought them into the world, and when had they come?" He answered me, that after God had made all things, He took a number of arrows . . .

> They are for the most part a people that have no law, and who believe that after God had made all things, he took a number of arrows . . .[60]

Cayet excises the elements of dialogue; his version contains no questions and answers. Also eliminated are the markers of who is speaking to whom, replaced with a generalized, objective voice. The *Chronologie*, that is, divorces the tales from their tellers, while making explicit, and damning, judgments about the Native stories. Cayet describes the Innus' concept of four divinities—God, a son, a mother, and the Sun—while leaving aside the rest of the exchange, inserting the statement, "they have an infinite number of other foolish beliefs."[61] Cayet does include Innu customs that might appear more in line with Christian attitudes; for example, he retains Champlain's statement that the Innus have marriage rituals that appear permanent, and he also notes their belief in the immortality of souls. Yet whereas in Champlain's account the religious discussion is knitted closely to the remainder of the encounter at Tadoussac, in the *Chronologie* this wider context is notably lacking. *Des Sauvages* suggests that the trading of stories constituted a fundamental part of the exchange: as with the trading of furs or the use of land, this barter of spiritual goods necessitated a rough intercultural consensus. By contrast, for Cayet, who interprets the 1603 voyage through the prism of the French Wars of Religion, religious debate might threaten, rather than support, the process of alliance formation.

By 1609, when lawyer and historian Marc Lescarbot looked back at *Des Sauvages* in his own colonial history, the colonial vision of Champlain's pamphlet, in which discussion shapes a Native-French alliance, may have come to appear too simplistic. Lescarbot's *Histoire de la Nouvelle France*, like Cayet's *Chronologie*, had a wide circulation in France, going through three editions; the text compiles previous French exploration accounts and also narrates Lescarbot's own brief sojourn in Acadia. While his *Histoire de la Nouvelle France* includes the complete first four chapters of *Des Sauvages*, Lescarbot inserts them into his summary of prior French voyages into the St. Lawrence River, coupling Champlain's voyage with those of Jacques Cartier, which had taken place seven decades earlier. In general Lescarbot seems uninterested in Champlain's story, except as source material for information on the St. Lawrence, and skeptical of the religious dialogue. He includes the debate, but in a printed marginal note placed alongside Champlain's account of God and the birth of Christ, Lescarbot writes: "I do not believe that this theology may be explained to these peoples, even if we were to understand their language perfectly."[62] His note slyly undercuts Champlain, suggesting that the 1603 account may be another "fiction of translation." In his next chapter, Lescarbot writes dismissively: "Let us now leave le sieur Champlain to have his Tabagie, that is, banquet, and to chat about Theology with the Sagamores Anadabijou and Besouat, and turn back to Captain Jacques Cartier."[63] Under no obligation to court intercultural understanding, Lescarbot characterizes the 1603 account as a farfetched conversion tale, one that disguises the likelihood that neither party understood the other at all.

Skeptical readers like Cayet and Lescarbot remind us of the range of interpretations of the early scenes of *Des Sauvages* available even to Champlain's own audiences. The significance of the religious discussion between Champlain and the sagamores must itself have been the subject of debate within French circles, with Lescarbot apparently taking the position that questions of religion were entirely separable from negotiations over political and economic alliances. Nevertheless, the French were continuing to listen to the Innus' stories, even if they argued over what they were hearing.

The tales emerge once more in Gabriel Sagard's *Le Grand voyage du pays des Hurons* (1632), repeated again in Sagard's 1636 *Histoire du Canada*. Sagard, a Recollet friar who had been in Canada in 1623–24 on a mission to the Hurons, includes the tales from *Des Sauvages* in a chapter addressing "the belief and faith of the savages in the Creator, and how they had recourse to our prayers in their necessities." He muses on the "diversity of opinions and belief" that exist among world peoples and the tendency of each of the "barbarous nations" to "forge a God suitable to its own place."[64] Turning to previous French accounts of Canada, he attributes to the Micmacs of the Port Royal region a set of beliefs suspiciously like those ascribed to the St. Lawrence Iroquois by Cartier in the mid-sixteenth century. He then addresses the "beliefs of the Souriquois," a Micmac subgroup: "The Souriquois (from what I have learned) truly believe that there is one God who has created everything and say that after he made all things that he took a number of arrows, and put them in the earth . . ."[65] By choosing to include these accounts in a section devoted to "barbarous" religion, Sagard writes in the tradition of earlier compilers of manners and customs; yet it is not clear why he assigns the stories to the Micmacs, who were likely not even present during the meetings of 1603. There is no evidence for the tale's presence in Micmac oral traditions, and the reassignment of the stories may simply exemplify the tendency of early ethnographers, as Gordon Sayre puts it, to present a "singular, generalized *sauvage américain*, overriding any specific observations about particular Native cultures."[66]

Sagard proceeds with the remainder of the sagamore's narrative in language almost identical to that of *Des Sauvages*. Here, though, the identities of both Champlain and Anadabijou are erased: in Sagard's version, "a Frenchman asked a Sagamore if he did not believe that there was any other than one God."[67] Sagard, unlike Lescarbot, removes all of Champlain's Christian responses, leaving his readers only the Native stories. He concludes by referring to the Natives' belief that "God is not very good," an opinion he—like Champlain—attributes to the fact that the "god" they have encountered is in fact a "Demon" bent on their damnation.[68] However, Sagard passes a different kind of judgment when he introduces the tale of the tobacco pipe, stating, "This Sagamore told and related again to this Frenchman this other pleasant tale."[69] Although the characterization of this tale as "pleasant" undercuts its function as a serious religious narrative, Sagard's suppression of Champlain's responses enables the Native stories to stand out in the text, without being contained by Christian orthodoxy. Somewhat ironically, then, the missionary Sagard seems to come closer than either Cayet or Lescarbot to valuing these narratives: if they are not, for him, serious religious accounts, they are at least stories worthy of inclusion for their own sake.

It might be tempting at this point to consider the *grand Sagamo*'s tales as literature in the genre of Chief Seattle's speech—words placed into Native mouths, only loosely connected to what a Native leader might actually have uttered.[70] And indeed, the reemergence of these stories in French texts does reveal more about French preoccupations than about Native beliefs (more work still needs to be done about the continuing presence of these stories among the Innus). At the same time, however, their multiple lives suggest the presence, already visible in *Des Sauvages*, of storytelling cultures on both sides of the Atlantic. As historians of early modern Europe like Natalie Zemon Davis and Carlo Ginzburg have demonstrated, sixteenth- and seventeenth-century European stories moved between high and popular cultures and ranged from conventional pardon tales to idiosyncratic cosmological visions.[71] We might conclude, then, by returning to 1603 and considering Champlain and Anadabijou, separated widely by culture, yet discovering their mutual interest in the performance of stories. Those that Anadabijou gave to the French would mark the emergence of new political relations in the Northeast, and over the years they would find an audience far larger, and a history far more complicated, than he could have imagined.

Notes

I would like to thank participants at the 2003 conference Champlain and His World: A Quartercentenary Exploration, for their insightful comments on an earlier version of this essay. My particular thanks to Professor Germaine Warkentin for her assistance and encouragement.

1. François Gravé Du Pont was a captain in the service of the holder of the French fur-trade monopoly, Pierre Chauvin de Tonnetuit. See Trudel, "Gravé Du Pont." For background on the voyage, see Trudel, *Histoire de la Nouvelle-France*, 1:252–69, and Heidenreich, "Beginning of French Exploration," 238–41.
2. The Innu people were referred to as the Montagnais by the French and are often known as Montagnais-Naskapi in the scholarly literature. I use the term Innu (plural Innus), following contemporary practice and tribal preference. See Gardette, *Les Innus*, 1–2, n. 1. Dickason attempts to distinguish more precisely between the Montagnais and the Naskapis when discussing the early colonial period: see Dickason, *Canada's First Nations*, 83. See also Rogers and Leacock, "Montagnais-Naskapi," 186. For a brief history of the Innus, see Beaulieu, "Du nomadisme aux réserves," 11–33. The Algonquins (Algonquin Nation, Ontario) sometimes refer to themselves as Anishinabek (also Anishinaabeg), as do Ojibwas and Odawas; I use the term Algonquins here, to make clear that I am writing of the Algonquin Nation rather than of the groups collectively. See Day and Trigger, "Algonquin," 792–97. Etchemin is a term "of unknown origin" used by the French to refer to the Maliseets and Passamaquoddies, who live in the New Brunswick and Maine regions (Erikson, "Maliseet-Passamaquoddy," 135).
3. Champlain, *Des Sauvages, ou, voyage de Samuel Champlain, de Brouage*. In this essay, I cite from the bilingual 1922 edition of *Des Sauvages*, in *The Works of Samuel de Champlain*, ed. Biggar, trans. Langton and Ganong (hereafter cited as Champlain, *Des Sauvages*), which preserves the original spelling of the 1603 edition. For a critical introduction to *Des Sauvages*, see Beaulieu and Ouellet. In 2010 the Champlain Society issued a new edition, *Life and Times*, shedding new light upon the text's publication and distribution.

4. Champlain, *Des Sauvages*, 98.
5. Rogers and Leacock, "Montagnais-Naskapi," 169–70. On the fur trade and Tadoussac, see Dickason, *Canada's First Nations*, 84. For the suggestion that the Native groups had assembled to be near the "trading post," see Lestringant, "Champlain," 236. For background on trading in early New France, see Turgeon, "French in New England"; Turgeon, "French Fishers"; and Axtell, "At the Water's Edge."
6. Champlain, *Des Sauvages*, 98–99. For some observations on the origin of the word *tabagie*, see 99, n. 2.
7. See Jury, "Anadabijou."
8. Champlain, *Des Sauvages*, 103.
9. Girard and Gagné, "Première alliance interculturelle."
10. Champlain, *Des Sauvages*, 100.
11. Champlain, *Des Sauvages*, 100–1.
12. Cheyfitz, *The Poetics of Imperialism*, 15.
13. Axtell, *The Invasion Within*, 88. Gustafson points out that "the native peoples who inhabited the continent had highly elaborated traditions of spoken eloquence that played central roles in religious life, government, and diplomacy, and they adapted these traditions to the new world of European colonialism" (*Eloquence Is Power*, xiv). See also Gustafson 33–35 for analysis of a similar passage in the writings of Roger Williams.
14. Still other historians are skeptical of the event's significance or ignore it altogether. Both Eccles and Delâge, though writing from very different points of view, skip over the 1603 encounter and focus their attention on the settlement of Acadia and Québec. Eccles states only that Champlain "had visited Tadoussac previously and had formed a very low opinion of its physical environment" (*French in North America*, 15). Delâge argues that the French sought to bypass Tadoussac and to trade directly with groups farther inland (*Bitter Feast*, 94–95).
15. Trigger, *Natives and Newcomers*, 173–74.
16. Dickason, *Canada's First Nations*, 83.
17. Dickason, *Canada's First Nations*, 83.
18. Beaulieu, "Birth of the Franco-American Alliance," 153, 155. Jacquin argues that the alliance had already taken shape *before* the 1603 encounter, as demonstrated by the Innus' offer of two young men to the French in 1602 ("Les Montagnais," 38–39).
19. Fisher, *Champlain's Dream*, 130–31, 134.
20. Girard and Gagné, "Première Alliance Interculturelle," 11–12.

21. Vincent, "Apparent Compatibility."
22. Vincent, "Apparent Compatibility," 135–38.
23. Vincent, "Apparent Compatibility," 144.
24. Morantz, "Plunder or Harmony?" 63, 65.
25. Seed, *Ceremonies of Possession*, 42–46. Seed's argument, important though it is, would have us read the Native participants at the 1603 meeting and later encounters as actors in a larger French drama, rather than the reverse.
26. Jehlen, "History before the Fact," 688–89. Another version of this argument has recently been advanced by Cohen, who analyzes accounts from early New England. Cohen asserts that in the cases he studies, "collaboration in the production of a text involves Native Americans" (*Networked Wilderness*, 15): it is possible, that is, to see texts like *Des Sauvages* as a text produced not just by the French but by the Innus as well.
27. See Jury, "Tessouat."
28. Champlain, *Des Sauvages*, 110.
29. Champlain, *Des Sauvages*, 111.
30. Champlain, *Des Sauvages*, 111–12.
31. Champlain, *Des Sauvages*, 112.
32. Champlain, *Des Sauvages*.
33. Champlain, *Des Sauvages*, 113–14.
34. Champlain, *Des Sauvages*, 115–16.
35. See, for example, Lestringant, "Champlain," 238.
36. Beaulieu, "Birth of the Franco-American Alliance," 158.
37. Deslandres, "Champlain and Religion," 193.
38. As Bruchac puts it, "When talking about an American Indian story you need to be specific about what particular Native nation owns that story. Always acknowledge the nation and the individual or individuals who have shared that story" (*Our Stories Remember*, 39).
39. Speck, *Naskapi*, 48; Speck's "Montagnais and Naskapi Tales" focuses primarily upon tales featuring Tseqa'bec.
40. Speck asserted that tobacco likely did not enter into widespread use among Innus until the eighteenth century (*Naskapi*, 225–26).
41. The literature, of course, is vast, and I cannot claim that my search has been comprehensive. See, for instance, Speck, "Montagnais and Naskapi Tales"; "Some Naskapi Myths"; and "Penobscot Tales." Other collections of tales from the region include Davidson, "Some Tete de Boule Tales"; and Jones, *Ojibwa Texts*. Vincent has worked to collect more recent Innu accounts: see, for example, Vincent and Bacon, "L'Arrivée des chercheurs de terre."

42. Thwaites, ed., *Jesuit Relations*, 6:156–59.

43. Leacock, "Seventeenth-Century Montagnais Social Relations," calls Le Jeune's accounts "the fullest record of everyday Montagnais life" (190). In chapter 13 of *Des Sauvages* Champlain records "another strange thing worthy of narration," the Micmac accounts of "a dreadful monster . . . Gougou." This monster reappears in tales collected later among the Micmac, like those gathered by the missionary Silas Tertius Rand; see *Des Sauvages*, 186–87.

44. Trudel, *Histoire de la Nouvelle-France*, 1:256, 260. In his article on Champlain for the *Dictionary of Canadian Biography Online*, Trudel asserts that "when he began his Canadian career in 1603 Champlain was a Catholic; this is proved by the doctrine he expounded at that time to the Tadoussac Indians" (Trudel, "Champlain, Samuel de").

45. Deslandres, "Champlain and Religion," 193–94.

46. Beaulieu and Ouellet, introduction to *Des Sauvages*, 56.

47. For analysis of Bakhtin's definition of the term *dialogism*, see Vice, *Introducing Bakhtin*, 46–59. I would also not wish to read this text as marking some kind of "hybrid" colonial subject, since colonization of the St. Lawrence had not even occurred in 1603. On the concept of hybridity in postcolonial theory, see Loomba, *Colonialism/Postcolonialism*, 173–83.

48. Cheyfitz has examined the ways in which colonial texts mistranslate or ignore fundamentally different Native understandings of property and kinship relations. In texts he studies, "The problem of translation, the complex interaction between cultures and histories, is at once announced and annulled" (Cheyfitz, *Poetics of Imperialism*, 7).

49. Mignolo's study focuses on New Spain, but he explicitly situates his work in a larger context of European-Native relations. The Spanish, Mignolo argues, employed their language and writing system as methods of control, erasing Native systems as they did so (*Darker Side of the Renaissance*, esp. 71–76).

50. Greenblatt, *Shakespearean Negotiations*, 37.

51. Susan Castillo sees in many early American texts "European and Native voices attempting to make sense of each other for a variety of pragmatic ends" and argues that "dialogical interaction whether in print or in actual embodied performance" was a fundamental vehicle for the "construction of group and individual identities" in many New World contexts (*Colonial Encounters in New World Writing*, 2, 14).

52. Richter, *Facing East*, 8–9.

53. On winter tales see Bruchac, *Our Stories Remember*, 35.
54. Leacock, "Seventeenth-Century Montagnais Social Relations," 194.
55. Cruikshank, "Oral History," 18–19.
56. Cruikshank, "Oral History," 21. Bruchac writes that stories are possessions; they belong to the people who tell them, they are part of the cultural heritage of "the nation and the individual or individuals who have shared that story." He also notes that stories can be given to their listeners to retell to others (*Our Stories Remember*, 39).
57. On Cayet, see Hoefer, ed., *Nouvelle biographie générale*, 9:307–9.
58. Cayet, *Chronologie*, 415r–415v. My translations, here and following.
59. Cayet, *Chronologie*, 415v.
60. Champlain, *Des Sauvages*, 111; Cayet, *Chronologie*, 417v.
61. Cayet, *Chronologie*, 417v.
62. Lescarbot, *Histoire*, 323. My translations, here and following.
63. Cheyfitz, *Poetics of Imperialism*, 15; Lescarbot, *Histoire*, 325.
64. Sagard, *Le Grand voyage*, 225. My translations, here and following.
65. Sagard, *Le Grand voyage*, 226. On the Souriquois, see Bock, "Micmac," 121.
66. On Micmac oral traditions see Bock, "Micmac," 116–17; Whitehead, *The Old Man Told Us*; Smith, *On the Trail of Elder Brother*; and Speck, *Beothuk and Micmac*. On Sagard's prose see Sayre, *Les Sauvages Américains*, 104–5.
67. Sagard, *Le Grand voyage*, 226.
68. Sagard, *Le Grand voyage*, 228.
69. Sagard, *Le Grand voyage*, 227.
70. On Chief Seattle's speech and its long literary life, see Kaiser, "Chief Seattle's Speech(es)." As Kinkade and Mattina have pointed out, the tale that circulates in these early French texts "might be called pseudo-narrative: speeches that have been concocted partly from native materials and largely from Euro-American ideas about what American Indians should have said" ("Discourse," 245).
71. Davis, *Fiction in the Archives*, 111–14. Ginzburg's *The Cheese and the Worms* describes the ways in which the miller Menocchio fashioned his own stories out of the varied literary and religious texts to which he had access.

Works Cited

Axtell, James. *The Invasion Within: The Contest of Cultures in Colonial North America*. New York: Oxford University Press, 1985.

———. "At the Water's Edge: Trading in the Sixteenth Century." In

Natives and Newcomers: The Cultural Origins of North America, 79–103. New York: Oxford University Press, 2001.

Beaulieu, Alain. "The Birth of the Franco-American Alliance." In *Champlain: The Birth of French America*, ed. Raymonde Litalien and Denis Vaugeois, trans. Käthe Roth, 153–62. Montréal: McGill-Queen's University Press, 2004.

———. "Du nomadisme aux réserves: Histoire et culture des Montagnais du Québec." In *Les Indiens montagnais du Québec: Entre deux mondes*, ed. Anne Vitart, 11–33. Paris: Editions Sépia, 1995.

Beaulieu, Alain, and Réal Ouellet. "Introduction." In *Des Sauvages*, ed. Alain Beaulieu and Réal Ouellet, 11–63. Montréal: Typo, 1993.

Bock, Philip K. "Micmac." In *Handbook of North American Indians*, vol. 15: *Northeast*, ed. Bruce G. Trigger, 109–22. Washington DC: Smithsonian Institution, 1978.

Bruchac, Joseph. *Our Stories Remember: American Indian History, Culture, and Values through Storytelling*. Golden CO: Fulcrum, 2003.

Castillo, Susan. *Colonial Encounters in New World Writing, 1500–1786: Performing America*. London: Routledge, 2006.

Cayet, Pierre. *Chronologie septenaire de l'histoire de la paix entre les roys de France et d'Espagne . . .* Paris: Jehan Richer, 1605.

Champlain, Samuel de. *Des Sauvages, ou, voyage de Samuel Champlain, de Brouage, fait en la France nouvelle, l'an mil six cens trios*. Paris: Claude de Monstroeil, 1603.

———. *Des Sauvages*. Ed. H. P. Biggar, trans. H. H. Langton and W. F. Ganong. Vol. 1 of *The Works of Samuel de Champlain*. Toronto: Champlain Society, 1922.

———. *Life and Times of Samuel de Champlain:* Des Sauvages *and Other Documents Related to the Period before 1604*. Ed. Conrad E. Heidenreich and K. Janet Ritch. Toronto: Champlain Society, 2010.

Cheyfitz, Eric. *The Poetics of Imperialism: Translation and Colonization from* The Tempest *to* Tarzan, expanded ed. Philadelphia: University of Pennsylvania Press, 1997.

Cohen, Matt. *The Networked Wilderness: Communicating in Early New England*. Minneapolis: University of Minnesota Press, 2010.

Cruikshank, Julie. "Oral History, Narrative Strategies, and Native American Historiography: Perspectives from the Yukon Territory, Canada." In *Clearing a Path: Theorizing the Past in Native American Studies*, ed. Nancy Shoemaker, 3–27. New York: Routledge, 2002.

Davidson, D. S. "Some Tete de Boule Tales." *Journal of American Folklore* 41 (1928): 262–74.

Davis, Natalie Zemon. *Fiction in the Archives: Pardon Tales and Their Tellers in Sixteenth-Century France*. Stanford: Stanford University Press, 1987.

Day, Gordon M., and Bruce G. Trigger. "Algonquin." In *Handbook of North American Indians*, vol. 15: *Northeast*, ed. Bruce G. Trigger, 792–97. Washington DC: Smithsonian Institution, 1978.

Delâge, Denys. *Bitter Feast: Amerindians and Europeans in Northeastern North America*, trans. Jane Brierley. Vancouver: University of British Columbia Press, 1993.

Deslandres, Dominique. "Samuel de Champlain and Religion." In *Champlain: The Birth of French America*, ed. Raymonde Litalien and Denis Vaugeois, trans. Käthe Roth, 191–204. Montréal: McGill-Queen's University Press, 2004.

Dickason, Olive Patricia. *Canada's First Nations: A History of Founding Peoples from Earliest Times*, 3rd ed. Don Mills, Ontario: Oxford University Press, 2002.

Eccles, W. J. *The French in North America*, rev. ed. East Lansing: Michigan State University Press, 1998.

Erikson, Vincent O. "Maliseet-Passamaquoddy." In *Handbook of North American Indians*, vol. 15: *Northeast*, ed. Bruce G. Trigger, 123–36. Washington DC: Smithsonian Institution, 1978.

Fisher, David Hackett. *Champlain's Dream*. New York: Simon and Schuster, 2008.

Gardette, Joëlle. *Les Innus et les Euro-Canadiens: Dialogue des cultures et rapport à l'autre à travers le temps (XVIIe–XXe siècles)*. Québec: Les Presses de l'Université Laval, 2008.

Ginzburg, Carlo. *The Cheese and the Worms: The Cosmos of a Sixteenth-Century Miller*, trans. John and Anne Tedeschi. New York: Penguin, 1980.

Girard, Camil, and Edith Gagné. "Première alliance interculturelle: Rencontre entre Montagnais et Français à Tadoussac en 1603." *Recherches amérindiennes au Québec* 25, no. 3 (1995): 3–14.

Greenblatt, Stephen. *Shakespearean Negotiations: The Circulation of Social Energy in Renaissance England*. Berkeley: University of California Press, 1988.

Gustafson, Sandra M. *Eloquence Is Power: Oratory and Performance in Early America*. Chapel Hill: University of North Carolina Press, for Omohundro Institute of Early American History and Culture, Williamsburg VA, 2000.

Heidenreich, Conrad E. "The Beginning of French Exploration out of the

St. Lawrence Valley: Motives, Methods, and Changing Attitudes towards Native People." In *Decentering the Renaissance: Canada and Europe in Multidisciplinary Perspective, 1500–1700*, ed. Germaine Warkentin and Carolyn Podruchny, 236–51. Toronto: University of Toronto Press, 2001.

Hodgen, Margaret T. *Early Anthropology in the Sixteenth and Seventeenth Centuries*. Philadelphia: University of Pennsylvania Press, 1971.

Hoefer, Jeon Chrétien Ferdinand, ed. *Nouvelle biographie générale depuis les temps les plus reculés jusqu'à nos jours*. Vol. 9. Paris: Firmin Didot Frères, 1855.

Jacquin, Philippe. "Les Montagnais et le Français aux XVIe–XVIIIe siècles," in *Les Indiens Montagnais du Québec: Entre deux mondes*, ed. Anne Vitart, 35–57. Paris: Editions Sépia, 1995.

Jehlen, Myra. "History before the Fact; or, Captain John Smith's Unfinished Symphony." *Critical Inquiry* 19 (1993): 677–92.

Jones, William. *Ojibwa Texts*. Ed. Truman Michelson. Publications of the American Ethnological Society, vol. 7, pt. 1. Leiden: E. J. Brill, 1917.

Jury, Elsie McLeod. "Anadabijou." In *Dictionary of Canadian Biography Online*. University of Toronto–Université Laval, 2000. June 6, 2009. http://www.biographi.ca/.

———. "Tessouat." In *Dictionary of Canadian Biography Online*. University of Toronto–Université Laval, 2000. June 6. 2009. http://www.biographi.ca/.

Kaiser, Rudolf. "Chief Seattle's Speech(es): American Origins and European Reception." In *Recovering the Word: Essays on Native American Literature*, ed. Brian Swann and Arnold Krupat, 497–536. Berkeley: University of California Press, 1987.

Kinkade, M. Dale, and Anthony Mattina. "Discourse." In *Handbook of North American Indians*, vol. 17: *Languages*, ed. Ives Goddard, 244–74. Washington DC: Smithsonian Institution, 1996.

Leacock, Eleanor. "Seventeenth-Century Montagnais Social Relations and Values." In *Handbook of North American Indians*, vol. 6: *Subarctic*, ed. June Helm, 190–95. Washington DC: Smithsonian Institution, 1981.

Lescarbot, Marc. *Histoire de la Nouvelle France, contenant les navigations, découvertes, & habitations faites par les François és Indes Occidentales & Nouvelle France* . . . Paris: Chez Jean Milot, 1609.

Lestringant, Frank. "Champlain, or the Empowerment of the Colonial Enterprise." In *Champlain: The Birth of French America*, ed. Raymonde

Litalien and Denis Vaugeois, trans. Käthe Roth, 233–38. Montréal: McGill-Queen's University Press, 2004.

Loomba, Ania. *Colonialism/Postcolonialism*. London: Routledge, 1998.

Mignolo, Walter D. *The Darker Side of the Renaissance: Literacy, Territoriality, and Colonization*. Ann Arbor: University of Michigan Press, 1995.

Morantz, Toby. "Plunder or Harmony? On Merging European and Native Views of Early Contact." In *Decentering the Renaissance: Canada and Europe in Multidisciplinary Perspective, 1500–1700*, ed. Germaine Warkentin and Carolyn Podruchny, 48–67. Toronto: University of Toronto Press, 2001.

Richter, Daniel K. *Facing East from Indian Country: A Native History of Early America*. Cambridge: Harvard University Press, 2001.

Rogers, Edward S., and Eleanor Leacock. "Montagnais-Naskapi." In *Handbook of North American Indians*, vol. 6: *Subarctic*, ed. June Helm, 169–89. Washington DC: Smithsonian Institution, 1981.

Sagard, Gabriel. *Le Grand voyage du pays des Hurons, situé en l'Amerique vers la Mer douce, és derniers confins de la Nouvelle France, dite Canada* . . . Paris: Chey Denys Moreau, 1632.

Sayre, Gordon M. *Les Sauvages Américains: Representations of Native Americans in French and English Colonial Literature*. Chapel Hill: University of North Carolina Press, 1997.

Seed, Patricia. *Ceremonies of Possession in Europe's Conquest of the New World, 1492–1640*. New York: Cambridge University Press, 1995.

Smith, Patricia Clark. *On the Trail of Elder Brother: Glous'gap Stories of the Micmac Indians*. New York: Persea Books, 2000.

Speck, Frank G. *Beothuk and Micmac*, ed. F. W. Hodge. New York: Museum of the American Indian, Heye Foundation, 1922.

———. "Montagnais and Naskapi Tales from the Labrador Peninsula." *Journal of American Folklore* 38 (1925): 1–32.

———. *Naskapi: The Savage Hunters of the Labrador Peninsula*. Norman: University of Oklahoma Press, 1977.

———. "Penobscot Tales and Religious Beliefs." *Journal of American Folklore* 48 (1935): 1–107.

———. "Some Naskapi Myths from Little Whale River." *Journal of American Folklore* 28 (1915): 70–77.

Thwaites, Reuben Gold, ed. *The Jesuit Relations and Allied Documents: Travels and Explorations of the Jesuit Missionaries in New France, 1610–1791*. 73 vols. Cleveland: Burrows Brothers, 1896–1901.

Trigger, Bruce G. *Natives and Newcomers: Canada's "Heroic Age" Reconsidered*. Montréal: McGill-Queen's University Press, 1985.

Trudel, Marcel. "Champlain, Samuel de." In *Dictionary of Canadian Biography Online*. University of Toronto–Université Laval, 2000. June 6, 2009. http://www.biographi.ca/.

———. "Gravé Du Pont, François." In *Dictionary of Canadian Biography Online*. University of Toronto–Université Laval, 2000. June 7, 2009. http://www.biographi.ca/.

———. *Histoire de la Nouvelle-France*, vol. 1: *Les Vaines tentatives, 1524–1603*. Montréal: Fides, 1963.

Turgeon, Laurier. "The French in New England Before Champlain." In *Champlain: The Birth of French America*, ed. Raymonde Litalien and Denis Vaugeois, trans. Käthe Roth, 98–112. Montréal: McGill-Queen's University Press, 2004.

———. "French Fishers, Fur Traders, and Amerindians during the Sixteenth Century: History and Archaeology." *William and Mary Quarterly* 3rd ser. 55 (1998): 585–610.

Vice, Sue. *Introducing Bakhtin*. Manchester: Manchester University Press, 1997.

Vincent, Sylvie. "Apparent Compatibility, Real Incompatibility: Native and Western Versions of History—The Innu Example." In *Figured Worlds: Ontological Obstacles in Intercultural Relations*, ed. John Clammer, Sylvie Poirier, and Eric Schwimmer, 132–47. Toronto: University of Toronto Press, 2004.

Vincent, Sylvie, and Josephine Bacon. "L'Arrivée des chercheurs de terre: Récits et dires des Montagnais de la Moyenne et de la basse Côte-Nord." *Recherches amérindiennes au Québec* 22, no. 2–3 (1992): 19–29.

Whitehead, Ruth Holmes. *The Old Man Told Us: Excerpts from Micmac History, 1500–1950*. Halifax, Nova Scotia: Nimbus Publishers, 1991.

[4]

Wendat Song and Carnival Noise in the Jesuit *Relations*

Olivia Bloechl

The Jesuit missionaries who worked in eastern Canada in the seventeenth century left extensive descriptions of Iroquoian and Algonquian ceremonial song and dance. These early ethnological writings were included as part of the Jesuits' annual *Relations* (1632–73), reports from the Canadian missions that were avidly consumed by religious and lay readers in France.[1] The Jesuits' accounts of Native ceremonial song are often more detailed and nuanced than those of other early ethnological writers. While they had little understanding of northeastern Native singing and instrumental performance, the priests did have some training in European music, and many of them composed music for use in the missions. However, anthropological or technical description of Native song was not a priority for them. Their aims were moral and spiritual, and their writings were thus mainly concerned with the ontological nature of the performances they witnessed.

Because the Jesuits assumed a universalist cosmology, they readily applied their own moral and metaphysical categories to Native cultures and religions, and this ethnocentric tendency influenced their rhetoric. Comparisons between Native and European cultures appear frequently in their writings, especially in passages describing Native ceremonial life. Although such comparisons were meant to help French readers better understand unfamiliar beliefs and practices, their function was rarely purely heuristic. Jesuit writers also exploited the humanist rhetorical convention of comparison for the moral truths it could convey.[2]

One of the Jesuits' recurring comparisons drew on readers' familiarity with French Carnival and other festivities, including their noisy and sometimes anarchic sound culture. This rhetorical convention was pragmatic, in that it helped readers connect the missionaries' labors to their own lives. Yet more fundamentally, it reflected the moral and ontological continuity that the missionaries perceived between certain kinds of festive or ceremonial performance on both sides of the Atlantic. The missionaries' comparisons with European Carnival also highlighted an organizational and methodological continuity between the Jesuits' Canadian missions and their missions in France.[3] A key component of the Jesuits' French missions, like those undertaken in France by other evangelical orders, involved the effort to reform or even eliminate popular festive practices deemed "superstitious," in the early modern Catholic sense of unorthodox beliefs or practices.[4] Similarly, all of the Catholic missionaries in eastern Canada worked to reform or root out Native beliefs or ceremonial practices that they found contrary to Christian life, although the Jesuits tended toward cultural adaptation rather than elimination.[5]

When Jesuit writers pointed to similarities between Native and European festive rites and their music, then, they were articulating what they perceived as a comparable degree of superstition. The charge of superstition was a serious one, demanding careful analysis: were these rites diabolical per se, or did they involve deception or madness? While we normally regard the latter two conditions from a secular and thus disenchanted perspective, early Jesuit missionaries, like other educated Catholics, understood their ultimate cause as demonological.[6] The Jesuits were characteristically cautious in attributing direct diabolical influence, yet their hearing, whether in France or in northeastern America, was always attuned to that possibility. Ritual performance mattered to them, in part, because it potentially manifested a diabolism that the Jesuits needed to combat in order to fulfill their mission of saving souls.[7]

As a means of examining the significance of ritual performance in this intercultural context, I survey comparisons between Wendat ceremonial song and French festive music in Jesuit *Relations* from the 1630s through the 1650s. I focus on Jesuit missions to the Wendat confederacy because the Jesuits conducted their most intensive and sustained missionary efforts in Wendake, the Wendat peoples' ancestral lands south of Georgian Bay (in present-day Ontario). The thirty years of writings discussed here document the first decades of interaction between the Wendats and the Jesuits in the context of established missions, the end date reflecting the disappearance of the confederacy in 1649 due to sustained Haudenosaunee (Iroquois) attacks and the subsequent dispersal of the survivors toward Québec and westward to the upper Great Lakes region.[8] During this period the Jesuits, extending the tradition of ecclesiastical and religious opposition to French festive life that began with the Catholic reformation in France, focused on the parallels between Carnival and three classes of Wendat healing ceremonies: *ononharoia*, *awataerohi*, and *otakrendoiae*. As I show, there were pragmatic reasons that Jesuit priests and their superiors thought this parallel important enough to highlight repeatedly in their reports: asserting the superstition of carnivalesque rites in France and in Canada justified the Jesuits' efforts in both mission fields, underscoring the urgency of the Canadian missions while emphasizing the importance of the Jesuits' ongoing work in France. Thus the Jesuits' rhetorical references to Carnival tell us a great deal about their relationship with laity on either side of the Atlantic; at the same time, those references offer us a glimpse of Native resistance to mission work. The Jesuits, I propose, may have found Carnival to be a powerful touchstone for their interpretation of Wendat ceremonies because those ceremonies served as occasions for traditionalist action in opposition to the missionaries and Wendat Christians. These temporal realities, together with the Jesuits' spiritual perspective, thus provided the intercultural performative matrix within which the missionaries heard in Wendat ceremonial song the raucous sounds of Carnival.

The Society of Jesus was prominent among the religious orders who established missions in French towns and rural areas in the period of Catholic reform, the mid-sixteenth and seventeenth centuries.[9] Like the Capuchins, Lazarists, Recollets, and other evangelical orders, Jesuit writers emphasized the impoverished state of religious belief and practice among the French, especially in rural areas. Indeed, many church officials, theologians, and members of the religious orders shared the opinion that in attempting to root out errant rituals and beliefs, reformers were faced with spiritual conditions not unlike those in the foreign missions. This conviction is borne out by frequent Jesuit references, appearing as early as the second half of the sixteenth century, to the villages and rural areas of France as "our Indies."[10]

While the Jesuits are better known for founding educational institutions during this period, pastoral care was an integral part of their work. In the course of their short-term missions they would preach, baptize, hear confessions, and instruct local residents in orthodox doctrine.[11] As part of the latter pedagogical effort, Jesuit missionaries staged morality plays and other theater, developed simple catechisms, and composed or adapted sacred songs (*cantiques spirituels*) to reinforce doctrine and to encourage penance.[12]

Jesuit missionaries also participated vigorously in the effort to reform French devotional practices and festive life. While clerical parodic feasts, especially the Feast of Fools, had been largely suppressed by the sixteenth century, lay festive life associated with Carnival and other occasions continued unabated through Louis XIV's reign, though often in altered form.[13] These festival occasions almost always included singing or instrumental performance, and Catholic reformers carefully scrutinized this musical aspect of festive life as a possible manifestation of superstition. As Stuart Clark's work has shown, in early modern Catholic theology the broad category of superstition always involved an ultimate diabolical cause, even when other more immediate causes—such as false belief—were involved.[14] Festive music was a ready target for such charges because of a predominant early modern ontology, shared among Catholics and Protestants alike, that regarded music as capable of conveying supernatural forces, to a much greater extent than ordinary language or the other arts.[15] Music performed in ceremonial or ritual contexts was thought particularly susceptible to superstition, if not carefully monitored, and it did not help that much festive music was parodic of Catholic sacred music or integrated Catholic and folk elements.

Even when superstition or diabolism per se were not at issue, Jesuits and other reformers commonly regarded such music as a holdover from a less civilized epoch, associated with rural people and with the third estate. This urbane, classed perspective on festive music becomes increasingly common from the 1630s onward and is predominant from the 1660s, following Louis XIV's assumption of personal rule. The words of Jesuit writer Claude-François Ménestrier are a case in point. Ménestrier's humanism generally moderated his perspectives on culture, yet in his *Représentations en musique anciennes et modernes* (1686) he dismisses Carnival music as "ridiculous" and praises its gradual suppression under Louis XIII and Louis XIV: "There were few towns that did not have these buffoonish spectacles in which ridiculous musics were performed, sometimes featuring singing asses, sometimes singing wolves, apes, or foxes, or other animals playing the flute; sometimes they sawed away at iron grills with rasps, in place of violins; and these follies were the usual diversions of Carnival, which more dignified customs have at last wisely abolished."[16]

A similar perspective emerges in the memoirs of the missionary Julien Maunoir, who documented the Jesuit missions to Brittany in the 1630s through 1650. Maunoir's retrospective account of the missions features extensive discussions of music and dance in Breton festive life, and he also composed music for use in the missions, including *cantiques* used in theatrical performances staged by the missionaries.[17] Following standard Jesuit protocol, Maunoir translated liturgical chants and catechisms into the local language of Breton and wrote new poems on doctrinal themes, which he set to existing or newly composed melodies. These songs and catechisms were meant to supplant traditional Breton festive music and dance, which the missionaries viewed as superstition.[18] In an episode from 1644 Maunoir reports that the missionaries succeeded in eliminating young people's round dances and "obscene" and parodical singing on Sundays and feast days in Plougastel, near the city of Brest:

> At that time the inhabitants of Plougastel lived in an unheard-of state of scandal and impiety. Nocturnal dances were organized in many public places, and, for half the year, young people of both sexes came from a league away to meet up there every night before

and after Sundays and feast days. When their parents could not see them, they played at licentious games. More troubling still, they mocked religion: amongst themselves they profaned the sign of the cross, intermingled the *Pater noster* and the *Credo* with impious cries and shouts, and shamelessly received young girls in confession, doing things with them that a Christian condemns. Nights were not enough for them: they devoted most Sundays and feast days to their lascivious dances. The rest of the week, they sinned as much as they could in speaking to one another, or in obscene songs. Our mission led them to abandon all these abominations, and our spiritual songs supplanted licentious conversation and songs in the hearts of the young people.[19]

Maunoir also reports that some of the missionaries' young converts acted to suppress the songs and dances associated with the hemp harvest at Plougastel: "In this same parish the hemp harvest was accompanied by dances performed to the sound of the flute. Seven young people arrived on the scene and decided to make a sacrifice of these instruments and these profane airs, replacing them with spiritual hymns. Accompanied by all the peasants, they began to sing the *Pater noster*, which I had translated into Breton."[20] If Maunoir's reports are to be believed, the Jesuits' cultural reform efforts in Brittany seem to have had their desired effect, at least in some communities.

The evangelizing religious orders were not alone in their opposition to festive music and dance traditions, especially those associated with the Carnival season. Members of the ecclesiastical élite, as well as some more zealous *curés* or lay priests, also worked to undermine superstitious or socially disruptive traditions of misrule in their districts, including traditions of music. For instance, Father Paul Beurrier, the curé of Nanterre, reported having put a stop to the performances of several *bâteleurs* (public entertainers) in his parish: "I remember that, having learned one feast day that some *bâteleurs* were performing a farce on a stage that they had built, I went there with some officers of justice, I went up on stage, I ripped the mask off the principal *bâteleur*, I took and broke the violin of the one who was playing and made them get off their stage, which I then had torn down by our officers; and since that time no more buffoons have dared to appear at Nanterre."[21] In a more serious and extended incident, the bishop of Alet, Nicolas Pavillon, took action against the custom of dancing on feast days by imposing public penance on the offenders, denying absolution to the fiddlers who accompanied the dances, and punishing parishes that refused to comply. Participants strongly resisted Pavillon's measures, and in 1660 members of a local *jeunesse*, or youth abbey, presented a list of grievances signed by six notables. However, several other bishops testified to the dances' indecency, and in 1662 the city council ruled in favor of Pavillon.[22]

As the incident at Alet illustrates, reformers' confrontations with parishioners over festive performance often had political overtones, inasmuch as their intervention threatened the existing balance of power among municipal authorities, royal agents, and the local seigniorial nobility. Moreover, as studies by Roy Ladurie, Natalie Zemon Davis, and others have shown, the license associated with feast days and the Carnival season could provide an occasion for social agitation and even insurrection by the least powerful members of French society.[23] At times such actions were supported by local leaders who resisted ecclesiastical or royal interference, as at Pamiers in the 1660s and '70s. For example, when the Jansenist bishop of Pamiers, François-Etienne Caulet, forced violin players, *jouglers*, and complicit innkeepers to leave the diocese and during Pentecost of 1662 imprisoned village dancers along with their oboists and drummers, local officials, notables, and the comte de Tréville appealed to the parliament of Toulouse against the bishop. The following year, during the feast of St. John the Baptist, the count himself authorized a protective escort for the dancers and musicians, who protested the bishop's actions by performing loudly on flutes and drums beneath his window. The bishop responded by displaying the consecrated host in order to drive the revelers off, reflecting the widespread ecclesiastical suspicion that such noisy music was diabolical in nature. The dispute continued until, in 1674, the governor ordered Caulet to tolerate the entertainers.[24]

In the seventeenth century, secular and ecclesiastical authorities increasingly targeted festivities sponsored by lay confraternities or abbeys of fools, fearing the disruptive potential of their parody and social satire. Music was almost always part of their rites, whether it was instrumental dance music, obscene or parodic songs, or music for satirical street theater.[25] The most important procession of the Infanterie Dijonnaise, one of the best known fool societies, took place during the last three days of Carnival, when nearly two hundred men would process through the streets in fools' costumes, accompanying one of their number who had been elected the *mère folle* (mother of folly).[26] The mère folle was often seated with her court on a large horse-drawn chariot, from which members of the company would perform satirical verse, songs, and plays at major intersections and in front of the houses of city officials.[27] According to the eighteenth-century historian Jean-Baptiste Lucotte du Tilliot, the Infanterie's spectacles and plays featured a band of violins and other musicians. A burlesque ballet performed by the company, the *Retour de la Mère-Folie*, included an entry for a musician, whose *récit* gives the flavor of their performances:

As for me, I bring my songs,
My airs, my notes, and my caprice
To make of these a fitting sacrifice

To the Mother of Fools, who revives our senses,
And to better sound the third and the fifth,[28]
We drink to her health the quart and the pint.

The Infanterie's performances were not, however, always so benign. The company was involved in decades of conflict with local authorities and with the crown as a result of their satire and, occasionally, their direct political action.[29] Louis XIII finally dissolved the abbey in 1630, following an uprising against royal tax officers that took place during a masquerade. Undaunted, the Infanterie survived this prohibition.[30]

A lighter perspective on the political indiscretions committed by fool societies appears in Esprit Fléchier's semifictional account of an incident at Clermont in January 1666. Fléchier had accompanied the royal commission of magistrates sent from Paris to hold the *Grands Jours* at Auvergne in 1665, and his celebrated *Mémoires*, in which this account appears, are based on his experiences there as a young cleric.[31] Fléchier reports that near the end of their residency in Clermont, the commissioners were confronted by a rowdy youth abbey dressed as fools, who were processing through the streets to the sound of drums and flutes. The festivities, he noted, went on in spite of Anne of Austria's recent death, and in defiance of the crown's imposition of mourning throughout the realm:

> In the morning we were astonished to hear all the drums of the province beating, whose confused sound, echoing through the narrow streets of the town, made a terrible racket that was varied only by the sound of several flutes. A troupe of young people followed whose costumes, mixing yellow and green, seemed a little extravagant. Mr. the *intendant* and Mr. [Denis] Talon found this public celebration very insolent at a time when the recent death of the queen should have suppressed all entertainments, and sent an order to the drummers to withdraw; but they responded proudly

> that they recognized no authority but that of the greatest prince in the world, whose faithful subjects they were, and they beat their drums even more loudly than before. This response obliged the *intendant* to summon the principal members of their troupe to account for this bold action, so contrary to the mourning and sorrow of the public. Two or three of these sirs, detaching themselves from the group, went up to the chamber of the *intendant* and greeted him in a truly mad fashion: "Know . . . that we are the officers of the Prince of High Folly, who will impose the usual tribute on a strange lord who comes to kidnap the most beautiful nymph of his realm. We have our voices [*Nous avons nos voix*]." They had hardly finished these words when all the drummers, entering into the court, made such a loud noise that nothing else could be heard in the house.[32]

Fléchier concludes on a gallant note, writing that members of the court burst into laughter and withdrew so as not to be deafened by the drumming.

The levity of Fléchier's account of festive music contrasts with the gravity of Jesuit missionary writings, yet his memoir also recognizes the disruptive potential of music in festive contexts. If the Jesuits characterized this potential in religious, and even demonological, terms, this is due to the different genre and context of their writings as well as to their soteriological aims—aims that also characterized their work in the American missions. Not surprisingly, then, an awareness of and emphasis on the danger of festive music figure prominently in the Jesuits' reports from the American missions.

References to Carnival rites and their music appear in some of the earliest French ethnological writings, including those by the explorer Samuel de Champlain. But they occur most consistently in reports sent back to France by Catholic missionaries in the field, especially the Jesuits. Such references responded to similarities that the missionaries perceived between certain aspects of Native and European ceremonial cultures. While the Jesuits' understanding of northeastern ceremonial life, song culture, and religion was limited, especially in the early years of the missions, their reports typically highlighted commonalities with Carnival practices: a similar ritual morphology, a shared moral character, or a parallel relationship to temporal power.

In the *Relation* of 1639 the superior of the Wendat missions, Jérôme Lalemant, described the Iroquoian ceremony of *ononharoia* ("one's head is agitated" or "the upsetting of the brain").[33] Ononharoia, as practiced within the Wendat confederacy, was a ceremony aimed at healing members of a community who were sick as a result of unfulfilled desires of the soul. Bruce Trigger writes that this soul-curing ritual was held at least once a year in every major settlement, either because a prominent person was ill or because many community members felt depressed or sick.[34] The ceremony Lalemant describes was held for a woman of the Attignawantan Nation who fell ill after having had a vision of the Moon as a beautiful woman who prescribed the ritual. In order to cure her, twenty-five or thirty fellow clan members arrived to carry her back to her home settlement of Ossossané, singing in procession the whole time, and a complex series of ritual actions spanning a period of three days followed their arrival. First, members of the community made gifts of everything she desired, and then the patient passed through the fires of the longhouse without feeling any pain. When night fell everyone ran wildly through all the cabins in Ossossané, breaking, burning, or overturning everything in their path. This "third act" of the ceremony, Lalemant wrote, "consists in a general mania of all the people of the village, who . . . undertake to run wherever the sick woman has passed, adorned or daubed in their fashion, vying with one another in the frightful contortions of their faces,—making everywhere such a din, and indulging in such extravagances, that, to explain them and make them better understood, I do not know if I should compare them to the most extravagant of our maskers that one has ever heard of, or to the bacchantes of the ancients, or rather to the furies of Hell."[35] The next day everyone went again through all the cabins, this time proposing riddles, singing songs, and gesturing in ways that hinted at what their souls desired, desires of which they had learned in dreams the night before. The whole community repeated this series of ritual actions on the remaining nights and days of the ceremony, which concluded when the sick woman asked for and received her soul's last desire.

Lalemant's account of the ononharoia ceremony proceeds cautiously in the face of the Wendats' altered-state ritual performance at Ossossané, and he offers several possible comparisons, evoking Carnival masqueraders in France, ancient adepts of Dionysus, and even a diabolical sabbath. What links these to ononharoia, for Lalemant, are their common components of manic behavior, visibly altered physicality, and noise. Lalemant's derogatory reference to participants' singing as "din" is particularly revealing, if characteristic of early American colonial literature. For seventeenth-century Europeans, the concept of "noise" involved more than a negative aesthetic judgment: it was essentially an ontological category, tying ungoverned sound to a state of temporal or spiritual disorder.[36] The Jesuits possessed ample experience evaluating the ontological and moral status of music in France, as well as in the global missions, and their discussions of Wendat song draw on this discourse.

In the 1656 *Relation* Claude Dablon also referred to Carnival in explaining the ononharoia ceremony to his readers, and his description is more explicit than Lalemant's about the singing and other vocalization that took place. Although Dablon refers to a ceremony performed at the Haudenosaunee

(Iroquois confederacy) settlement at Onondaga, it is clearly a variant of the ononharoia ceremony shared by many Iroquoian-speaking nations in the seventeenth century, including the Wendats. Here the ononharoia ritual was performed as part of the midwinter ceremonial, in preparation for war against the Cat nation. "Not only do they believe in their dreams," Dablon wrote, "but they also hold a special festival to the demon of dreams. This festival might be called the feast of fools, or the Carnival of wicked Christians; for, in both, the devil plays almost the same part, and at the same season."[37] Dablon was referring specifically to Mardi Gras, since he writes that the ononharoia ceremony began on February 22. He also, by characterizing the ceremony participants as "masqueraders" and emphasizing their extravagant costuming and vocalization, especially their singing, evoked the masked processions that the lay confraternities held during the Carnival season. The participants' singing, as Dablon appears to have recognized, formed an important part of their attempts to communicate the desires revealed in their dreams: "it sometimes happens that one is not bright enough to guess their thoughts; for they are not clearly put forth, but are expressed in riddles, phrases of covert meaning, songs, and occasionally in gestures alone."[38] To this end, a man whom he describes as a Satyr "marched about our cabin, singing and howling at the top of his voice" before accompanying two women dressed as "Megaeras" (or Furies) through the settlement, "their hair flying, their faces coal-black, their persons clothed with a couple of Wolfskins, and each armed with a handspike or large stake." A female warrior entered the priests' cabin next, "armed with an arquebus which she had obtained through her dream. . . . She was shouting, howling, and singing, saying that she was going to war against the Cat Nation, that she would fight them, and bring back some prisoners. . . . This Amazon," Dablon recalls, "was followed by a [male] warrior, who came in carrying his bow and arrows and bayonet. He danced and sang, shouted, and threatened; and then suddenly rushed at a woman who had entered to view this comedy."[39] Dablon describes groups as well as individuals processing through the settlement, including some who "march about in companies, and perform dances with contortions of body that resemble those of men possessed." He concludes that "during the three days and three nights in which this nonsense lasts," such a "din" prevailed that "scarcely a moment's quiet" could be had.[40]

Dablon interrupts his narration with a reflection that specifically recalls the festivities held during the Carnival season by the Infanterie Dijonnaise: "If it be true that every one has some grain of folly,—since *Stultorum infinitus est numerus* ["Folly is infinite and universal"]—then these people must be acknowledged to possess more than half an ounce apiece."[41] The Latin reference is to Ecclesiastes 1:15, "Perversi difficile corriguntur et stultorum infinitus est numerus," but it was also a well-known maxim that served as the motto of the Infanterie.[42] Dablon reiterates his references to Carnival several times in the same chapter and wraps up his account by moralizing, "It is not in America alone that people seem to take pleasure in being deceived, but in Europe also."[43]

Similarly disdainful comparisons with Carnival also appear in the missionaries' discussions of the *awataerohi* ceremony. Jean de Brébeuf drew such comparisons in the *Relation* of 1636, written when he was the superior of the Wendat mission at Ihonatiria. *Awataerohi* ("hot cinders dance") was a healing ceremony performed to cure the disease of the same name, which was caused by a spirit (also known as Awataerohi) that had lodged itself in the body of the patient. The most general remedy the Wendat possessed for curing illnesses, awataerohi, like many other such healing ceremonies, was the specialty of a single medicine society; as was typical of Wendat healing ceremonies, the ceremony was performed if the sick person dreamed that it would be the cure or if a shaman prescribed it.[44] The ceremony centered on a feast, during which an adept would sing and play the turtle rattle to the spirit responsible for the sickness and would handle fire and sometimes apply hot cinders or stones to the patient. Other members of the medicine society or the community would also sing and dance in the presence of the patient.

Brébeuf's account focuses on a man named Ihongwaha who was seeking to become an *arendiwane* ("his supernatural power is great"), the general term for a shaman.[45] In late January Ihongwaha was invited to participate in an awataerohi feast, which involved him breaking the thirty-day fast that he was then observing in order to become an arendiwane. Ihongwaha evidently agreed to do so because he was one of the few people who could sing the awataerohi songs needed to heal the sick person: indeed, according to Brébeuf, he "was one of the masters."[46] Ihongwaha's entranced singing was so vigorous that he fell into a frenzy and afterward needed to have many feasts performed for his own healing. It was this manic quality of Ihongwaha's singing, together with his use of the turtle rattle, that led Brébeuf to compare him to a Carnival fool: "He allowed himself, at last, to be so carried away, and ate so heartily and sang with so much vehemence that he left the feast with his brain in a sling. See him then with the turtle, or more correctly, with the *marotte* in his hand, in the most trying season of winter,—naked as when he was born, running about in the snow, and singing night and day."[47] The marotte was one of the most ubiquitous European icons of the fool. It had a number of forms but typically was either a rattle or a wooden club topped with a fool's head, including the characteristic jester's cap. From the perspective of seventeenth-century

Wendat culture, Brébeuf's comparison of the turtle rattle with the marotte was particularly unfortunate, not to mention inaccurate, since the turtle rattle was a sacred, animate instrument, related to the Turtle clan and to Wendat origin myths, and as such an integral part of most major ceremonies.[48]

Lalemant acknowledged the instrument's connection with Iroquoian origins three years later, in the *Relation* of 1639: "This Turtle [rattle]," he wrote, "is not a real Turtle, but only the shell and skin so arranged as to make a sort of drum; having thrown certain pebbles into this, they make from it an instrument like that which children in France use to play with. There is a mysterious something, I know not what, in this semblance of a Turtle, to which these peoples attribute their origin."[49] Historian Georges E. Sioui (Wendat) recounts one version of the myth as follows: "The Wendats believed, as did the Iroquois, that the land on which all humankind lived was an island to which a woman named Aataentsic had descended from a celestial world. This woman landed on the back of the Big Turtle, who welcomed her at the request of the animals (who were all aquatic at this time). The humblest of these, the toad, dove into the water and was able to gather some silt, which the Small Turtle spread over the Big Turtle's shell. This island grew until it formed the world (America) as it is known to the Amerindians."[50] In this light Brébeuf's characterization of the turtle rattle as a marotte desacralized the instrument by removing it from its original mythic-ceremonial context and trivializing it as a European fool's bauble. Yet in another sense, Brébeuf's cultural translation of the turtle rattle for his readers can be understood as an exchange of one sacred context for another, if profoundly foreign, one. Such an act of spiritual recontextualization does not diminish the conceptual violence of his rhetoric, but it does help us better understand its stakes, since the fool was anything but a disenchanted figure for Brébeuf and his colleagues. The missionary's evocation of the fool aligns Ihongwaha's singing and the awataerohi ceremony itself with a category of festive rites that the Jesuits feared were often superstitious (and thus diabolical) in nature.

Later in the same chapter Brébeuf extended this Carnival analogy in a passage describing Ihongwaha's induction into a different medicine society, the Atirenda.[51] The society, which had to be brought in from another village, specialized in *otakrendoiae*, a dance in which participants mimicked poisoning each other, then recovering from the poison. The Atirenda performed the otakrendoiae ceremony for Ihongwaha in order to cure him of the lingering mania or madness he had suffered since breaking his thirty-day fast.[52] The society first diagnosed Ihongwaha's illness, in a dance that Brébeuf describes as follows: "The dance being ended, because [Ihongwaha] had fallen over backward and vomited, they declared him to belong entirely to the confraternity of fools [*confrérie des fols*]; and came to the remedy therefore which is usual in this disease, and which would be sufficient to make them pass for fools, even if they were the wisest men in the world."[53] Possessing little understanding of Iroquoian medicine societies, Brébeuf compares the Atirenda to the French confraternities of fools, with their parodic traditions. A similar lack of comprehension marks his discussion of the events following Ihongwaha's initiation into the society, when the Atirenda perform the otakrendoiae dance itself. Watching the society's members perform, Brébeuf can do little more than condemn the Atirenda's proceedings as Bacchic debauchery: "never did frenzied Bacchantes of bygone times do anything more furious in their orgies."[54] The missionary may not have understood what was going on in Wendat terms, but he thought he recognized in the performers' frenzied state a diabolical manifestation with roots extending back, through contemporary France, to classical antiquity.

The Jesuit writers discussed here were particularly concerned with song that occurred in Wendat healing ceremonies, and nearly all their references to Carnival appear in this context. This focus is partly explained by Wendat arendiwanes' use of trance performance—as in the case of Ihongwaha—as part of the ensemble of healing practices associated with a particular ceremony: the perceptibly altered embodiment that Europeans associated with trance always posed an ontological conundrum for the missionaries. Entranced vocalization, in particular, demanded analysis and intervention, because as already noted, Europeans believed well into the seventeenth century that the voice was a vehicle for the spiritual forces that animated it. The diabolical agency that the Jesuits heard in Wendat trance performance could easily have connected it to the similarly charged performance that Catholic reformers worried was endemic in French festive life. Yet while altered-state performance was part of many Wendat ceremonies, French Carnival performance did not itself involve the kind of skilled trance that arendiwanes practiced. Perhaps a better explanation for the Jesuits' focus on healing ceremonies is the presence of manic behavior, including frenzied singing and dancing. Real or simulated mania *was* a component of Carnival masquerades or other fool processions, and just as important, it was also a primary factor in the social or political disruption that sometimes occurred.

A similar connection between ceremonial performance and traditionalist resistance to priestly authority obtained in the Wendat context. Iroquoian and Algonquian communities throughout the region accorded real prestige and power to skilled healing shamans, and thus it is unsurprising that the arendiwanes and the healing societies were at the forefront of efforts to discredit and undermine the missionaries' efforts to intervene in traditional ceremonial life. Indeed, many of the

Native communities in which the Jesuits worked came to suspect that the priests were themselves powerful shamans or sorcerers, and rivalries flared between Wendat shamans and Jesuit priests. Trigger argues that the refusal of the missionaries and their converts to participate in traditional healing ceremonies was partly responsible for the suspicions of witchcraft that surrounded them. In a similar fashion, the Christians' repudiation of traditional ceremonial life was blamed for the string of calamities that occurred in the 1630s and 1640s, including severe epidemics, bad harvests, and devastating warfare.[55]

In the context of such traditionalist suspicion of Jesuit influence, the arendiwanes and Wendat headmen used the most important healing ceremonies, such as ononharoia, to spur communal action against the Jesuits, especially in the 1640s, when a strong traditionalist movement developed. In the 1639 ononharoia ceremony at Ossossané, for example, Lalemant writes that the missionaries were repeatedly "attacked" and pressured to contribute whatever the participants' dreams required, which they refused. And Trigger reports that when Ossossané celebrated ononharoia in the winter of 1641–42, the headmen again tried to convince every Christian in town to participate, using coercion as necessary, although they backed down when the converts resisted.[56]

At Teanaostaiaé the traditionalists' hostility toward the Christians was so severe that several Christians were attacked in the Jesuits' chapel when ononharoia was celebrated in 1645–46.[57] Father Ragueneau reported that one recent convert, Laurent Tandoutsont, ran toward the commotion in the chapel singing songs that Wendat captives sang when they were about to be ritually tortured, which suggests that Tandoutsont viewed the traditionalists' aggression as an act of warfare against fellow villagers. In contrast, Ragueneau represented the ononharoia attacks in hierarchical political terms, as an act of "sedition" against the Jesuits' authority. Tandoutsont's response more accurately reflected the nature of the conflict as rooted in internal tensions within Wendat society, which resulted partly from social and cultural changes that Christianization had introduced. Regardless, both men recognized the relationship between ononharoia and the traditionalists' resistance, even if their understanding necessarily differed.

For the missionaries, Carnival's unstable mixture of social conservation and anarchy provided an apt parallel for the temporary license and, sometimes, violence sanctioned by ononharoia ceremonies. Indeed, it is tempting to ask whether the Jesuits heard Wendat healing chants as noise because they suspected the devil's influence in Native music, or whether the priests' demonological explanations stemmed from an ingrained response to what they heard as noise, and to its association with disorder. In this respect, although the Jesuits' tendency to hear the echoes of Carnival in Wendat ceremonial performance certainly disregarded Wendat traditionalists' own understanding of their songs, the Jesuits' misreading recognized a deeper affinity between Native and European communal song traditions in the seventeenth century: their common utility as occasions for resistance to cultural interference by outsiders armed with an expansionist religious and political ideology. The parallels the Jesuits perceived between Wendat and French Carnival song, in other words, reflected their fears of both the sinister religious charge and the temporal threat that both traditions posed. The Jesuits' rhetoric thus highlighted the potential of song or music in both situations as a medium for contesting collective social realities and powers of self-determination, whether in actual performance or, as in the Jesuit *Relations*, in polemical representation.

Notes

1. Greer, introduction to *Jesuit Relations*, 1–19; and Thwaites, introduction to *Jesuit Relations* (hereafter *JR*), 1:1–44.
2. Lyons, *Exemplum*, 33–65.
3. See Châtellier, "Les Campagnes européennes," 315–17; Clossey, *Salvation and Globalization*, 234–35; and Deslandres, "Mission et altérité."
4. On early modern "superstition" see Clark, *Thinking with Demons*, 472–88; and, in relation to music, Bloechl, *Native American Song*, 35–57.
5. Châtellier, *Le Catholicisme en France*, 255–56.
6. See Clark, *Thinking with Demons*, 389–400 and passim; and Clossey, *Salvation and Globalization*, 130–35.
7. Clossey, *Salvation and Globalization*, 245.
8. For the Wendats' history during this period, see Trigger, *Children of Aataentsic*, 2:725–840.
9. See Broutin, *La réforme pastorale*; Châtellier, *Le Catholicisme en France*, 231–56; Delumeau, *Catholicism between Luther and Voltaire*, 175–202; Hsia, *World of Catholic Renewal*, 194–209; Le Goff and Rémond, *Histoire de la France religieuse*; and Mullett, *Catholic Reformation*. Invaluable for any discussion of Catholic reform in France are the volumes of the *Histoire des diocèses de France* and the *Histoire religieuse des provinces de France*.
10. See Clossey, *Salvation and Globalization*, 232–33; Dompnier, "La Compagnie de Jésus"; and Martin, *Jesuit Mind*, 213.
11. On the Catholic domestic missions see Châtellier, *Religion of the Poor*, 1–90; Deslandres, "Mission et altérité"; Dompnier, "La Compagnie de Jésus"; and Pérouas, "Essai sur l'histoire des missions."
12. Launay, *La Musique réligieuse*, 191–201.
13. See Davis, *Society and Culture*, 97–123.
14. Clark, *Thinking with Demons*, 389–400 and passim.
15. Bloechl, *Native American Song*, 35–106; Tomlinson, *Music in Renaissance Magic*, 44–66, 101–44.
16. Ménestrier, *Des Représentations*, 56. All English translations are my own unless otherwise noted.
17. Maunoir, *Miracles et sabbats*, 68.
18. Maunoir, *Miracles et sabbats*, 29, 39, 41, 48, 51, 60, 68–71, 75, 88, 98.
19. Maunoir, *Miracles et sabbats*, 70.
20. Maunoir, *Miracles et sabbats*, 70.

21. Father Paul Beurrier, "Mémoires," Bibliothéque Sainte-Geneviève, MS 1885, fol. 252, cited in Ferté, *La Vie réligieuse*, 292.
22. Bercé, *Fête et révolte*, 157–58.
23. See Davis, *Society and Culture*, 97–123; Ladurie, *Peasants of Languedoc*; and Ladurie, *Carnival in Romans*.
24. Bercé, *Fête et révolte*, 158.
25. See Brown, *Music in French Secular Theatre*, 80–109.
26. Women were never members of the abbeys: the officers with female identities—including the *mère folle* herself, as well as her ladies-in-waiting—were cross-dressed men.
27. Du Tilliot, *Mémoires*, 63–66.
28. In music theory the "third" and the "fifth" are the pitch intervals that make up a triad, the basic chord of Western harmony.
29. Ménestrier reports similar satirical spectacles, also called "la Mère-folie," performed during Carnival at Dijon, in which "persons of quality disguised as vintners, and mounted on festival cars, sang songs and satires, which were like the public censure of that time" (*Représentations en musique*, 52).
30. Davis, *Society and Culture*, 119, 307 n. 89. Du Tilliot transcribed documents pertaining to the Infanterie, including the royal edict of 1630 (*Mémoires*, 111–12).
31. On the *grands jours*, see Mousnier, *Institutions of France*, 2:491–501.
32. Fléchier, *Mémoires sur les Grands-Jours*, 387.
33. See Trigger, *Huron*, 115. On the *ononharoia* ceremony see also Tooker, *Ethnography of the Huron*, 110–14; Tooker, *Iroquois Ceremonial*, 84–103; and Trigger, *Children of Aataentsic*, 1:83–84.
34. Trigger, *Children of Aataentsic*, 1:83. Sioui (*Les Wendats*, 309 n. 330) and Trigger (*Huron*, 115) note that the ceremony could also be held when the community was in serious danger.
35. *JR*, 17:176–177. English translations from the *Jesuit Relations* are adapted from the Thwaites edition.
36. Bloechl, *Native American Song*, 33–106.
37. *JR*, 42:153.
38. *JR*, 42:155.
39. *JR*, 42:159–61.
40. *JR*, 42:163.
41. *JR*, 42:159.
42. Dablon's colleague at the Onondaga mission, Father Chaumonot, was born and reared near Châtillon-sur-Seine in Burgundy, and he

certainly would have heard of the Infanterie Dijonnaise, since he spent time in and around Dijon as a young man (Chaumonot, *Un Missionnaire des Hurons*, 3–4).

43. *JR*, 42:175.
44. Tooker, *Ethnography of the Huron*, 103–6, 109; Trigger, *Huron*, 116–17; Trigger, *Children of Aataentisic*, 1:80–81.
45. The Iroquoian word *arendiwane* is a compound of *arendi* or *orenda* ("supernatural power") and *wane* or *wanen* ("large" or "powerful"). Hewitt ("Orenda," 43) notes that the root of this word, *orenda*, is also the only word that signified "to sing" or "to chant" in seventeenth-century Iroquoian, and it is related to anything used as a charm or amulet as well as to hoping, praying, or submitting. See also Tooker, *Ethnography of the Huron*, 91–92; and Trigger, *Huron*, 107, 134–35.
46. *JR*, 10:197.
47. *JR*, 10:197–99.
48. Diamond et al., *Visions of Sound*.
49. *JR*, 17:157. See Sioui, *Les Hurons-Wendats*, 16; also Tooker, *Ethnography of the Huron*, 79, 151–53.
50. Sioui, *Les Hurons-Wendats*, 33.
51. Brébeuf (*JR*, 10:205) writes that the Atirenda society possessed about eighty members at that time, including six women. On the society and its ceremonies see Tooker, *Ethnography of the Huron*, 98–99; and Trigger, *Children of Aataentisic*, 1:80–81.
52. According to Brébeuf (*JR*, 10:203), this was the first time the *otakrendoiae* ceremony was performed in an Attignawantan ("Bear" Nation) settlement, and Tooker (*Ethnography of the Huron*, 99 n. 92) speculates that it was adopted from Anishinaabe (Ojibwa) Midéwiwin healing societies in the nearby Great Lakes region.
53. *JR*, 10:205.
54. *JR*, 10:205–207.
55. Trigger, *Children of Aataentsic*, 2:589–96, 831–32.
56. *JR*, 17:171, 23:41–57.
57. *JR*, 30:99–101; Trigger, *Children of Aataentsic*, 2:714–22.

Works Cited

Bercé, Yves-Marie. *Fête et révolte: Des mentalités populaires du XVIe au XVIIIe siècle*. Paris: Librairie Hachette, 1976.

Bloechl, Olivia A. *Native American Song at the Frontiers of Early Modern Music*. Cambridge: Cambridge University Press, 2008.

Broutin, Paul. *La réforme pastorale en France au XVIIe siècle: Recherches sur la tradition pastorale après le concile de Trente.* 2 vols. Tournai: Desclée and Company, 1956.

Brown, Howard Mayer. *Music in the French Secular Theatre, 1400–1550.* Cambridge: Harvard University Press, 1963.

Châtellier, Louis. *Le Catholicisme en France (limites actuelles) 1500–1650*, vol. 2: *Le XVIIe siècle, 1600–1650.* Paris: Sedes, 1995.

———. "Les Campagnes européennes au temps de la Réforme catholique: Pays de mission ou centres missionnaires?" In *La Christianisation des campagnes: Actes du colloque du* CIHEC*, 25–27 August 1994*, ed. Jean-Pierre Massaut and Marie-Élisabeth Henneau, 311–32. Brussels: Institut historique belge de Rome, 1996.

———. *The Europe of the Devout: The Catholic Reformation and the Formation of a New Society.* New York: Cambridge University Press, 1989.

———. *The Religion of the Poor: Rural Missions in Europe and the Formation of Modern Catholicism, c. 1500–c. 1800.* Trans. Brian Pearce. Cambridge: Cambridge University Press; Paris: Editions de la Maison des sciences de l'homme, 1997.

Chaumonot, Pierre-Joseph-Marie. *Un Missionnaire des Hurons: Autobiographie du Père Chaumonot.* Ed. Henri Martin. Paris: H. Oudin, 1885.

Clark, Stuart. *Thinking with Demons: The Idea of Witchcraft in Early Modern Europe.* New York: Oxford University Press, 1997.

Clossey, Luke. *Salvation and Globalization in the Early Jesuit Missions.* Cambridge: Cambridge University Press, 2008.

Davis, Natalie Zemon. *Society and Culture in Early Modern France.* Stanford: Stanford University Press, 1975.

Delumeau, Jean. *Catholicism between Luther and Voltaire: A New View of the Counter-Reformation.* Philadelphia: Westminster Press, 1977.

Deslandres, Dominique. "Mission et altérité: Les missionnaires français et la définition de l' 'Autre' au XVIIe siècle." In *Proceedings of the 18th Annual Meeting of the French Colonial Historical Society*, ed. James Pritchard, 1–13. Montreal: French Colonial Historical Society, 1992.

Diamond, Beverley, M. Sam Cronk, and Franziska von Rosen. *Visions of Sound: Musical Instruments of First Nations Communities in Northeastern America.* Chicago: University of Chicago Press, 1994.

Dompnier, Bernard. "La Compagnie de Jésus et la mission de l'intérieur." In *Les Jésuites à l'âge baroque, 1540–1640*, ed. Luce Giard and Louis de Vaucelles, S.J., 155–79. Grenoble: Éditions Jérôme Millon, 1996.

Ferté, Jeanne. *La Vie religieuse dans les campagnes parisiennes (1622–1695)*. Paris: Librairie Philosophique J. Vrin, 1962.

Fléchier, Esprit. *Mémoires sur les Grands-Jours tenus à Clermont en 1665 et 1666*. Ed. B. Gonod and Eric de Bussac. Clermont-Ferrand: Porquet, 1844; reprint, Clermont-Ferrand: Éditions Paleo, 2007.

Greer, Allan, ed. *The Jesuit Relations: Natives and Missionaries in Seventeenth-Century North America*. New York: Palgrave Macmillan, 2000.

Hewitt, John N. B. "Orenda and a Definition of Religion." *American Anthropologist* 4 (1902): 33–46.

Histoire des diocèses de France. Paris: Letouzey et Ané; Beauchesne, 1967–.

Histoire religieuse des provinces de France. Chambray-lès-tours: CLD, 1978–.

Hsia, R. Po-Chia. *The World of Catholic Renewal 1540–1770*. Cambridge: Cambridge University Press, 1998.

Ladurie, Roy. *Carnival in Romans*. Trans. Mary Feeney. New York: G. Braziller, 1979.

———. *The Peasants of Languedoc*. Trans. John Day. Urbana: University of Illinois Press, 1974.

Launay, Denise. *La Musique réligieuse en France du Concile de Trente à 1804*. Paris: Société Française de Musicologie, 1993.

Le Goff, Jacques, and René Rémond, eds. *Histoire de la France religieuse*, vol. 2: *Du Christianisme flamboyant à l'aube des Lumières*. Paris: Seuil, 1988.

Lyons, John D. *Exemplum: The Rhetoric of Example in Early Modern France and Italy*. Princeton: Princeton University Press, 1989.

Martin, A. Lynn. *The Jesuit Mind: The Mentality of an Elite in Early Modern France*. Ithaca: Cornell University Press, 1988.

Maunoir, Julien, S.J. *Miracles et sabbats: Journal du Père Maunoir, Missions en Bretagne—1631–1650*. Trans. (from Latin) Anne-Sophie and Jérôme Cras. Ed. Éric Lebec. Paris: Les Éditions de Paris, 1997.

Ménestrier, Claude-François. *Des Répresentations en musique anciennes et modernes*. Paris: René Guignard, 1686; reprint, Geneva: Minkoff, 1972.

Mousnier, Roland E. *The Institutions of France under the Absolute Monarchy, 1598–1789*. 2 vols. Trans. Arthur Goldhammer. Chicago: University of Chicago Press, 1994.

Mullett, Michael A. *The Catholic Reformation*. London: Routledge, 1999.

Pérouas, Louis. "Essai sur l'histoire des missions à l'intérieur de la

France." In *La mission générale: Dix ans d'expérience du* CPMI, ed. J.-F. Motte, 39–57. Paris: Les Editions du Cerf, 1961.

Sioui, Georges E. *Les Hurons-Wendats: Une civilsation méconnue*. Sainte-Foy, Canada: Presses de l'Université Laval, 1994.

Thwaites, Reuben Gold, ed. *The Jesuit Relations and Allied Documents: Travels and Explorations of the Jesuit Missionaries in New France, 1610–1791*. 73 vols. Cleveland: Burrows Brothers, 1896–1901.

Tilliot, Jean-Baptiste Lucotte du. *Mémoires pour servir à l'histoire de la fête des foux, qui se faisoit autrefois dans plusieurs églises*. Lausanne: Marc Bousquet, 1741.

Tomlinson, Gary. *Music in Renaissance Magic: Toward a Historiography of Others*. Chicago: University of Chicago Press, 1994.

Tooker, Elisabeth. *An Ethnography of the Huron Indians, 1615–1649*. Bureau of American Ethnology Bulletin 190. Washington DC: Smithsonian Institution, 1964.

———. *The Iroquois Ceremonial of Midwinter*. Syracuse: Syracuse University Press, 1970.

Trigger, Bruce G. *The Children of Aataentsic: A History of the Huron People to 1660*. 2 vols. Montreal: McGill-Queen's University Press, 1976.

———. *The Huron: Farmers of the North*. 2nd ed. Fort Worth TX: Harcourt, 1990.

[5]

"I Wunnatuckquannum, This Is My Hand"

Native Performance in Massachusett Language Indian Deeds

Stephanie Fitzgerald

On September 8, 1683, Wampanoag queen sachem Wunnatuckquannum conveyed a parcel of land on the eastern section of Noepe, or modern day Martha's Vineyard, to David Okes, a member of her constituency.[1] Ritually enacted on site, the ceremonial passing of land from one hand to another was just one part of a gathering that likely included diplomatic encounters, transmission of tribute goods and gifts of wampum, and even the arrangement of marriages.[2] The ritual revolved around Wunnatuckquannum, for as sachem she served as the site of legal, political, and social authority. Lengthy discourses punctuated by "emphaticall speech and great action" by the queen sachem and other high-ranking members would have accompanied the events, as "skilled speech and status were interrelated" in this coastal Algonquian society.[3] Such performances often included a ritual reciting of the genealogy of the land in question and mapping out the land through Native toponyms, with those present serving as witnesses. Thus Wunnatuckquannum's conveyance to Okes was not just a redistribution of land but a strategic performance of the sachem's power, wealth, and beneficence that served to cement bonds of kinship and allegiance in a time of political and hierarchical transition.

However, the story of the land in question, Pachatickquset Neck on the west side of Edgartown Great Pond, does not end with Okes. Five years later, on July 15, 1688, Okes in turn conveyed the land to fellow Wampanoag Isaak Tuhkemen. Both records remained firmly entrenched in the Wampanoag oral tradition, and were not entered into the colonial English legal record until July 23, 1707, both written in the same hand on the same sheet of paper. Even then, the deeds were not penned in English but in the Massachusett language.[4] In this way the land transfers at Pachatickquset Neck generated a number of texts (both oral and written) and performances that represent the divide between oral and print cultures and Wampanoag and Anglo-American legal systems—a divide that is bridged by the performing body of the sachem. Each text, each act, was followed by another, linked together by Wunnatuckquannum's initial performance as the "symbolic embodiment" of the sachemship.[5] This embodiment was echoed through Wunnatuckquannum's choice of metonymic language in her ritual performances. In the first extant deed, dated 1683, she signed, ritualistically, as her own witness: "I Wunnatuckquannum, witness; my hand." With the words "I Wunnatuckquannum, this is my hand" in a subsequent deed, she invoked the power of the sachemship as a whole.[6]

Reconstructing Indian performance in the seventeenth century is a complicated act in itself, obliging us to draw on disparate sources such as accounts of early colonists and explorers, archival documents in a variety of languages, and oral histories and traditions of contemporary tribes, our access to which is always mediated. As mediated accounts, they must be approached with a certain amount of caution. In this discussion I proceed under a definition of Wampanoag legal performance as a ritualized act that transmits "social knowledge, memory, and identity."[7] Ritual is a dynamic force, always changing, synthesizing, and transforming. It orders the relationship between the everyday and the other-worldly as well as the political, social, and religious order of a community. Traditional Wampanoag legal practice was inextricable from the political, social, and ceremonial implications that made up the performance. Supernatural figures such as the thunderbird and the horned serpent, as well as other abstract designs, have been found on pre-contact amulets and pictographs, reinforcing the relationship between the Wampanoag and their cosmos.[8] When Wunnatuckquannum redistributed land to David Okes in a ritualized legal performance, she reordered a series of relationships—between herself as sachem and her followers, between the land and the people, and between the collective group and the cosmos—as well as transmitting that knowledge to the witnesses and participants.

Catherine Bell's definition of ritual as "a type of critical juncture where some opposing social or cultural forces come together" is particularly useful for this discussion.[9] For Wunnatuckquannum and her followers, seventeenth century Noepe was the site of this "critical juncture." Wunnatuckquannum ruled during a time of transition, one in which English cultural values began to entwine themselves with traditional Native practices, and the Wampanoag land base was slowly but surely moving into English hands. Accordingly, the Wampanoags used, adapted, and transformed objects and systems from "opposing social or cultural forces" into their own. One such example is the way that the inhabitants of Noepe took to literacy in the vernacular, using it to their own purposes and fashions. Church officials kept birth, death, and marriage records in Massachusett, and Thomas Waban, the town clerk of Natick, kept official records in the vernacular. Beginning writers used the margins of books, especially Bibles, to inscribe names and other personal information, in the process interacting with new forms of literacy.[10] Such examples demonstrate the ways Native people adapted to both alphabetic literacy and English legal customs and practices. In a similar vein, the legal performances spawned by Wunnatuckquannum's original land conveyances drew as much from pre-contact cultural memory as they did from recent contact with English colonists and English common law.

Wunnatuckquannum's 1683 land transfer to David Okes is one of a number of similar transactions the queen sachem undertook in the latter part of the seventeenth century with both English colonists and her fellow Wampanoag. The written conveyances take the form of what Elizabeth Little has identified as "Indian deeds," an often slippery term that encompasses both Indian-to-Indian land transactions written by Indians in the vernacular and Anglo-Indian land transactions in English. Little's study concludes that deeds beginning with "'Neen' or 'I' followed by the name of the grantor" were written by Indians. English deeds differ from their Indian counterparts in their use of the English language and legal terms such as "this witnesseth" and "heirs and assigns."[11] Indian deeds were unstable on a number of registers. Conflict arose between sachems and their followers over land sales to the English. Anglo-Indian deeds, as Peter Leavenworth reminds us, often went "unrecorded for decades" and were particularly susceptible to forgeries.[12] Francis Jennings explains that "an Indian 'deed' was not a deed at all as that term is understood in Anglo-American law. When it was written in favor of an English government it was a deed of cession, and when it was written in favor of a private person it was a quitclaim rather than a conveyance." And New England Governor Edmund Andros is said to have remarked in 1688 that Indian deeds were worth "no more than the scratch of a bear paw."[13] Scholarship on colonial era land deeds largely focuses on Anglo-Indian transactions, which recount a familiar narrative of land loss and colonization.[14] I hope to chart an alternative path, one that takes into consideration the history of the early Wampanoag people and their own performative practices relating to land and law. In this essay I foreground three types of ritualized legal performances: those embodied by Wunnatuckquannum in the ritual land conveyances, Indian-to-Indian land transactions written by Indians in the vernacular Massachusett language, and the filing of the written documents with the colonial courts. Specifically, I examine four extant Massachusett language Indian deeds attributed to Wunnatuckquannum as both embodied and textual encounters that highlight the tensions between the materiality of the written deeds and the Native performances that produced them.

What little we know about Wunnatuckquannum and her tenure as queen sachem is gleaned from archival sources such as the legal documents mentioned. While reports from English colonists help us define the roles and responsibilities of the sachems, even the Mayhews, so prominent in the history of Martha's Vineyard, paid little attention to her in their writings. Her people, the Wampanoags, call themselves the "People of the First Light," referring to their geographic position on the eastern seaboard. The sociopolitical body of the Wampanoags was the sachemship, which, as Kathleen J. Bragdon describes, "was made up of those who defended it," and whose "loyalty . . . rested with the sachemship as an ongoing social grouping, to whom one's ancestors had belonged and to which one's own posterity would be loyal." The sachemship itself was highly stratified, headed by the sachem, a council made up of "principal men," commoners, and a servant or slave class. Kinship relations and their accompanying reciprocal rights and responsibilities bound the sachemship together and were vital to the maintenance and survival of the group as a whole.[15]

By the time Wunnatuckquannum assumed her role as sachem, her grandfather and predecessor Tawanquatuck had already paved the way for English colonization and evangelization of the island and its inhabitants by selling land in his district of Nunepog to Thomas Mayhew in 1641. This land sale and its accompanying migration of English colonists set the stage for the epidemics that swept the island in 1643 and 1645, reducing the Wampanoag population by half, leaving gaps and fissures in the social and political hierarchy. The kinship system with its reciprocal rights and responsibilities began to weaken. Wampanoag leaders such as Tawanquatuck himself converted to Christianity, and his sachemship soon followed. As Christianity took hold, old customs such as curing rituals, the blackface rite, the ritual painting of bodies, and mourning ceremonies were left behind. While the island Wampanoags were largely spared the violence and strife their mainland kin experienced during King Philip's War of 1675–1676, their relationships with the English on the island were strained, resulting in a reordering of the political and social systems. As Ann Marie Plane has pointed out, "sachems found their autonomy diminished and women found their opportunities for formal leadership reduced."[16] Wunnatuckquannum would be the last sachem of Nunepog and the last queen sachem of Noepe.

Conversion to Christianity required English-style clothing, houses, and manufactured goods, and many Wampanoags, including Wunnatuckquannum, found themselves indebted to island merchants. By 1683, the same year she deeded land to David Okes, Wunnatuckquannum had fallen fifty shillings in debt to Joseph Daggett.[17] A combination of mounting consumer debt, lawsuits, and loss of tribute payments from her constituents due to the epidemic of 1690 led her to sell land to English settlers "at least eight times between 1670 and 1690," displacing her own people to the opposite side of Edgartown Great Pond via what historian David Silverman interprets as "fee simple sachem rights."[18] The lands conveyed by four of these fee simple sachem rights found their way into the colonial archive in the form of Indian deeds.

The Indian deeds I discuss here belong to a larger body of early vernacular Native writing that has been largely overlooked by scholars, a genre that includes political and legal documents such as petitions and treaties. This genre has its roots in Indian ritual performance, which privileges the oral over the written text, yet becomes attached to it through writing. As Craig Womack has argued, such indigenous writings "were used as a *complement* of oral tradition rather than a *replacement*."[19] Within such a system, the oral and textual traditions become synthesized and intertwined. Acquisition of vernacular literacy on Martha's Vineyard began with Thomas Mayhew, who built upon John Eliot's invention of a Roman-based Massachusett orthography and success in educating Native converts in the Massachusetts Bay Colony. Evidence from this period suggests that writing was "inherently social, and . . . reading and writing were 'inextricably' linked to speech," as Native converts were known to read to one another.[20] Further, the choice to write and keep records in Massachusett rather than English designates this practice as an early example of what Scott Lyons has called rhetorical sovereignty, or "the inherent right and abilities of *peoples* to determine their own communicative needs and desires in this pursuit, to decide for themselves the goals, modes, styles, and languages of public discourse."[21] In this way the Native inhabitants of Martha's Vineyard chose vernacular literacy as their means of public discourse in the ritual performances I discuss here.

In coastal Algonquian societies, Bragdon suggests, "the *act* of writing itself can be seen as another type of ritual, the goal of which was the acquisition of personal power." This personal power took the form of *manit*, a "spiritual force" that was integral to Wampanoag cosmology. Accounts from early colonists reinforce this idea of writing as power, as Roger Williams observed: "especially of Bookes and Letters, they will end thus: *Manitôwock*, They are Gods." Bragdon argues that "books and writing were endowed with [spiritual] significance" in the Wampanoag worldview.[22] In his analysis of a Pequot medicine bundle containing a page from a seventeenth-century King James Bible, Kevin McBride asserts that the "original meaning [of the page] was essentially transformed in order to accommodate a Native perspective on manitou and power."[23] Reports of the linked relationship between writing and power are easily extended to performance as well. As performance scholar Diana Taylor has noted, "writing and embodied performance have often worked together to layer the historical memories that constitute community." While there is no historical evidence for Wunnatuckquannum as "writer," she is the "author" of the legal performances embodied in the Indian deeds bearing her mark. It is Wunnatuckquannum herself, the "symbolic embodiment" of her sachemship, who bridges the divide between the oral and the written, the performance and the text, and thereby constitutes her community.[24]

By placing the four extant deeds attributed to Wunnatuckquannum, from 1683 to 1700, in conversation with each other, we can map out the journey of a Wampanoag legal practice that moves from oral performative acts to their transcriptions in the vernacular Massachusett to one entwined with written deeds filed with the English colonial courts, with each performance adding a layer of complexity and awareness of the parallel English legal system. The original performative acts are fleeting and ephemeral, and exist only in the collective memory of the community. As Jan Vansina describes, "the utterance is transitory, but the memories are not."[25] Enacted on the site of the land to be deeded, the performances require the presence and participation of a number of parties: the sachem and principal men, the grantee and a large number of witnesses as well as those who might be called "rememberers," charged with the responsibility for memorizing and recalling the transaction in detail upon demand. The rememberers act as the community's oral archive; the textual form of the deeds belongs to another type of archive, both linked by performance.[26] The tensions inherent in both appear in the gaps and silences, in what remains unsaid.

The Indian deeds themselves are the written representations of the original ritual performances, with the scribes' identities unknown, and are marked at the edges by anxiety about the future. As the siting of the conveyances and their political, social, and historical contexts change, so do the internal structures of the written deeds. For example, the first extant deed, dated 1683, is fairly simple, consisting of a declaration of agreement, a brief topographic description of the lands in question, and signature and witness lines. It begins with a statement of authority, "I Wunnatuckquannum have bargained with David Okes," that alludes to the ritualistic power of speaking. This statement serves as a transmission of social knowledge as well as a means of reordering relationships within the Nunepog community and is suggestive of a dialogue between Wunnatuckquannum and Okes. Yet at the same time, this statement tends to obscure the depth and tenor of the "bargaining." Such a phrase may have served as a mnemonic device for the extent of the agreement. Perhaps what needs to remain in the collective memory is the fact that a bargain was struck and the parties agreed to it. Short and terse, the deed outlines in the present tense the land to be conveyed: "He owns land at Pachatickquset, seven acres. What he has is around my house and up from the water, and to the swamp and part of the swamp."[27] The switch to present tense confirms the granting of land to Okes: he now *owns* the seven acres at Pachatickquset. The catalogue of topographic features points toward the way the Wampanoags oriented themselves spatially—"up from the water" and "to the swamp." Bodies of water, including oceans, estuaries, marsh, and swampland play important roles in the history and culture of the Wampanoags and other New England tribes. They not only provided food sources and raw materials but figure prominently in Wampanoag oral tradition. For example, Noepe and other nearby islands are said to have been formed by the culture hero Moshup as he walked across the land.[28]

The written deed concludes with the queen sachem's signature line and mark: "I Wunnatuckquannum, witness; my hand (X)," as well as those of two witnesses. In signing the document "witness," she "witnesses" her own hand or mark, validating the authenticity of the document and the legal agreement it encompasses. She is *the* witness, as opposed to the other two witnesses, who state "I am a witness, Paquatauwashon, my hand," and "[And] Moimminnuiwit, a witness (X)." As Little as well as Goddard and Bragdon have demonstrated, the Massachussett phrases "Neen Wunnatuckquannum," or "I Wunnatuckquannum," and "I Wunnatuckquannum, this is my hand" denote this document as Indian authored, and likely a direct transcription of the original ritual performance, as they appear in many similar deeds and petitions of the same era.[29] In the move from oral performance to textual act, the validity and authenticity of Wunnatuckquannum's words are essential to the legitimation of traditional Wampanoag legal practices and are its link to vernacular literacy and English colonial law. Further, the significance of Wunnatuckquannum's authorship of the deed ties it to her political performance as sachem and the reordering of relationships within the community.

Wunnatuckquannum's more detailed 1686 deed to Joshua Sasimmin begins with an archaic form of Massachusett ritual address—"Wunnatuckquannum neen"—that highlights the way vernacular Massachusett incorporates earlier, ritualized oral forms of speech. The queen sachem conveys one section of land known by the native toponym Paquaik, located between modern day Oyster and Paqua ponds. While the original meaning of Paquaik or Paqua is lost to us today, toponymic practice, as Margaret Wickens Pearce observes, tells us that it refers to that specific site "in terms of its physical appearance, the way in which the land is used, the people who use the land, or a story or historical event that occurred" there. Thus, toponymic mapping practices have both cultural and ecological functions. William Cronon has noted that "the purpose of such names was to turn the landscape into a map which, if studied carefully, literally gave a village's inhabitants the information they needed to sustain themselves." This particular deed also reflects native mapping techniques, which Pearce has described as "word maps"[30]: "I convey one section, it is called Paquaik, as far as Tahkuppasesuh, that corner, part of *nishwapasquash*, from that straight towards the northeast as far as the crooked path extends and from that straight towards the south, it is named Mashpootacheh, between that corner. And all completely of this section I convey into the hand of Joshua Sassimin. I am Wunnatuckquannum, this is my hand. (X)."[31] This word map is much more detailed than the one found in the earlier deed from 1683. Such internal changes perhaps reflect the anxieties over land tenure and the legitimacy of Indian deeds in both the Wampanoag and English communities. In her descriptions Wunnatuckquannum deviates from the earlier emphasis on toponymic features as cultural and spatial orientations. Instead, she relies on orthogonal spatial dimensions and detailed descriptions of cardinal points, perhaps an adaptation to Western-style descriptions of land. Still, the deed adheres to Williams's observation that "the *Natives* are very exact and punctual in the bounds of their Lands, belonging to this or that Prince or People, (even to a River, Brooke &c.)."[32] Wunnatuckquannum's deeds demonstrate her knowledge of Nunepog terrain, down to the mention of "the crooked path," and Native place names for which the significance and location have been lost to us.

In addition, her signature line subtly diverges from the form found in the prior deed, stating emphatically "I am Wunnatuckquannum, this is my hand (X)," asserting her personal sovereignty as queen sachem of Nunepog during a time of political and social anxieties over land tenure and leadership. The second part of the signature line functions as a metonymic reference to the hand standing in for the sachem, who in turn represents the sachemship as a whole, suggesting there is consensus in the land sale. Wunnatuckquannum's textual performance here takes the form of both change and continuity: the reference to the hand reflects her attempt at maintaining the office of sachemship and the bonds of kinship and allegiance it entails, while her affirmation "I am Wunnatuckquannum" serves to anticipate challenges to the same office.

Similarly, the third deed from 1687 highlights yet another type of performative and textual act, one in which Wunnatuckquannum is joined by husband Jacob Washamun to convey jointly a section of land known as Koinokawake to the Christian minister John Momanequin, land that her grandfather

Tawanquatuck had previously "conveyed away." The presence of a joint male authority is indicative of challenges to Wunnatuckquannum's tenure and changes in Wampanoag social structure. The document begins, "This is our confirmation of land, of us, Jacob Wahshaman and Wunnatuckquannum. We say, 'Truly it is thus, and John Mommanequin, owns land at Pahchatuckquissut.'"[33] The internal structure of this third deed changes with the use of this direct quotation and a subsequent one in the written record, an indication of a literal transcription of the original words spoken by the two parties. Instead of "bargaining" or "conveying" land, this deed speaks of a "confirmation of land" and, in the present tense, echoes the second deed. In each successive deed, the toponymic mapping becomes more geographically detailed. Wunnatuckquannum joins with Washamun in asserting and confirming her right to distribute the land within the bounds of her sachemship.

It is in the third section that the internal structure of the deed deviates most dramatically from the earlier ones. This section reads: "And firmly he owns it and forever, and (his) posterity firmly own it. We and our posterity shall not have the power to alter it. This is firm. And no one (shall) have the power to alter it. Because I am a sachem." Here, posterity in the early Wampanoag sense refers to descendants, both of Momanequin, who will own it outright, and those of Wunnatuckquannum herself, which includes the possibility of a future sachem. This final rhetorical gesture is suggestive of anticipated challenges to the conveyance, which were becoming more and more common as Wunnatuckquannum sold Nunepog land and displaced members of her sachemship. The second direct quotation in the deed belongs to the grantee, John Momanequin: "And I John Momanequin give fifteen pence every year," an indication of the tribute in coin he will pay to the couple every year in exchange for the land. The signature line for Washamun appears above the queen sachem's standard signature "I Wunnatuckquannum, this is my hand (X)."[34] As a female Native leader in a time when English social structures began to supplant traditional Native ones, Wunnatuckquannum would have needed to establish further and solidify her power base through an alliance with a male partner or ally. The reversal of the order of signatures is a literal and textual performance of such an alliance.

Wunnatuckquannum's final appearance in the historical record lies in her Indian deed of March 29, 1700, to Caleb (Callab) Ahteohoo of lands at Watcha between Watcha and Oyster ponds. It begins with the forceful phrase "Know all you men at this time that I Wunnatuckquannum have divided land on behalf of Callab Ahteohoo." From this deed we can glimpse the political forces at work in 1700. There is no "bargaining" to be done, no "confirmation of land," no tribute paid to the queen sachem. We can deduce that there is less land available, hence the "division" of land in favor of Ahteohoo. The deed adheres to the common internal structure by mapping out the land to be divided, but it stands apart from Wunnatuckquannum's earlier deeds in her use of the word "boundary": "The boundary partly that *posohkaak* goes towards about the northwest up to that great path lying *bohkak*, as far as that, and from that corner at Mattuhtuqussesut, it goes toward as the *sonkittamm*—direction up to the end of Wattishut, named Onsanneh, as far as that is that boundary. From that, straight *booshpane* as far as to Nashonkkanisse, that corner." By paying close attention to such word usages, we can map out the changes in both Wunnatuckquannum's performance and the resulting text, as English real property legal terms begin to creep into Wampanoag legal practices. Such changes become even more apparent in an examination of the deed's final wording:

> Therefore, I divide this for him, this much land, lovingly, for my brother Callab Ahteohoo. Peacefully he (shall) own it and all his posterity, as long as it comes from him. I Wunnuttoohquanmanmau have conveyed this land. Therefore I shall not alter it, nor my defenders, nor they who succeed to my sachemship. They shall not do it from this time and as long as the earth remains. March 29, 1700. At this time I sign it and I seal it with my seal, I sachem Wunnuttoohquanmanmau.[35]

The tensions inherent in the land situation on Noepe come to a head in this deed to Ahteohoo. Caleb Ateohoo may or may not have been Wunnatuckquannum's brother; with *cousin*, *brother* was a metaphorical kinship term often used in deeds and petitions that bound the parties together in a kinship relationship, with the potential for aiding one another in times of need. Similarly, the adjective "lovingly" was often used in deeds to reflect the bonds between grantor and grantee and the relationship they have entered into by way of the deeds. This usage marks a fundamental difference between the way the colonial era Wampanoags viewed land transactions and the English colonists viewed them.[36] The word "peacefully" further invokes the tensions between the Wampanoag and colonists, and when coupled with the phrase "all his posterity, as long as it comes from him," underscores the intent behind the deed: that Ateohoo may convey the land to his descendants, but no one else can change the meaning of the transaction. The phrase "as long as the earth remains" is representative of the language found in later treaties between tribes and the U.S. government, possibly indicating an early use of the phrase. Its use here points out what is at issue in this deed: the slow but increasing erosion of Wunnatuckquannum's land base, and with it, the rituals, kinship systems, and ordering of the cosmos. This final deed is the only one of the four in which Wunnatuckquannum does not make her mark, but rather "signs" it with her seal, itself a performative act that reflects the entwining of English legal practice with Wampanoag customary law and underscores the turbulent times of Wunnatuckquannum's tenure. As the validity of Indian deeds became increasingly challenged, Native people chose to combine English legal practices with their own in order to strengthen and preserve their own land holdings.

The filing of the transcribed deeds with the colonial court commemorates a third type of ritual performance, one that combines traditional Wampanoag legal practice with English common law. Changes in colonial law in 1666 required all conveyances of real property, including Indian deeds, "to be acknowledged and endorsed by a magistrate and recorded by the County or Shire clerk within six months of the transaction." The clerk was responsible for the copying of the deed, yet another performative act, which served as the legal record. As the filing dates of the deeds suggest, these laws were not always followed to the letter. In her final performative acts, Wunnatuckquannum appeared twice before Justice of the Peace Matthew Mayhew, in 1686 and 1687, acknowledging the Sassimin and Momanequin deeds "to be her act and deed," language that reflects the blending of the two legal systems.[37] The 1683 and 1688 Pachatickquset deeds to David Okes and Isaak Tuhkemen were not recorded until 1707, and then with the magistrate's notation written in English in an otherwise Massachusett language text. And Wunnatuckquannum's final extant deed to Caleb Ahteohoo was not entered into the record until February 21, 1744, likely long after her death. Similar to the original ritual performances that produced the texts, the performative acts of the court filings are ephemeral, reduced to the magistrate's notation on the page. The concrete act of recording the deeds draws attention to the two competing legal systems, Wampanoag and English, which come together in the written documents.

As ritualized performances, the Indian deeds "authored" by Wunnatuckquannum took place at a "critical juncture" in Wampanoag history and recount a narrative of a political leader and community in transition from an Indian world to one dominated by English colonists and their customs. Through a careful reading of Wunnatuckquannum's Indian deeds, we can trace the progression of a shift in Native relationships to land, law, and literacy. The decision to transcribe the land conveyance ceremonies into textual form is but one example of the ways the Wampanoags grappled with new systems of literacy that entered their world. These new systems were adapted and transformed to meet the needs of the community as a form of rhetorical sovereignty. Wunnatuckquannum's texts and performances were similarly adapted and transformed, reframing the manner in which Wunnatuckquannum and other community leaders dealt with the increasing role of English law in Wampanoag life. The filing of the documents with the colonial courts fulfilled the requirements of English law; it may also have protected Wampanoag land from unscrupulous speculators. While sales to the English undoubtedly disrupted Wampanoag relationships to their land, the narratives attached to topological features such as the Aquinnah Cliffs and the Devil's Bridge remain to this day within the collective consciousness. The textual and historical evidence of Wunnatuckquannum's performative acts and other Massachusett language documents exemplify the ways in which literacy was an active, ritual force in seventeenth-century Wampanoag life and, at the same time, demonstrate the permeability of the complex divide between oral and print traditions.

Anishinaabe scholar Gerald Vizenor has asked: "What did it mean to be the first generation to hear the stories of the past, bear the horrors of the moment, and write to the future?"[38] Vizenor is referring to the Wounded Knee Massacre of 1890, but his words hold true even reaching back as far as Martha's Vineyard in 1690. What did it mean to be one of the few survivors of a series of wars, epidemics, and land and language loss that tore the social fabric of a community? What does it mean for Indian people to "write to the future?" A preoccupation with future generations is evident in Massachusett language Indian deeds from the seventeenth and eighteenth centuries through the use of the word "pumeetyuwôk," meaning descendants, generations, or, as in the deeds themselves, "posterity."[39] The Massachusett language texts are a legacy from past generations to modern Wampanoag people, serving as the foundation for the Wôpanâak Language Reclamation Project, a collaborative effort of the Wampanoag Nation and linguists at MIT. These writings are a legacy to Wampanoag people today, offering a way to recover the Wôpanâak language in the twenty-first century. The archival Indian deeds hint at something far greater than the legal documents themselves; they suggest what is at stake in these performative acts: the social, political, and ceremonial life of a people.

Notes

1. With the lack of a standard orthography for the Massachusett (Wampanoag) language, Wunnatuckquannum's name also appears in the historical record as Natuckquanum, Wunnattuhquanummou, and Wunnattuhquanmow. In this essay I use the simplified spelling of Wunnatuckquannum.
2. See Keary, "Retelling the History," 255; Salisbury, *Manitou and Providence*, 41–43; Bragdon, *Native People*, xv.
3. Williams, *Key*, 55; Bragdon, "Interstices of Literacy," 122. Bragdon suggests that high status individuals were trained in oratory from an early age.
4. The original document is archived in the Dukes County Registry of Deeds, Martha's Vineyard (DD 2:3388). Transcriptions and a

facsimile copy can be found in Goddard and Bragdon, *Native Writings*, 104–9. According to Goddard and Bragdon, "the speakers of Massachusett comprised the groups commonly referred to as the Massachusetts, the Pokanokets (or Wampanoags), and the Nausets," and their contemporary name is Wampanoag (*Native Writings*, 1).

5. Bragdon, *Native People*, 155.
6. Goddard and Bragdon, *Native Writings*, 81, 123.
7. Taylor, *Archive and the Repertoire*, 2.
8. See Bragdon, *Native People*, 187, for a discussion of Wampanoag relationships to the cosmos.
9. Bell, *Ritual Theory*, 16. The foundational work on ritual is that of Turner, who theorizes that the processual structure of rituals closely follows the unfolding of social dramas. More recently, Bell has engaged in reworking ritual studies. See Turner, *Forest of Symbols* and *Ritual Process*, and Bell, *Ritual Theory*, especially 13–66.
10. Goddard and Bragdon, *Native Writings*, 18. For examples of marginalia, see pages 375–471.
11. Little, "Three Kinds of Indian Land Deeds," 62, 65. The three types of land deeds Little identifies are English deeds, which encompass land sales to colonists by Indians using a distinctly English legal style; Indian deeds, which include Native phrasing; and recorded oral land transfers, which are oral transcriptions of testimony regarding deeds.
12. Leavenworth, "'Best Title That Indians Can Claime,'" 291. See Silverman, *Faith and Boundaries*, especially chap. 4, for a discussion of the conflicts between the inhabitants of Noepe over Indian deeds.
13. Jennings, *Invasion of America*, 130; Andros qtd. in Baker, "Scratch with a Bear's Paw," 235. The first quotation comes from a chapter titled "The Deed Game"; Jennings, of course, is writing of Anglo-Indian deeds.
14. See, for example, Baker, "Finding the Almouchiquois," 73–100; "Scratch with a Bear's Paw," 235–56; Leavenworth, "'Best Title That Indians Can Claime,'" 275–300. Although Leavenworth argues for Native agency in land sales to the English, he notes "the loss of territory was permanent for Indians and had been accomplished much more often at the point of a pen than of a sword" (276).
15. Wampanoag Tribe of Gay Head, "Other Stories and Information"; Bragdon, *Native People*, 141. In my discussion of the Wampanoags' social body, I draw from Silverman, *Faith and Boundaries*, especially 121–56, as well as Bragdon, *Native People*, 140–68.
16. Plane, "Putting a Face on Colonization," 157.

17. Dukes County Deeds (1:15).
18. Silverman, *Faith and Boundaries*, 136. Silverman reports that in 1698, Nunepog had a population of only eighty-four inhabitants, thereby drastically reducing the amount of tribute that was possible to be paid to Wunnatuckquannum.
19. Womack, *Red on Red*, 15–16. For a discussion of early Native petitions and treaties, see Brooks, *Common Pot*, 51–105.
20. Bragdon, "Interstices of Literacy," 123. For a discussion of Native women's reading practices, see Monaghan, "'She Loved to Read,'" 508, 514.
21. Lyons, "Rhetorical Sovereignty," 449.
22. Bragdon, "Vernacular Literacy," 30; Silverman, *Faith and Boundaries*, 27; Williams, *Key*, 191.
23. McBride, "Bundles, Bears, and Bibles," 141. The recovery, analysis, and reburial of the medicine bundle was authorized and sanctioned by the Mashantucket Pequot Tribe.
24. Taylor, *Archive and the Repertoire*, 35; Bragdon, *Native People*, 155.
25. Vansina, *Oral Tradition as History*, xi.
26. For a discussion of the role of rememberers in Northeastern Algonquian society, see Brooks, *Common Pot*, 229.
27. Goddard and Bragdon, *Native Writings*, 81. See Austin, *How to Do Things with Words*, 12–24, for more on the performative power of speech acts.
28. Wampanoag Tribe of Gay Head, "Other Stories and Information."
29. Goddard and Bragdon, *Native Writings*, 21.
30. Pearce, "Native Mapping," 159, 161; Cronon, *Changes in the Land*, 65–66.
31. Goddard and Bragdon, *Native Writings*, 107.
32. Williams, *Key*, 167.
33. Goddard and Bragdon, *Native Writings*, 108–9.
34. Goddard and Bragdon, *Native Writings*, 107, 123.
35. Goddard and Bragdon, *Native Writings*, 131. In the first quotation, italicized words represent those for which there are no known translations.
36. Silverman, *Faith and Boundaries*, 41. The terms *brother* and *sister* are still used by Native people today to reflect these "metaphorical kinship" relations.
37. Goddard and Bragdon, *Native Writings*, 15–16, 23, 105.
38. Vizenor, *Manifest Manners*, 51.
39. Richards, "Wôpanâak Language Reclamation Project."

Works Cited

Austin, J. L. *How to Do Things with Words*. Cambridge: Cambridge University Press, 1962.

Baker, Emerson W. "A Scratch with a Bear's Paw: Anglo-Indian Deeds in Early Maine." *Ethnohistory* 36 (1989): 235–56.

———. "Finding the Almouchiquois: Native American Families, Territories, and Land Sales in Southern Maine." *Ethnohistory* 51 (2004): 73–100.

Bell, Catherine. *Ritual Theory, Ritual Practice*. Oxford: Oxford University Press, 1992.

Bragdon, Kathleen J. "The Interstices of Literacy: Books and Writings and Their Use in Native American Southern New England." In *Anthropology, History, and American Indians: Essays in Honor of William Curtis Sturtevant*, ed. William L. Merrill and Ives Goddard, 121–30. Washington DC: Smithsonian Institution, 2002.

———. *Native People of Southern New England, 1500–1650*. Norman: University of Oklahoma Press, 1996.

———. "Vernacular Literacy and Massachusett World View, 1650–1750." In *Algonkians of New England: Past and Present*, ed. Peter Benes, 26–34. Boston: Boston University, 1993.

Brooks, Lisa. *The Common Pot: The Recovery of Native Space in the Northeast*. Minneapolis: University of Minnesota Press, 2008.

Cronon, William. *Changes in the Land: Indians, Colonists, and the Ecology of New England*. New York: Hill and Wang, 1983.

Dukes County Deeds (1:15), Dukes County Registry of Deeds, Dukes County Courthouse, Edgartown MA.

Goddard, Ives, and Kathleen Bragdon. *Native Writings in Massachusett*. Philadelphia: American Philosophical Society, 1988.

Jennings, Francis. *The Invasion of America: Indians, Colonialism, and the Cant of Conquest*. Chapel Hill: University of North Carolina Press, 1975.

Keary, Anne. "Retelling the History of the Settlement of Providence: Speech, Writing, and Cultural Interaction on the Narragansett Bay." *New England Quarterly* 69 (1996): 250–86.

Leavenworth, Peter S. "'The Best Title That Indians Can Claime': Native Agency and Consent in the Transferal of Penacook-Pawtucket Land in the Seventeenth Century." *New England Quarterly* 72 (1999): 275–300.

Little, Elizabeth. "Three Kinds of Indian Land Deeds at Nantucket,

Massachusetts." In *Papers of the Eleventh Algonquian Conference*, ed. William Cowan, 61–69. Ottawa: Carleton University, 1980.

Lyons, Scott Richard. "Rhetorical Sovereignty: What Do American Indians Want from Writing?" *College Composition and Communication* 51 (2000): 447–68.

McBride, Kevin A. "Bundles, Bears, and Bibles: Interpreting Seventeenth-Century Native 'Texts.'" In *Early Native Literacies in New England: A Documentary and Critical Anthology*, ed. Kristina Bross and Hilary E. Wyss, 132–41. Amherst: University of Massachusetts Press, 2008.

Monaghan, E. Jennifer. "'She Loved to Read in Good Books': Literacy and the Indians of Martha's Vineyard, 1643–1725." *History of Education Quarterly* 30 (1990): 492–521.

Pearce, Margaret Wickens. "Native Mapping in Southern New England Indian Deeds." In *Cartographic Encounters: Perspectives on Native American Mapping and Map Use*, ed. G. Malcolm Lewis, 157–86. Chicago: University of Chicago Press, 1998.

Plane, Ann Marie. "Putting a Face on Colonization: Factionalism and Gender Politics in the Life History of Awashunkes, the 'Squaw Sachem' of Saconet." In *Northeastern Indian Lives, 1632–1816*, ed. Robert S. Grumet, 140–65. Amherst: University of Massachusetts Press, 1996.

Richards, Norvin. "Wôpanâak Language Reclamation Project." May 27, 2009. http://web.mit.edu/norvin/www/wopanaak.html.

Salisbury, Neal. *Manitou and Providence: Indians, Europeans, and the Making of New England, 1500–1643*. New York: Oxford University Press, 1982.

Silverman, David J. *Faith and Boundaries: Colonists, Christianity, and Community among the Wampanoag Indians of Martha's Vineyard, 1600–1871*. Cambridge: Cambridge University Press, 2005.

Taylor, Diana. *The Archive and the Repertoire: Performing Cultural Memory in the Americas*. Durham: Duke University Press, 2003.

Turner, Victor. *The Forest of Symbols: Aspects of Ndembu Ritual*. Ithaca: Cornell University Press, 1967.

———. *The Ritual Process: Structure and Anti-Structure*. Chicago: Aldine, 1969.

Vansina, Jan. *Oral Tradition as History*. Madison: University of Wisconsin Press, 1985.

Vizenor, Gerald. *Manifest Manners: Postindian Narratives of Survivance*. Lincoln: University of Nebraska Press, 1999.

Wampanoag Tribe of Gay Head (Aquinnah). "Other Stories and Information." February 15, 2009. http://www.wampanoagtribe.net/Pages/Wampanoag_Way/other.

Williams, Roger. *A Key into the Language of America*, ed. John J. Teunissen and Evelyn J. Hinz. Detroit: Wayne State University Press, 1973.

Womack, Craig S. *Red on Red: Native American Literary Separatism.* Minneapolis: University of Minnesota Press, 1999.

[6]

In a Red Petticoat

Coosaponakeesa's Performance of Creek Sovereignty in Colonial Georgia

Caroline Wigginton

In 1733 the Creek trader Coosaponakeesa donned a red stroud petticoat and stationed herself on a bluff overlooking the Savannah River. Along with her husband, a group of local Yamacraw Indians, and the Yamacraw leader Tomochichi, she awaited the appearance of the first Georgian colonists and their governor, James Oglethorpe. At last seeing the colonists, the Yamacraws "saluted them with a volley of gunfire."[1] The Georgians returned the greeting, and the two groups approached each other. Then, as the Yamacraws watched, Coosaponakeesa mediated and interpreted the first of many friendly diplomatic conversations between Tomochichi and Oglethorpe.

From the perspective of Oglethorpe and the other colonists, Coosaponakeesa "then appeared to be in mean and low Circumstances, being only Cloathed with a Red Stroud Petticoat and Osnabrig Shift."[2] As this description suggests, to them her selection of clothing for the first encounter accentuated that she was a woman but an Indian one. On the one hand, as garments typically worn by English women, the petticoat and shift were familiar and declared femininity. On the other hand, as a petticoat and a shift were frequently undergarments and as she was bareheaded, she appeared strange and perhaps improper.[3] Moreover, her outfit may have evoked for them the economic motivations behind their colony, an extension of Britain's mercantile empire. Stroud, a woolen rag cloth usually used to make blankets for trade with Indians, would have demonstrated that she was willing to participate in trade for English manufactures and to adapt those objects for her own purposes through sewing or other material interventions.[4] In the preceding account the anonymous white author, writing sixteen years after the meeting and describing her appearance as indicating "mean and low Circumstances," attests to the vividness of the moment even as he couches her difference in terms of poverty and inferiority. After encountering a woman attired in the objects of European trade, fluent in English and Creek, and experienced as an Indian trader, the colonists may have seen Coosaponakeesa as embodying their hopes for the new colony, a figure of raw potential awaiting the adornment of prosperity. After all, they depended upon her skills and her opinion throughout their early years in Georgia, even when they found her motives suspect.

Yet this image of Coosaponakeesa in her spare, unusual clothing spoke of more than Georgia's promise. To herself and to the Yamacraws observing this encounter, her choice of the color red likely announced a particular stance toward this first diplomatic meeting. As a culture whose cosmology centered upon dualities and balance, the Creek Nation—and by extension the Yamacraw band, composed mainly of Creek exiles—structured political relationships around the duality of red and white (roughly translated as war and peace).[5] The *talwa*, or main Creek political unit, and individual male Creek leaders had permanent identifications as red or white.[6] During local and national councils those who were red argued from a red or war stance and those who were white argued from a white or peace stance. Additionally, a man could identify himself as on the red or white path in terms of a relationship with another person or group.[7] Unlike men, women may have belonged to a red or white talwa, but otherwise they maintained balance in the cosmos "behind the scenes."[8] Red and white alignments structured political engagements, but according to Katherine E. Holland Braund, women's "considerable impact" on political matters derived from their privately influencing public opinion through "tears, ridicule, and other methods to persuade husbands, brothers, uncles and sons. This was especially true of matters of war and peace."[9] In choosing a red petticoat, Coosaponakeesa began her first diplomatic meeting vibrantly adorned in the Creek diplomatic "male" color of war—quite the opposite of the exploitable poor and female subject the Georgians read in Coosaponakeesa's strange apparel.

Coosaponakeesa's color choice did not automatically indicate that she was declaring war upon the colonists. In explicating Creek duality, George E. Lankford explains that balance instead of competition defines the relationship between dual categories: "As seems to be true of most dual oppositional thought, the goal is to maintain a workable balance between the opposing forces or worlds. The opposition is not one which is envisioned as temporary, with one to become a victor over the other, but a permanent tension of opposites which need to be kept in balance."[10] In this respect, while she chose a red petticoat, Coosaponakeesa's subsequent willingness to mediate between the Yamacraw *mico* Tomochichi and Oglethorpe, an act that helped lead to a partnership between the two groups and a Georgian settlement on Yamacraw land, stressed her readiness to adapt her behavior to the future actions of the colonists. At the same time her red attire sent a signal to her people that she would continue to advocate for their interests. Having experienced firsthand the costly Tuscarora and

Yamasee wars of the 1710s—wars caused in part by traders' abuse of Indians throughout the region—and now seeing their interpreter in red, the observing Yamacraws would conceivably have recalled the potential for economic mistreatment from traders. Coosaponakeesa's diplomatic actions after Oglethorpe's arrival occurred in the presence of that memory and perhaps reassured her Yamacraw and eventual Creek allies that she, too, would fight for fair and vigorous trade.

To the scholarly eye reading cultural and historical context, this confluence of meaning in a single object of red apparel suggests Coosaponakeesa's experience as an active participant in trade, her personal willingness to declare war, her ability to push the quotidian limits of gender roles—Creek as well as English—and her claiming of an uncommon (though not unheard of) leadership role. In other words, her wearing of the red petticoat was and remains a charged performative act, one that she supplemented in following years and one that can be traced in her diplomatic and legal writings. By examining these writings, one can see how the red petticoat's symbolic suggestions pervade her textual choices. Integrating Creek concepts of community with English words and genres, Coosaponakeesa's texts materially create and structure relationships between Creeks and Georgians and thereby intervene in the region's emergent mercantile economy. She asserts a vision of economic exchange that relies upon Creek ways of relating. Yet when the colonial government does not fulfill its obligations, she exploits the flexibility of Creek kinship to reformulate and even threaten those same relationships.[11]

In reading Coosaponakeesa's works in this way, I depend upon a definition of Indian performance that directly opposes a reading of Native assumption of English tools and roles as acculturation, and that rejects the implication of inauthenticity that can accompany descriptions of performative acts, especially in the cases of marginalized peoples. Instead I argue that Indian performance informs ongoing, active sovereignty. If performance is self-conscious assertion, an Indian performance must be an act of sovereignty because it necessarily depends upon the agency and presence of its actors. Under this definition Indian performance is clearly related to *survivance*, Gerald Vizenor's (Anishinaabe) term for survival-plus-resistance. As Vizenor writes, *survivance* means "more than endurance or mere response; the stories of survivance are an active presence."[12] For Coosaponakeesa, however, the phrase *Indian performance* rather than the term *survivance* may best evoke the possibilities of her time and place, when the avenues for survival and resistance available to mid-eighteenth-century Creeks perhaps appeared numerous and assured and when negotiation, trade, and friendship with European colonists were adaptive continuations of pre-contact Native life.[13] This definition also suggests that Indian performance has a genealogy. In identifying sovereignty instead of simulation as the foundational component, I seek to link Coosaponakeesa's Indian performance to a genealogy of sovereignty and thereby to differentiate it from non-Native Indian performance and its emphasis upon imitation and invention. That is not to say that Indians do not engage in fakery or fabrication or that in doing so they are somehow less "Indian"; rather it is to insist upon the underlying continuity of Native acts, even as the North American stage was radically changing.

Born early in the eighteenth century, Coosaponakeesa was the daughter of Edward Griffin, a Euro-American trader, and a Tuckabatchee Creek woman.[14] After spending her early years among the Creeks, she "was brought Down by her Father from the Indian Nation, to Pomponne in south Carolina [and] There baptized, Educated and bred up in the Principles of

Christianity." Her education there was likely similar to most Christian education given to Indians. Margaret Connell Szasz speculates that Carolina schoolmasters "would have instructed the young Indians in the English language, in reading and writing (probably by means of a New England Primer), and perhaps in ciphering."[15] Coosaponakeesa's education would thus have been beneficial to her as a diplomat and interpreter for the English and as an Indian trader.

When Oglethorpe encountered her on the Yamacraw bluff in 1733, she and her first husband, the mixed-blood Creek John Musgrove, had been operating their trading post since 1732. Coosaponakeesa played an active role in Georgia-Creek relations during Oglethorpe's tenure and a somewhat less active, but still prominent, role under subsequent leaders. Besides interpreting and helping Oglethorpe relate to the Yamacraws and the Creeks, she ran several trading posts, assisted during trade and land negotiations, and helped enlist (or delay) Creek military support for British struggles with other Indian tribes and European powers in the region.

Coosaponakeesa had influence and standing with the Lower Creeks as well as the English colonists. Her matrilineal relationship to prominent Creek leaders in Coweta, a relationship that she told the colonists made her a "Rightfull and Natural Princess," added to her influence.[16] By helping to produce written versions of land claims and schedules of prices for traded goods, she stabilized Creek talwas and expanded trade. Lower Creek micos gave her authority in negotiating land settlements on their behalf and trusted her during negotiations to relate and explain the contents of English-language documents. Ultimately, various Lower Creek micos (though not all) rewarded her by granting her territorial claims to several coastal islands—Ossabaw, St. Catherine's, and Sapelo—south of Savannah and at the fringes of Creek territory.

These islands became the focus of a long legal battle between Coosaponakeesa and Georgia's administrators. In the mid-1740s, shortly after marrying her third husband Thomas Bosomworth, a white Englishman and ordained Anglican minister, she filed the first of many memorials with the colonial government and requested restitution for her services to the colony. The "Bosomworth Controversy," as it is known to historians of Georgia, occupies much paper and archival space. In addition to these memorials Coosaponakeesa and her husband filed copious articles of documentation (including transcriptions of colonial records, letters, and government journals as well as affidavits from Creek leaders, fellow translators, and Indian traders). The couple threatened Georgia by accompanying a delegation of somewhat hostile Creeks to Savannah in order to underscore their claims. Eventually Governor Henry Ellis settled with Coosaponakeesa by giving her the proceeds from the sale of two of the islands as well as the deed to St. Catherine's. Coosaponakeesa died soon after.[17]

Most scholarship about Coosaponakeesa, especially prior to the twenty-first century, represents her as a figure of Georgia history. Such scholarship praises her invaluable services as diplomat, mediator, and interpreter during her early years and deplores the controversy surrounding her restitution claims in later years. In these histories her name is almost invariably associated with her "disruptive" and "greedy" suits; in discussions of the Bosomworth Controversy, she is regularly painted as a pawn of Bosomworth.[18] Despite these numerous (if not always thorough) historiographic treatments, no one has closely analyzed her writings; even Craig Womack's (Muskogee Creek/Cherokee) *Red on Red: Native Literary Separatism* (1999), a book dedicated to recovering Creek authorship, overlooks Coosaponakeesa, perhaps because he was unaware of her extant writings or because he chose to focus on later centuries.[19] Yet a sifting of colonial archives, much of it published, reveals a variety of documents bearing Coosaponakeesa's varying signatures.[20] She leaves behind a letter to Oglethorpe written in July of 1734; various restitution memorials, the first from August 10, 1747; interpreter reports, some of which she co-signs; and two 1752 letters to James Glen, colonial governor of South Carolina. Along with these documents Coosaponakeesa translated talks by the Yamacraw mico Tomochichi and the Coweta mico Chikelly; in addition, she participated in various treaty conversations. Especially in a period lacking Creek-English dictionaries and deep cultural contact to provide guidance in linguistic and cultural translation, we must consider these latter documents—translations, interpreter reports, and treaties—as acts of authorship as surely as Coosaponakeesa's formal correspondence.

In my reading of this woman who must be counted as one of the first Native authors in English, I focus on her earliest documents, when her rhetorical strategies most actively shaped Georgia-Creek relations. My project does not, however, seek to justify or condemn her actions, which, in addition to being acts of sovereignty on behalf of the Creeks, also at times included undermining other Indian Nations' economies in order to promote her own, selling alcohol to her fellow Creeks, enlisting Creek military support against other tribes who fought on the side of Britain's imperial rivals, and in some ways advancing British colonization in Georgia and South Carolina. Nor, as a means of bringing her writings into the Anglo-American literary canon, do I seek to defy her self-identification as Creek and her people's unquestioned acceptance of that identity. Instead I follow Womack's model, which "emphasizes unique Native worldviews and political realities, searches for differences as often as similarities, and attempts to find Native literature's place in Indian country, rather than Native literature's place in the canon."[21] By considering Coosaponakeesa as a Creek woman who has acquired English tools—paper, pen, and alphabetic literacy—I argue that she promotes a vibrant trade environment for her Creek community by inserting the idiom of Creek kinship into diplomatic and legal texts. Since relatively few documents by Coosaponakeesa or other Creeks remain from this period and our knowledge of Creek culture is necessarily limited, I use folklore studies, historiography, and anthropology to read this material deeply and imaginatively, believing that only in this way can we recover the historically influential and rhetorically powerful performances that Coosaponakeesa and other Creeks enacted in colonial America.

One of the earliest of Coosaponakeesa's such performances occurred in 1733, when she helped negotiate "Oglethorpe's First Treaty with the Lower Creeks at Savannah" through her role as diplomat and interpreter. These "Articles of Friendship and Commerce" formalize the trade affiliation between Georgia and the Lower Creeks and involve promises on both sides.[22] While many portions are adaptations of other treaties with South Carolina, the fourth or land settlement clause of the treaty specifically addresses British territory acquisition and is unique to this treaty. The land settlement clause is also unique in the context of the treaty as a whole. Copied from previous documents, other clauses in this treaty have more clearly identifiable goals and fewer references to Creek beliefs. They include price schedules and provisions for criminal justice, treaty violations, and runaway slaves. However, in the fourth clause, Creek kinship and understandings of land form the logical foundations. This clause archives a Creek infiltration into an English legal document.

As chief interpreter during this portion of the negotiation, Coosaponakeesa chose the English translations that would encapsulate what the Lower Creek leaders wanted embedded in this contract.[23] She may even have encouraged Creek leaders to negotiate for a formal land agreement since experience with whites' understanding of land as property may have indicated the value of such a clause. She undoubtedly observed encroachment upon Indian land by white settlers in South Carolina, where no such treaty clauses existed. Because it emerged under Coosaponakeesa's linguistic and diplomatic guidance and can provide insight into her vision of intercultural trade and relationships, I provide the land settlement clause in its entirety:

> Fourthly. We the Head Men of the Coweta and Cussita Towns in behalf of all the Lower Creek Nation being firmly persuaded that He who lives in Heaven and is the occasion of all good things has moved the hearts of the Trustees to send their Beloved men among us for the good of us our Wives and Children and to Instruct us and them in what is Streight do therefore declare that we are glad that their People are come here, and though this Land belongs to us the Lower Creeks yet we that we may be instructed by them do consent and agree that they shall make use of and possess all those Lands which our Nation hath not occasion for to use and we make over unto them their Successors and Assigns all such Lands and Territories as we shall have no occasion to use, Provided always that they upon Settling every New Town shall set out for the use of ourselves and the People of our Nation such Lands as shall be agreed upon between their Beloved Men and the head men of our Nation and that those Lands shall remain to us forever.[24]

The article begins by expressing satisfaction that contact has occurred between English and Creeks, especially Creek women and children, and desire for those contacts to continue. The article then formalizes an agreement that the English may occupy lands that the Lower Creeks "hath not occasion for to use" so long as the English settlements continue to reserve an adjacent portion, to be agreed on by the English and Creek leaders, that "shall remain to us forever."[25] This opening underscores interpersonal relationships and therefore implies that sustainable trade arises from the kind of personal knowledge that defines mutually beneficial communitarian interaction. By moving from relationships to the topic of land, the clause subtly connects relationships and trade to geographic proximity.

The nature of these envisioned connections, moreover, emerges pointedly from Creek culture. In emphasizing that the whites are "among us," including "Wives and Children," the clause establishes for the record that the colonists are moving into the Creek homeland. To detect an underlying element of the Creek worldview in this phrasing, it is important to recall that Creek culture is matrilineal: when a man and a woman marry, the man moves in with the woman's household or compound, any children who result from the union belonging to the wife's matrilineage and, by extension, her clan.[26] While fathers retain much material responsibility and emotional connection to their children, the wife's male relatives in her matrilineage, especially her brothers, are the most important male figures in the children's lives. In the Creek matrilineal culture, matrilineages directly and indirectly govern cropland distribution, residences, inheritances, hunting territories, justice, social responsibilities, leadership, and marriages through kinship and clans. From this perspective, then, the reference to "Wives and Children" within the land settlement clause demonstrates that the Creeks can already begin to claim a form of modified kinship with white settlers since some whites have been in contact with their women and children, the units through whom kin attachments are made and claimed. I call this modified kinship "friendship," the term used in the treaty. In calling for continued contact with women and children and for portions of land to be set aside for Creeks alongside white settlements, the clause institutes a mechanism through which this friendship will continue.

Interestingly, the land settlement clause also establishes a difference between land that "belongs to us the Lower Creeks" and the "possess[ion]" of land. The implication here is that the land will *always* belong to the Creeks even as English colonists temporarily possess and use it. This distinction seems to place colonists in the position of Creek husbands, whose contributions to the community never gain them full right to their wives' matrilineages but whose entrance into already established Creek territorial divisions helps bind clans, families, and communities. As a Creek woman, Coosaponakeesa has not only inserted the concept of modified Creek kinship into a colonial document but has also formulated relationships that seem markedly feminine in their placement of matrilineage at their foundation. This interpretation is further supported by Coosaponakeesa's role as mediator instead of as public political leader: her role in these negotiations emerges from traditional Creek womanhood, which seeks to influence through relationships and to impel and perhaps shame male leaders into acting as the women desire.

Ultimately, what this clause argues is that *proximity* is a crucial component of stable, prosperous trade. Proximity leads to personal acts of exchange. Personal acts of exchange lead to familiarity. Familiarity leads to intimacy. Intimacy leads to friendship. This trajectory toward friendship would have been particularly apparent and reasonable to Coosaponakeesa, a mixed-blood woman who spent significant portions of her life residing at Indian trading posts.

Another document from this period, a familiar letter from Coosaponakeesa to Oglethorpe, similarly understands and structures trade through kinship. On July 17, 1734, Coosaponakeesa wrote a letter to Oglethorpe about a diplomatic discussion between some Choctaws and English colonists. According to this band of Choctaws, trade with the French had stagnated, and so they were looking for a new European trading partner. Since the Choctaws had a decades-long history of trading with and militarily supporting the French, these talks appeared to be a crucial turning point in the region's balance of colonial power.[27] Oglethorpe could not be present for these talks because he was in England at the time, where he was reporting to the colonial trustees and shepherding Tomochichi and other Yamacraws on a state visit. Because the Choctaw meeting could not have been interpreted by Coosaponakeesa—she did not speak Choctaw as far as we know—and she was not a key player in discussions, the reason for her writing this letter is unclear. Perhaps it is the only surviving portion of a series of letters she wrote to Oglethorpe to keep him informed during his absence.

Coosaponakeesa begins the letter by establishing an intermediary position for herself. She announces, "I make bold to acquaint You that Thos. Jones is returned from the Choctaws and according to your Honours Desire he has brought the Choctaws down and they have received great favours."[28] Coosaponakeesa's position as writer and communicator appears in the fact that she is "acquaint[ing]" Oglethorpe instead of acting on his behalf or on the Indians' behalf, Choctaw, Creek, or Yamacraw. This opening sentence lends the letter a tone of impartiality toward the outcome of the talks and implies that her comments are disinterested.

The remainder of the paragraph, however, subtly ridicules the Choctaws, elevates the Creeks, and flatters the colonists. This process begins with a description of the Choctaws' happiness in talking with the English: "The Choctaws are so glad that some white People whom they call'd their Masters has taken such Care of them as to send for them and they was very glad of the opportunity to come for they lived very poor before and now they are in good hopes to live as well as the other Indians do, for they had nor have no Trade with the French and their Skins lye by them and rot."[29] Through her authorial choices Coosaponakeesa characterizes the Choctaws as weak. In the first place, according to her, they have admitted inferiority to the colonists by gladly calling them "Masters." By choosing this word Coosaponakeesa underscores the lack of value in this potential connection, as she draws a line of relationship, but not of kinship, between Choctaws and colonists. Kinship means obligation; with no kinship, there is little or no obligation. As such, when she subsequently claims that the Choctaws need someone to care for them, she implies that the English, being under no obligation to fulfill their need, can choose whether or not to do so solely on practicality. And since, as she goes on to suggest, it would in fact be impractical to trade with the Choctaws—who, unlike other Indians, "live very poor[ly]" and, in perhaps their greatest transgression, have so ineptly negotiated in trade and are so unaware of the value of their commodity that their deerskins "lye by them and rot"—Coosaponakeesa's meaning is clear: while she acknowledges Oglethorpe's "Desire" to establish friendly ties with the Choctaws, she subtly criticizes that desire by demonstrating the unworthiness and untrustworthiness of the Choctaws.[30]

In contrast, the letter also hints at the wisdom of Oglethorpe's maintaining a primary trade relationship with her people. Coosaponakeesa begins this argument in the preceding quotation when she states that the Choctaws do not "live as well as the other Indians do." In Savannah the other Indians are Creeks. The fact that Creeks live well demonstrates that the current trading partnership is a prosperous one. A few sentences later Coosaponakeesa directly establishes a distinction between the

Choctaws and the Creeks. She writes, "The Choctaws are all amazed to see the Creeks drink as they do, and they think the Creeks are saucy to the white People."[31] Her reference to her fellow Creeks' behavior sounds boastful. Such a tone, especially in light of the other sentence, results in a nuanced contrast: the Creeks do not consider the English colonists to be their masters and therefore are capable of standing in a kinship relation to them, with its mutual and binding obligations, in ways the hapless and subordinate Choctaws cannot.

While others have mined the quoted paragraph for historiographic insight into Indian-Anglo relationships, I would argue that the remainder of the letter is crucial to a full understanding of how these subtle distinctions between Choctaws and Creeks become an argument for a continued trade relationship between Creeks and Georgians.[32] In the second paragraph, discussing various events, Coosaponakeesa abandons the topic of the Choctaws and emphasizes her connection to Oglethorpe. She writes, "The Colony is in good health and I hope your Honour and all your family is in good health and my Husband is the same, and I beg your Honour will take great Care of him."[33] Here she claims kinship to Oglethorpe through textual and real proximity: the textual proximity of the various references to familial components—"I," "your Honour," "all your family," "my Husband"—highlight the real proximity of Oglethorpe's family with her Husband. This places Oglethorpe and her into a kinship by extension; their families are connected. And since kinship means obligation in Creek culture, this sentence reminds Oglethorpe of his obligation to care for her husband: by writing the letter, she has honored her obligations and provided him with information, and now, presumably, he is obliged in return. In moving from the topic of Choctaws, Creeks, and Georgia to the familiar, even intimate language of family, Coosaponakeesa's letter implies that primary trade between Creeks and Georgians is not only practical but natural due to the special kinship bond of friendship.

Coosaponakeesa produced these texts during a period of peace with Oglethorpe and Georgia. A decade later, after Oglethorpe returned to England and she received neither immediate recognition of her land claims nor monetary compensation for her services to the colony, she began to write letters more personally and less communally motivated. However, even in those letters, she continued to refer to kinship and friendship to support her demands. Most of the letters took the form of memorials, documents that were expressions of facts in support of a petition.[34] One early (and perhaps the earliest) memorial is "TO the Honourable Lieutenant Collonel Alexander Heron Commander in Chief of his Majestys Forces in the Province of Georgia," dated August 10, 1747. In this memorial she begins by formalizing her kinship to the leaders of the Lower Creek Nation. She next emphasizes both the loyalty of the Creeks to the British in the past and the continued importance of Creek friendship "to the British Interest."[35] She reminds Heron of her centrality in establishing and maintaining that friendship, then goes on to provide a detailed personal history that includes her childhood, marriages, and various services to Georgia. In the context of this history she makes note of her financial investments and frequent losses, often incurred after sacrificing personal interests to British interests. She then tallies her exact investment at £5,714 17s 11p and requests remuneration. After this narrative and culminating calculation, Coosaponakeesa suggests how Heron can help, justifies her anger and indignation at Britain, and concludes with a not-so-veiled threat to disally the Creeks with the British, an act that would leave the colony open to attack from other Indian and European nations.

The fact that previous documents established a (constructed) *friendship* instead of a true (natural) *kinship* between Creeks and Georgians is the rhetorical linchpin of this document. Now that Coosaponakeesa is clearly on the red path with Georgia's government, she chooses to undermine that friendship and show its tenuousness. Her first step in doing so is to align herself, through *un*tenuous kinship, with the Creeks. Her opening paragraphs explain that she "was born at the Cowetaw Town on the Oakmulgee River which is a branch of the Alatamaha, and the Chief Town of the Creek Indian Nation. That She is by Descent on the Mothers Side, (who was Sister to the Old Emperor) of the Same Blood of the Present Mico's and Chief's now in that Nation, and by their Laws, and the Voice of the Whole Nation is esteemed their Rightfull and Natural Princess." These lines not only declare her familial relationship to Creek leadership but underscore that *this* kinship is through her matrilineage. Soon after, she reminds her reader that the "Friendship and Alliance" between the Creeks and the Georgians is based on "Several Treaties." The ephemerality of paper documents contrasts with the "Natural" relationship Coosaponakeesa claims with the Creeks and the land.[36]

Significantly, when Coosaponakeesa subtly threatens the British government in the next paragraph by reminding her reader of the importance of the Creek alliance in maintaining the regional balance of power with the French and Spanish colonial forces, she asserts that these forces "Have for some time past, and are at this Juncture, Labouring by all the Artifices Imaginable to seduce that Nation from their Alliance with his Majestys Subjects, which will certainly be a great Addition and Increase of Territory Strength and Power to his Majestys Enimies."[37] The allusions to "Artifices" and "seduc[tion]" suggest again that the colonists are like husbands entering a matrilineage's settlement, where their right to remain is indeed tenuous. As Charles Hudson notes: "Among the Creeks as among other matrilineal people, marriages were somewhat fragile and divorce was rather common."[38] Like that of a husband, the colonists' right to reside on the land lasts only so long as they maintain a mutually contented relationship with their Creek partners.

Despite all these veiled threats to sever ties between her community and Georgia, Coosaponakeesa still insists that Georgia can avoid losing its Creek alliance. Though by natural law she is a Creek, she reminds her reader that "your Memorialist by the Laws of Great Britain is a Subject of that Crown." She then supports Britain's responsibility to her by listing in detail the "many Signal Proofs of her Zeal and Loyalty."[39] For example, she writes "that after the War with Spain the services of the Indians were so frequently required that no Advantage could Possably be made by the Trade there; that she Constantly employed her Interest to bring Down her Friends and Relations from the Nation to fight against his Majestys Enemies which since the War they have so much Annoyed that they have been a strong Barrier and Defence of the Country against the Designs of the Spaniards as must be universally Allowed by every Unprejudiced Person."[40] As in many other examples, she is careful to note how her services to the community have both negatively impacted her personal assets and contributed to the colony's safety.

The most crucial moment in the document, however, occurs after Coosaponakeesa has offered these rhetorical reminders that she is a natural Creek and a valuable subject of Britain. In this subsequent section, she invokes British abuse of her friendship to justify her current paper war and a possible future war between nations, promoted through her Creek influence:

> AND Lastly your Memorialist cannot Help repeating with an equal Mixture of a Real Grief of Heart, and Indignation; that her Injuries and Oppressions have been such, as she believes; have been scarce

> paralleled under a British Government. Language is too Weak to Represent her present Deplorable Case; She at present Labours under every sence of Injury; and Circumstance of Distress; Destitute of even the Common Necessaries of Life, being Insulted, Abused, contemned and Dispised by those ungratefull People who are indebted to her for the Blessings they Injoy.
>
> The Only Returns she has met with for her past Services, Generosity, and Maternal Affection (she has at all times shewn for the whole Colony) has been injust Loads of Infamy and Reproach; Branded and Stigmatized with the Odious Name of Traytor, for Making any Pretensions to those Rights she is Justly entitled to by the Laws of God and Nature (as her ancestors were the Natural born Heirs Sole Owners and Proprietors of every Foot of Land which is now his Majestys Colony of Georgia,) tho she has in Vain made Application for a Grant from the Crown, and is Desireous and Willing to hold What Posesions she is there entitled to by the Laws of Nature and Nations, as a Subject of great Britain.[41]

Through these words, Coosaponakeesa initiates a rhetorical shift of relationship between herself and Georgia. Her "Real Grief of Heart, and Indignation" personalize Georgia's abuses and indicate that they are no longer wrong merely because of an abstract understanding of British justice. Her description of language as "too Weak" underscores the implication that paper laws and rights are meaningless compared to feeling. Her usage of "Labours" in the next sentence—labor suggesting not only work but childbirth—begins to suggest that Britain's abuses of her as a woman are particularly heinous. Her statement that the people of Georgia are "indebted to her for the Blessings they Injoy" helps categorize Georgia as her child, the result of her "Labour." This claim widens when she dramatically mentions her "Maternal Affection" in the next paragraph. British violations of the "Laws of God and Nature" now appear to be acts of matricide—a particularly heinous crime in a matrilineal culture like that of the Creeks. In committing matricide, Coosaponakeesa strongly suggests, the colonists have severed their claims to kinship and clanship and should be treated as outcasts.

Coosaponakeesa's writings—from those that structure a Creek-Georgian friendship to those that linguistically assert her maternal rights, declare personal war on her own child, and even threaten infanticide—offer considerable insight into the Native presence and Native agency in early America, for through them, Coosaponakeesa consistently wrote Creek culture into colonial documents. Her writings can thus be seen as performances of national and personal sovereignty that must be read with attentiveness to tribal specificity. As evidence of national sovereignty, these documents underscore that Creeks were not inevitably and tragically swept away by British colonialism. Rather, they acted as economic and military partners, took advantage of new trade opportunities to adjust and strengthen their communities, and labored to promote the British presence in an effort to increase their own claims to power. As evidence of personal sovereignty, these documents show how Coosaponakeesa used her linguistic skills and cultural knowledge to become a vivid and active presence in the region. They expose the fallacy behind the colonists' first impression of her as an impoverished, exploitable female in strange attire. Her gender, she proved, was not a limitation, forcing her to remain on the sidelines, but a flexible identity through which she structured her interventions into Creek and Georgian communities and furthered what she saw as Creek interests. Ultimately she played a vital part in performing Creek sovereignty through an independent voice grounded in her gender, her intercultural skills, and her subtle, powerful acts of trade and diplomacy.

Notes

The author would like to thank Joanna Brooks, Matt Cohen, James H. Cox, Lisa L. Moore, William J. Scheick, and the editors of this volume for their assistance in crafting this essay.

1. Fisher, "Mary Musgrove," 55.
2. Candler, *Colonial Records*, *Proceedings*, 6:272.
3. According to the OED, a petticoat could be a skirt worn externally or underneath another skirt or dress. It could also be a short, tight-fitting undercoat worn by men or women for warmth, though this definition was increasingly rare by this point in time. By the eighteenth century a shift meant a woman's "body-garment" or "underclothing." While traditional winter dress for Creek women was a short deerskin skirt and a fur or cloth coat, Yamacraw women dressed similarly to Coosaponakeesa.
4. Osnabrig is also a cloth acquired by trade. This coarse, durable cloth is made from linen and is used for clothing, tents, sacks, and so on. American slaves were often given osnabrig clothing. See "osnabrig" and "stroud" in the OED.
5. Since Creek culture continues to thrive and adapt, my discussion of eighteenth-century specifics is written in the past tense. However, dualities remain core components to Creek ideology.
6. A *talwa* is roughly translatable as town. *Mico* is the Creek term for a talwa's leader associated with peace. A talwa had a separate leader for war concerns, called the *tastanagi thlako* (war chief). The mico had more power than the war leaders and acted as the primary leader for the talwa (Lankford, "Red and White," 57–58).
7. Because red and white occur at various structural points, many Creek men would transition between red and white mindsets, relating to a situation not only through personal character and desires but also through assigned roles. As Lankford clarifies, "The point is not to be red or white, but red and white" ("Red and White," 78).
8. C. Hudson, *Southeastern Indians*, 187.
9. Braund, "Guardians of Tradition," 242. A small number of women achieved the official status of beloved woman or chief after being recognized for their achievement of peace.
10. Lankford, "Red and White," 77.
11. In using the term *kinship*, I refer to Daniel Heath Justice's (Cherokee) definition: "Kinship isn't a static thing; it's dynamic, ever in motion. It requires attentiveness; kinship is best thought of as a verb rather

than a noun, because kinship, in most indigenous contexts, is something that's done more than something that simply *is*" (Justice, "'Go Away Water!,'" 150).

12. Vizenor, *Fugitive Poses*, 15.
13. Because Coosaponakeesa's writings at times performed Creek sovereignty at the expense of non-Creek tribes and because tribal specificity is so crucial to their interpretation, they resist easy categorization as "Indian" documents. As Mielke reminds us in her introduction to this volume, some Natives "resisted or forcefully rejected the category of Indian." Coosaponakeesa's writings highlight this fraught nature of the term *Indian performance*.
14. Baine, "Myths," 432. Tuckabatchee was located at the bend of the Tallapoosa River in Georgia where it moves northward. Baine provides perhaps the most considered account of Coosaponakeesa's early life, correcting other authors who have unquestioningly repeated fabrications begun by Coosaponakeesa and her third husband, Thomas Bosomworth, as well as by some of Georgia's historians.
15. Juricek, *Early Documents, Georgia Treaties*, 11:141 (hereafter cited as *Georgia Treaties*); Szasz, *Indian Education*, 141.
16. Juricek, *Georgia Treaties*, 140.
17. For an especially detailed biography and discussion of the Bosomworth Controversy, see Fisher, "Mary Musgrove." For an example of a filing that includes multiple memorials and affidavits, see Candler, *Colonial Records, Original Papers*, 26:465–502.
18. For an example of a scholar emphasizing Coosaponakeesa's "disruptiveness," see Coulter, "Mary Musgrove." For a moderate treatment see Corry, "Bosomworth Claims." A recent impressive collection, *Feminist Interventions in Early American Studies*, includes an essay on the history of Coosaponakeesa as a cultural figure; see A. Hudson, "Imagining Mary Musgrove." For romanticized treatments see Todd, *Mary Musgrove*; and Mueller's work of historical fiction, *Angry Drum*.
19. For a possible exception see Harris's brief introduction in *American Women Writers* to what she believes is Coosaponakeesa's only surviving text, a 1734 letter to Oglethorpe (118).
20. See Candler, *Colonial Records*. The thirty-six volumes of *The Colonial Records of the State of Georgia* have different editors and publishers at different points, but they are usually referred to collectively.
21. Womack, *Red on Red*, 11.
22. Juricek, *Georgia Treaties*, 15.

23. In his introduction to these early documents, Juricek describes how "this treaty was closely patterned after the Creek treaty negotiated in 1717 by Oglethorpe's friend and collaborator, Governor Johnson of South Carolina" (*Georgia Treaties*, 4). Article four, in which the two groups lay out terms for future transfers of territory from Creeks to English colonists, has no counterpart in the 1717 treaty. Juricek also reasons, "If [Coosaponakeesa] was not the chief interpreter for the formal conference, she evidently was the interpreter for the land agreement" (4).
24. Juricek, *Georgia Treaties*, 15.
25. Unsurprisingly given English cultural attitudes, not all English settlements honored this agreement, which led to conflict throughout the early years of the colony.
26. According to Braund, "clans were composed of matrilineages that possessed a common, though distant and usually mythical, ancestor" (*Deerskins and Duffels*, 11). For more in-depth discussions of kinship, clans, and matrilineages see *Deerskins and Duffels*, 3–25; and C. Hudson, *Southeastern Indians*, 184–257.
27. The Choctaws referenced in this letter were likely a group of tribal outlaws seeking refuge. The relationship between French and Choctaws remained fairly close until the Seven Years' War in the mid-1750s.
28. Coleman and Ready, eds., *Colonial Records, Correspondence to the Trustees, James Oglethorpe, and Others*, 20:63 (hereafter cited as *Oglethorpe Papers*).
29. Coleman and Ready, *Oglethorpe Papers*, 63. According to the official translation and account, the Choctaw "King" said, "[W]e are very glad that the English have taken notice of us. We have wanted an opportunity to make peace: but being come a great way we were not able to bring any presents. I belong to a great Nation and all my People are ready to confirm what I say, we are very glad you have sent so good a Man as Thomas Jones [official Georgia representative] to us. We are surrounded with White People and the French are building Forts which we do not like. We are come to see who are our friends and whose Protection we may rely on. We desire a trade very much that a Path may be kept betwixt you and us. And that you may see we come with good hearts we have brought our Women with us" (Juricek, *Georgia Treaties*, 36).
30. Coleman and Ready, *Oglethorpe Papers*, 63.
31. Coleman and Ready, *Oglethorpe Papers*, 63.

32. For an example, see Juricek, *Georgia Treaties*, 28–29.
33. Coleman and Ready, *Oglethorpe Papers*, 64.
34. See "memorial" (definition 5.b) in the OED.
35. Juricek, *Georgia Treaties*, 140.
36. Juricek, *Georgia Treaties*, 140.
37. Juricek, *Georgia Treaties*, 140.
38. C. Hudson, *Southeastern Indians*, 200.
39. Juricek, *Georgia Treaties*, 141.
40. Juricek, *Georgia Treaties*, 143.
41. Juricek, *Georgia Treaties*, 144–45.

Works Cited

Baine, Rodney M. "Myths of Mary Musgrove." *Georgia Historical Quarterly* 76 (1992): 428–35.

Braund, Kathryn E. Holland. *Deerskins and Duffels: The Creek Indian Trade with Anglo-America, 1685–1815*. Lincoln: University of Nebraska Press, 1993.

———. "Guardians of Tradition and Handmaidens to Change: Women's Roles in Creek Economic and Social Life during the Eighteenth Century." *American Indian Quarterly* 14 (1990): 239–58.

Candler, Allen D., ed. *The Colonial Records of the State of Georgia*, vol. 26: *Original Papers, Trustees, President and Assistants, and Others, 1750–1752*. 36 vols. Atlanta: Chas. P. Byrd, 1916.

———. *The Colonial Records of the State of Georgia*, vol. 6: *Proceedings of the President and Assistants from October 12, 1741, to October 30, 1754*. 36 vols. Atlanta: Franklin, 1906.

Coleman, Kenneth, and Milton Ready, eds. *The Colonial Records of the State of Georgia*, vol. 20: *Original Papers, Correspondence to the Trustees, James Oglethorpe, and Others 1732–1735*. 36 vols. Athens: University of Georgia Press, 1982.

Corry, John Pitts. "Some New Light on the Bosomworth Claims." *Georgia Historical Quarterly* 25 (1941): 195–224.

Coulter, E. Merton. "Mary Musgrove, 'Queen of the Creeks': A Chapter of Early Georgia Trouble." *Georgia Historical Quarterly* 11 (1927): 1–30.

Fisher, Doris. "Mary Musgrove: Creek Englishwoman." Ph.D. diss., Emory University, 1990.

Harris, Sharon. *American Women Writers to 1800*. New York: Oxford University Press, 1996.

Hudson, Angela Pulley. "Imagining Mary Musgrove: 'Georgia's Creek

Indian Princess' and Southern Identity." In *Feminist Interventions in Early American Studies*, ed. Mary C. Carruth, 112–25. Tuscaloosa: University of Alabama Press, 2006.

Hudson, Charles. *The Southeastern Indians*. Knoxville: University of Tennessee Press, 1976.

Juricek, John T., ed. *Early American Indian Documents: Treaties and Laws, 1607–1789*, vol. 11: *Georgia Treaties, 1733–1763*. Gen. ed. Alden T. Vaughan. 20 vols. Frederick MD: University Publications of America, 1989.

Justice, Daniel Heath. "'Go Away Water!': Kinship, Criticism and the Decolonization Imperative." In *Reasoning Together: The Native Critics Collective*, ed. Craig S. Womack, Daniel Heath Justice, and Christopher B. Teuton, 147–68. Norman: University of Oklahoma Press, 2008.

Lankford, George E. "Red and White: Some Reflections on Southeastern Symbolism." *Southern Folklore* 50, no. 1 (1993): 53–80.

Mueller, Pamela Bauer. *An Angry Drum Echoed: Mary Musgrove, Queen of the Creeks*. St. Simon's Island GA: Piñata, 2007.

Szasz, Margaret Connell. *Indian Education in the American Colonies, 1607–1783*. Albuquerque: University of New Mexico Press, 1988.

Todd, Helen. *Mary Musgrove, Indian Princess*. Marietta GA: Larlin, 1981.

Vizenor, Gerald. *Fugitive Poses: Native American Indian Scenes of Absence and Presence*. Lincoln: University of Nebraska Press, 2000.

Womack, Craig S. *Red on Red: Native Literary Separatism*. Minneapolis: University of Minnesota Press, 1999.

[7]

Playing John White

John Wompas and Racial Identity in the Seventeenth-Century Atlantic World

Jenny Hale Pulsipher

In September 1679 John White died and was buried in London, a city more than three thousand miles from his home. His birthplace, as English ears heard and transcribed it, was Assenham East-stock—Hassanamesitt to New English ears and pens. This town was located in the Nipmuc country of central Massachusetts, and "John White, alias Wompas" was a Nipmuc Indian.[1] How he came to take the name John White and die in the largest city of the English empire offers both a compelling story in its own right and a window into a transitional period in the history of race. Recently scholars have argued that until the late seventeenth century, racial identity had less to do with color than culture: while prejudice certainly existed between cultural others, behavior and beliefs divided them much more than skin.[2] John Wompas lived his early life during a time when the possibility of an Indian becoming part of the English world seemed open. The openness of this period, before the erection of laws restricting Indian freedoms, allowed Wompas to present himself as Indian or English—whichever best suited his audience and his interest. He consistently claimed the benefits of both Indian and English culture, with little remark or opposition from either. That changed near the end of his life, a time of tremendous decline in Indian power and presence in New England and, most significantly, of war between Indians and English colonists. The violence of King Philip's War led to a hardening of racial lines, embodied in postwar regulations targeting Indians. Examining Wompas's life thus grants us a view into a time when skin color began to replace culture as the defining element in being an Indian.

"Being" Indian or English has been a subject of considerable scholarship, most of it focusing on the centuries after Wompas lived.[3] This temporal focus is unsurprising: race-based restrictions from the late seventeenth century onward helped create distinct, bounded racial groups with shared histories of oppression, characteristics we associate with the modern concept of "identity." The lack of color-based categories of race in Wompas's time, by contrast, makes identity as a static category problematic.[4] Indeed, it is worth reminding ourselves that Wompas was unlikely to have recognized the concept of *identity* as a fixed state at all. He manifested no anxiety over adhering to a set of expectations associated with an ethnic, racial, or religious group; he simply performed whatever role lent him the legitimacy to accomplish his ends. In other words, he did what worked, using either Englishness or Indianness strategically as his situation demanded. What is intriguing about his story is that what he did *stopped* working, at the same time that race and the imposed identity it created began to be fixed and regulated by law. Wompas died at a time when the world, or at least the Atlantic world, began to demand that people who looked like Indians *be* Indians.[5]

John Wompas began his education in acting English at a very young age. He was born a Nipmuc Indian in central Massachusetts around the year 1637. While he was still a young child, his father, Old Wompooas, accepted the teachings of

John Eliot and his colleagues at Nonantum and became a "Praying Indian," and later one of the chief proponents of gathering a dedicated community of Indian Christians. Determined that his own son would accept English ways early, Wompooas asked Eliot to find a godly English home in which to raise him. Eliot demurred at first, but within a short time, young John Wompas was living with Isaac Heath, the ruling elder of the Roxbury Church.[6]

Living in the Heath home in Roxbury, Wompas became fluent in English and well acquainted with English ways. No records reveal what his status was in the Heath home, whether it was closer to that of a child or a servant. But both children and servants, under Puritan teachings about the obligations fathers and mothers owed their household, would have come in for regular religious teaching as well as instruction in reading so they would have access to the written word of God.[7] John Wompas was no older than his early teens when he went to live with the Heaths, and he had already spent several years hearing the regular preaching of Eliot and his colleagues. It is likely he would have absorbed one of Eliot's more frequent messages: that Indians and English were equal in God's eyes. Indeed, the English had once been "as ignorant of God and Jesus Christ as the *Indians* are, but by seeking to know him by reading his booke, and hearing his word, and praying to him, *&c.* they now know Jesus Christ." Similarly, the Indians could move from ignorance to knowledge of God by casting off their unsettled life, learning to read and pray, and adopting other English patterns of civility.[8]

Because their teachers equated Englishness with Christian belief and behavior, it is not surprising that some of the Praying Indians identified themselves as English. In a 1648 letter to his colleague Thomas Shepherd, Eliot recorded one convert's prediction: he "thought that in 40 yeers more, some *Indians* would be all one *English*, and in a hundred yeers, all *Indians* here about, would so bee."[9] Converted residents of Hassanamesitt, Wompas's home village, likewise seem to have thought that their belief and behavior, not their appearance, made them English. In response to Massachusetts agents inquiring about their loyalty immediately after the outbreak of King Philip's War, Thomas Wihtasuksacupin declared, "They do account themselves as English men and therefore they will not fight against themselves."[10]

Modern readers, remembering four hundred years of oppression and discrimination against Native peoples, might question whether such cultural characteristics could make Indians "English." In the earliest years of contact, however, differences of skin color between Indians and English were often considered to be acquired, the result of a different climate, application of dyes, or other secondary causes.[11] Thus at the time of settlement the colonists seem to have believed the Indians were, in the words of seventeenth-century court records, "of one blood" with themselves, descended from "but one father," Adam.[12] English settlers judged themselves superior to the Indians not because of race, then, but because of religious and cultural distinctions. They allowed that the English had once been "savage" themselves, but they had acquired civility. The natives might do the same.[13]

Such ideas may explain why John Wompas seems to have felt entitled to all the perquisites of English as well as Indian culture. By the time he reached adulthood he had spent nearly as much time in English as in Indian society; he spoke English fluently, was a Christian, and undoubtedly had followed the promptings of his mentors and adopted English dress and hairstyle.[14] In 1661 he followed yet another English practice and was married before a colonial magistrate in Boston to Anne Praske, an Indian woman from Connecticut.[15] Five years later Wompas purchased a house and land bordering on Boston Common, next door to Hudson Leverett, the son of the future governor of the colony.[16] It was also at this time, according to Samuel Eliot Morison, that Wompas attended the Indian College at Harvard, a school with the purpose of training Indians to minister to their own people.[17] Wompas, however, did not follow the path laid out for him. He neither joined the ministry nor returned to live among the Indians. Instead, he went to sea.

Wompas's work as a sailor probably began sometime in the late 1660s. By 1671 he was using the terms *seaman* or *mariner* to identify himself.[18] Wompas's entry into this still largely English field may have encouraged him to take on yet another trapping of Englishness—a new name. From 1672 on, Wompas identified himself by the name John White.[19] The irony of such a name strikes the modern reader forcibly. In Wompas's time, however, racial terms like *white*, *black*, and *red* were not in regular use.[20] Instead, cultural labels like English, Indian, or Christian—all three of which Wompas could have claimed—were common. Nor was Wompas unique in taking an English name; many Indians did so, whether to ease their interactions with English colonists or, following Native practice, to symbolize a new stage in their lives. Among the most familiar examples of this practice are Wamsutta and Metacom, Wampanoag sachems who requested new, English names from the Plymouth magistrates and were known thereafter as Alexander and Philip.[21] The vast majority of Indians who followed this practice, however, took only first names, as did the sachem Josias Wampatuck.[22] Wompas was thus somewhat unusual not only in embracing both an English given name *and* surname but in supplementing his birth name rather than replacing it: "John White, alias Wompas," or "John Wompas, alias White" was how he typically referred to himself.

There is little evidence that contemporaries found these efforts to act English unusual, much less risible. The strongest suggestion that anyone questioned his performance appears in a copy of Cicero's *de Officiis*, possibly owned by Wompas while a student at Harvard and containing the inscription "John Wompowess his booke" on the inside cover; on the opposite endpaper, in a different hand, appear a sketch of a meetinghouse and an inscription: "John Savage his meeting house the king of it I say."[23] This second phrase might have been the work of an English student teasing the "savage" who aspired to become a minister, the "king" of a meetinghouse. Or it may have been the gentle mockery of a fellow Indian student, much in the way modern minorities use racial epithets that would be offensive from outsiders. It reads like such teasing, but there may have been an underlying criticism as well. Was Wompas trying too hard to be English? Were his peers telling him, in mocking fashion, not to forget his origins?

While Wompas's classmates may have challenged his desire to act English, the majority of Massachusetts colonists seem to have accepted him without remark. Indeed, there was little to distinguish him from an Englishman; he was fluent in English, had a comfortable acquaintance with English legal and business ways, and dressed in the English style (as did his wife). He seems, in fact, to have been largely accepted as English. Dozens of Indians appear in the *Records of the Suffolk County Court* in the decade of the 1670s, including Wompas and his wife, Anne, but the two appear to be the only ones without the label "Indian" appended to their names.

While Wompas did portray himself as English, to the point that court records seem to have seen him as distinct from the other Indians who appeared in court at the time, he did not restrict himself to that role. When it was to his advantage, Wompas claimed to be Indian as well, as seen most clearly in his participation in land sales. From 1666, when Wompas and his wife purchased their property in Boston, to his death in 1679, Wompas bought and—mostly—sold dozens of plots of land amounting to hundreds of thousands of acres. The only way he could claim title to this land was through his lineage as an Indian.

The selling of land was a deeply contentious issue in seventeenth-century New England, Indian and English conceptions of ownership differing to such an extent that misunderstanding and outright fraud were always possibilities. Yet while instances of fraud and coercion in transfers of land from Natives to Europeans certainly occurred, it was not always the English duping the Indians.[24] Sometimes, as the case of John Wompas makes clear, the Indians did the duping. Wompas became a land speculator in Massachusetts on a scale that would not have been possible without his dual role as Indian and English, which gave him the legitimacy in English eyes to claim ownership of land, and the facility with English law and language to sell it.

The first recorded instance of Wompas selling land in the Nipmuc country occurred in 1671, when Wompas, identified as an "Indian and Seaman of Boston," deeded one hundred acres of land between Marlborough and Mendon to a fellow mariner, Thomas Stedman of New London. This land, Wompas declared, was part of a fourteen-square-mile tract of land "appertaineing unto me . . . as my proper right & inheritance."[25] Unlike most seventeenth-century Indian deeds, which named from several to over a dozen Indians as owners, Wompas was the only Indian selling this land. Doing so represented yet another example of Wompas adopting an English pattern of behavior, claiming the kind of exclusive right typical of English, not Indian, land usage.[26] It is perhaps for this reason that the deed contains language suggesting that Wompas knew his exclusive right could be questioned: following the words "my proper right & inheritance" is the phrase "or one third part thereof." Wompas's father, Old Wompooas, had died in 1651, but his father's brothers, Tom and Anthony Tray, were still living in 1671, and according to Indian custom their consent was needed before land they lived on and used could be sold.[27] There is no evidence that Wompas asked his uncles to consent to his land sale or that they shared in the purchase price. He seems to have imposed an English pattern on the land, dividing it among the heirs and claiming exclusive right to one portion.

Wompas's familiarity with English law and his fluency with the language had earlier persuaded his kin to ask him to represent them—and, presumably, protect them—in land dealings with the English.[28] It is unclear how early he began representing fellow Nipmucs, but it was probably well before his 1671 sale of land to Thomas Stedman. Such a position of trust would have made it easier for Wompas to make sales that benefited himself; it would also have facilitated more blatant fraud. He could, for instance, have acted as a translator between his relatives and English buyers, arranging for a certain price for a parcel of land, then paying less than that amount to the Indians and retaining the difference. Such fraud, invisible on the records, would help explain two things: first, how John Wompas found himself flush with money on several occasions in the mid-1660s and mid-1670s; and second, why his kin petitioned the Massachusetts magistrates in 1677 to prevent Wompas from representing them in any future land dealings, asking that he "be forbidden to put forward claims or interfere with their affairs."[29]

Wompas's first recorded purchase may have been funded by the fraud that later convinced his kin to break off any financial dealings with him. Wompas and his wife purchased their home and lot in Boston in 1666 for thirty-seven pounds and ten shillings, equivalent to over three years' wages for an ordinary seaman. Even if Wompas had risen to the position of "able seaman," which paid as much as thirty-eight shillings per month in the 1660s, it would have been difficult for him to save enough money to buy his Boston home outright.[30] In addition, given the evidence that Wompas was a student at Harvard in 1666, it is unlikely he was then employed as a mariner. There is no record of him selling any land in his own name before 1666, so unless he was able to borrow that substantial sum, skimming it from Indian land sales seems a likely source for the money. Even more strikingly, Wompas had a similar sum on hand in 1668, just two years after purchasing his home. In that year Wompas mortgaged his house for almost its full value and then repaid it within the year, preventing foreclosure.[31]

Wompas might have been able to keep this game going, trading on his acceptance in both English and Indian societies, had his access to easy money not given him access to another English trade article: alcohol. His kin would later blame drinking for his fraudulent actions, saying he had sold lands "to gett money to be drunk."[32] Drinking also disrupted his domestic life. In the spring of 1673 John got into a fight with his wife, the court charging him with being drunk and her with "abuseing & strikeing of her husband." Even if, as the record implies, John lost the fight, it created enough of a disturbance that a public officer ordered the couple to appear in court and required John to post a bond ensuring their appearance. John duly presented himself on April 29, 1673; but because Anne did not, the court retained the bond (probably ten or twenty pounds), fined John ten shillings, laid a forty-pound bond for good behavior on top of the other charges, and committed him to prison until the charges were paid.[33]

This was yet another substantial sum, and there is no record of how Wompas paid it.

John Wompas's attempts to straddle both the English and Indian worlds in Massachusetts had succeeded for a time, but his drinking and fraud eventually undermined his standing with both cultures. Unable to maintain his dual act on the local stage, Wompas took it on the road. From the spring of 1673, when he was imprisoned for drunkenness, to the spring of 1677, Wompas was absent from any record in Massachusetts. He did, however, appear on several records in London from late 1675 through 1676, and it is possible he was there from 1674 on. Though we know little of his day-to-day activities during these years, we do know that he landed in a London debtors' prison in 1676 and that he secured his release by capitalizing on his Native identity. In August of that year he sent a petition to King Charles II, in which, writing as a "poor Indian," he pleaded for the king's aid.[34] His Indianness, as Wompas no doubt knew, made him stand out from the hundreds of other supplicants to the king.[35] It was probably this quality that enabled Wompas to secure a royal audience at a time when Charles II had sharply restricted access to his presence.[36] Wompas had spent years using an English name, blending almost imperceptibly into an English world, so this apparently conscious choice to emphasize his Indian identity is striking. King Charles was known to have a taste for the exotic, something Wompas may have learned while living in London. He played the Indian card in his petition, and the portals of Whitehall opened for him.

Wompas also capitalized on the common perception that Indians were oppressed by the Massachusetts government. Complaints of Massachusetts's mistreatment of Indian subjects had reached the king before, and Wompas well knew that the colony's magistrates were in precarious standing with the crown.[37] In his petition he blamed his current poverty on the fact that the Massachusetts magistrates had denied him the freedom to sell his land, and he begged the king to order the colony to confirm his sales so he could free himself from prison.[38] At the same time, however, to underline his faithfulness as an English subject in contrast to the fractious and independent New Englanders, Wompas took the Oaths of Allegiance and Supremacy, which acknowledged the ultimate authority of the crown. In claiming the status of subject, Wompas also claimed the right to royal protection against the abuses of the king's English subjects, an approach that the Narragansetts had used successfully in 1644 and 1664.[39] Such a strategy demonstrated a keen understanding of the differences between colonial perceptions of native status—subjects, but beneath the colonial authorities—and the metropole's idealized view of Indians as equal subjects of the crown. The king granted his petition, sending a letter directing Massachusetts Governor John Leverett to do justice to "our subject," John Wompas.[40]

Within months Wompas borrowed enough money to repay his debt and took a ship to Massachusetts. He arrived, bearing the king's letter, in the spring of 1677. His timing could not have been worse. While he was away, King Philip's War had devastated the colony and dramatically altered Indian-English relations. Where Indians had once made up 25 percent of the population, wartime deaths from combat, disease, and starvation had reduced them to less than 10 percent.[41] Many Indians had fled the region, taking up residence in reserves in Canada or New York. Those remaining, including many Christian Indians who had fought as allies of the English in the war, found their freedoms tightly restricted. Indian policy after the war treated all Indians, regardless of their belief or behavior, as potential threats to the colony's safety.[42] For someone like Wompas, who continued to insist on all the rights of an English subject, to arrive in Massachusetts at such a time was like tossing a match into a powder keg.

Wompas's first errand in New England was to the colony's governor, to whom he presented the king's letter and demanded confirmation of his land sales.[43] There was nothing the Massachusetts magistrates liked less than appeals over their heads to the royal government, particularly during a time when the crown was investigating the colony for abuses of its charter authority. In the past, the colony's magistrates had severely condemned and punished such challenges.[44] Thus their decision to refer the case to a lower court overseen by the Indian superintendent seems restrained. But it was also an explicit categorization of Wompas's case as something "other," an indication that attitudes toward even the most English of the Indians had shifted. At the Indian court, the magistrate in charge was Daniel Gookin, the Indian superintendent of the colony and a man well acquainted with many of Wompas's kin. He summoned them to court to give testimony about Wompas's right to the land and, after hearing their judgment that Wompas "could not prove or demonstrate any Right he had in lands more than other common Indians had," ruled against him.[45] Wompas's petition to the king had conveniently omitted any mention of other Indians with rights to Nipmuc lands.[46]

Wompas refused to accept defeat. While colonists had stopped seeing him as English, he continued to claim both cultural roles. Documents record Wompas broadcasting his complaints in several different settings in the summer and fall of 1677. Two Cambridge residents testified that Wompas "boasted of his Being the king's subject," a status he implied raised him above the English colonists. When one protested that "they were his majesties subjects as well as he," Wompas said "he questioned that, . . . as if they were not legal subjects to his majesty."[47] Wompas made this allusion to the colony's precarious standing abundantly clear in another visit to an English household, the Cambridge Village home of Daniel Meade. While there Wompas described in great detail his audience with the king in England, where he had also observed the colony's agent, William Stoughton, on his knees begging for the renewal of the Massachusetts charter. In response to this plea, the king chided Stoughton for Massachusetts's repeated violations of English law and declared that, though "his grand father had [given] them their patent, . . . they had forfeited it & acted contrary to it." Wompas's claims that he was a true subject of the king and that the English of Massachusetts Bay were not "legal subjects to his majesty" rested on these observations. Speaking on another occasion to Hannah Meade and Goodwife Mann, Wompas declared, "New England hath lost the day and . . . it is knowne in old England."[48] By voicing his private knowledge that New England's independent authority was all but lost, Wompas raised the specter of the crown acting against the colony, a possibility that the presence in the colony of royal official Edward Randolph and recent letters from the king had made very real.[49]

Wompas added to his threats by playing up his Indian connections and appearance. One English resident noted Wompas's stirring up trouble among his Indian kin, telling them the English had cheated them out of the benefit of their lands.[50] Worse, Wompas, acting as if he spoke for the Indians as a whole, hinted that their discontent might turn to violence. While King Philip's War had ended in southern New England by the fall of 1676, fighting was still going on in Maine and New Hampshire, and rumors of Indian attacks kept the colony anxious and suspicious of Indians among them. Just such a rumor led to an alarm in September 1677. When Cambridge residents gathered at the meetinghouse for news, John Wompas came, too. The appearance of an Indian at such a time led to enough discomfort among the townspeople that Wompas asked "whether they never saw an Indian before?" When someone replied that yes, of course they had, Wompas intoned, "You shall feel them too."[51]

Wompas's speech here sounds oddly formulaic. His words were, of course, reported by Englishmen, one of whom made a point of saying that Wompas delivered the lines in a "surly manner." Both the threatening words and the "surly" delivery evoke the kind of stereotypical "savage" the Cambridge villagers had come to expect over the course of a bloody, destructive war. Yet it may also be that Wompas chose these particular words as a means of reflecting the villagers' fears back to them. In either case, it is striking that these accounts of Wompas's words and actions identify him explicitly as "Indian." Though Wompas had been absent from the colony during the most critical months of the war and had never participated in attacks on the English, the colonists clearly saw him as the embodiment of the Indian threat. Other incidents that autumn deepened the identification of Wompas with a generalized Indian menace: he threatened to shoot a Cambridge woman if he got a gun, continued to stir up discontent among his relatives, and gave "out expressions [rendering] him justly to be suspected of conspiring with ye enemy against us."[52] Such threats, on the heels of a devastating war, terrified the colonists.

Wompas chose the worst possible moment to play the part of the hostile Indian. Absent from the colony for most of the war, he may not have fully appreciated the collapse of Indian power and autonomy by its end and the impact the war had on English-Indian relations. During his time abroad, those who had once held out hope for Indians to become like the English had abandoned this hope, in anger or despair. Sudbury minister Edmund Browne, who had supported and briefly assisted with missionary work to the Natives, condemned their "trecherous and cruell proceedings against the English that sought their good" and declared them "unworthy of the grace of the Gospel."[53] To be sure, some, like John Eliot, maintained that it was the English who had fallen short of their professed ideals, writing, "the prophane Indians prove a sharp rod to the English, & the English prove a very sharp rod to the praying Indians."[54] But Browne's attitude proved more common than Eliot's, and postwar regulations made all Indians, Christian or otherwise, a separate, subordinate, and restricted class.

Restrictions on Indians after the war made the kind of double life John Wompas had lived virtually impossible. After the war, Indians, friendly or otherwise, were confined to five, later three, Praying Towns, changing what had been refuges into reservations. Indians were prohibited from carrying guns in the presence of the English, were liable to be shot if they failed to put down weapons when encountering English in the woods, and were banned from English towns until long after the war. When, years later, Indians once again began appearing in Boston records, they were almost always listed as servants, and were increasingly identified with another oppressed minority—African slaves. Over time Indians and African slaves came to share similar laws, such as curfews, and by 1798, both were prohibited from intermarrying with whites.[55] The postwar period thus witnessed the categorization of Indians according to appearance, not behavior, the beginnings of institutionalized racism.[56]

Even if Wompas had understood the postwar change in English attitudes toward Indians, he may have been too overwhelmed with anger and grief to curb his outbursts. He had come home from England to find his wife dead and his Boston home in the hands of an English family.[57] Many friends had been killed or had lost their homes in the war, and all Indians, Christian or otherwise, had come under a deep cloud of suspicion and had lost their mobility and their rights. Had this harsh new reality brought him at last to identify explicitly with his Indianness? In *Medicine Bundle*, Joshua David Bellin argues that "the natural, the necessary, condition of intercultural encounter is that one forms oneself by performing one's other."[58] Wompas had spent years acting like an Englishman and had returned to the colony to apply royal English power to his land problem. Now, however, he was blocked from participating in the English land market, English colonists viewed him with fear and distrust, and his kin had been scattered, demoralized, and killed. It is not surprising that in a time when English rights were denied him, Wompas increasingly identified with his Indian roots.

One relationship in particular shows this connection. On at least one recorded occasion during the summer of 1677, Wompas found company with Andrew Pittimee, another Indian convert and one who had suffered grievously during the war.[59] By the time Wompas returned from England, six of Andrew's close kin, including his wife and sisters, had been murdered by Englishmen while innocently foraging for berries.[60] Andrew's kinsman Swagun attempted to avenge the murders by attacking a passing Englishman, "saying that he must kill an English man." Andrew's brother made a similar attempt.[61] While we do not know whether Andrew also tried to avenge the deaths, his grief and anger must have been substantial. Wompas probably knew these women and children, and given his documented association with Pittimee, he probably also knew how he and his relatives felt about the tragedy. Wompas's threats against the English reflect an anger that events like the Pittimee family murders might have fueled.

We cannot know whether Wompas's threatening speech to the Cambridge English was an ironic pose, a political expedient, or a deep expression of renewed identification with his people.

Whatever the case, the conjunction of his lawless behavior, his threats of Indian violence, and the postwar anxiety that had led colonists to see all Indians as enemies made Wompas a focus of deep prejudice. In response, colonists asked the magistrates to do what they had done to other Indians guilty of "imbruing their hands in English blood": send him out of the country as a slave.[62] Though the magistrates did not comply with this extreme demand, they threw Wompas in jail. In fact, Wompas's railing, "drunkenness and evil carriage," and threats landed him in three separate prisons over the course of a year. He escaped from one, secured his release from the others, then fled the region altogether.[63] It was clear he was not welcome in English Massachusetts, and his claims of Native right would not be honored there, whatever threats he might make to back his demands with Indian or royal force.

By 1679 Wompas was back in London, and by the fall of that year he had died, but not before once more playing his Indian identity to his advantage. In return for "various considerations," perhaps food and assistance with the costs of medical treatment in his final illness, John Wompas deeded to an English victualler, Edward Pratt, a vast tract of land in the Nipmuc country of Massachusetts. He justified this sale by claiming to be "a sachem," a status many English, ignorant of the nuanced and consensual nature of Indian land holding, believed conferred absolute right to alienate property.[64] Wompas may have tried this tactic earlier; at the same time that his Nipmuc kin revoked his right to represent them, they told the Massachusetts magistrates that Wompas was "no sachem, and had no more right . . . to any lands in the Nipmuk Country . . . than other comon Indians."[65] Massachusetts magistrates would reject this deed, as they had Wompas's earlier land sales, but Pratt and those to whom he sold shares were remarkably persistent. By 1704 they or their heirs had secured eight square miles of land once the possession of the Indians of Hassanamesitt.[66]

By any measure John Wompas lived a remarkable life. His appeals to the crown, his residence in the heart of Boston, his life as a sailor, and his career in land fraud challenge our preconceptions of what was possible for an Indian in seventeenth-century New England. But his story tells us as much about what was not possible for Indians, at least by the end of the century, as what was possible early on.

Reading the largely legal documents of Wompas's life, some patterns emerge. Both Wompas himself and the English with whom he interacted generally ignored the fact that he was an Indian during times when he seemed a law-abiding citizen and the colony was at peace with Indians. Even after his misbehavior closed off access to profitable land sales, Wompas had no difficulty securing work as a sailor, a largely English occupation at the time, and traveling to England. Once there Wompas exhibited his Indianness openly, describing himself as a "poor Indian" on his petition to the crown and claiming to be a "sachem" on land deeds he recklessly distributed. In England, where Indians were far more unusual than in the Bay Colony, Indian identity conferred both legitimacy and exoticism that Wompas used to his advantage. When, however, he continued to perform this identity on his return to the politically and racially altered landscape of Massachusetts, his attempts to frighten English settlers with his claims that they would "feel" the Indians "ere long" backfired, lumping him with all other Indian "hostiles" and getting him booted from the colony.

The change encapsulated in Wompas's life—from Indian identity seeming almost irrelevant to its becoming a threatening and defining fact—paralleled the breakdown in English-Indian relations in late seventeenth-century Massachusetts and the erection of legal barriers between Indians and English based on race. In their discussion of identity, Rogers Brubaker and Frederick Cooper argue that "setting out to write about 'identifications' as they emerge, crystallize, and fade away in particular social and political circumstances may well inspire a rather different history than setting out to write of an 'identity,' which links past, present, and future in a single word."[67] The war, and the actions of the government in its aftermath, had transformed Indian identity from a malleable set of behaviors that invited cross-cultural passage to a fixed racial category that firmly divided English and Indians. Could someone like Wompas have operated in Massachusetts after that event? It seems unlikely. But perhaps it was still possible to do so in England—or at least, Wompas thought it was. The final document in his life was his will, crafted while he was "weak in body but sound in mind." In it, he named himself "John White, alias Wompas, late of Boston, mariner."[68] He claimed both an Indian and an English name and trade, but he said nothing about race. For Wompas, Indianness and Englishness persisted in being what he performed, not who he was. And he doggedly continued granting Indian land until he died, claiming to the last the perquisites of both Indian and English cultures.

Notes

1. The two most complete accounts of John Wompas's life are Humes, "John Wampas"; and Connole, *Indians*, 122–37.
2. See Shoemaker, "How Indians Got to Be Red" and *Strange Likeness*, 125–40; Chaplin, "Race"; Cogley, *John Eliot's Mission*, 7–9; Hanaford, *Race*, xii–xv, chaps. 6 and 7; and Vaughan, *New England Frontier*, 20, 62–63, 324, and *Roots of American Racism*, chaps. 1, 2, and 8.
3. See, for example, Deloria, *Playing Indian*; Clifton, ed., *Being and Becoming Indian*; Brown, "Métis"; and Garroutte, *Real Indians*.
4. Brubaker and Cooper argue that "identity," as it has developed in the last several decades of scholarly discourse, has become something

of a catch-all, including both popular notions of essentialism and contradictory scholarly claims of fluidity, contingency, and multifacetedness, and that the concept would be more useful analytically if replaced with more precise terms (Brubaker and Cooper, "Beyond Identity").

5. Wompas offers a parallel example to the experience of Anthony Johnson and other black men in mid-seventeenth-century Virginia. They, too, lived during a time of transition from a world in which they functioned as free planters to one in which black men were, by definition, slaves (Breen and Innes, "*Myne Owne Ground*").
6. Clark, ed., *Eliot Tracts*, 95–96, 223–24.
7. Morgan, *Puritan Family*, chaps. 4 and 5.
8. Cogley, *John Eliot's Mission*, 6–9, 126–31; Clark, ed., *Eliot Tracts*, 85–86.
9. Clark, ed., *Eliot Tracts*, 124.
10. Massachusetts Archives Collection, 30:169, Massachusetts State Archives, Columbia Point, Boston (hereafter cited as Mass. Archives).
11. Kupperman, *Indians and English*, 58–59.
12. Shurtleff, ed., *Records of Plymouth Colony*, 5:66; Clark, ed., *Eliot Tracts*, 89.
13. Kupperman, *Indians and English*, 59–62.
14. Clark, ed., *Eliot Tracts*, 116. The estate inventory of Wompas's wife Anne demonstrates that she adopted English dress and other cultural trappings (Humes, "John Wampas," 25).
15. Appleton, ed., *Boston Births*, 81.
16. Suffolk Deeds, 5:490–91.
17. Cogley, *John Eliot's Mission*, 219–24; Morison, *Harvard College*, 342–58.
18. Suffolk Deeds, 8:421. Histories of New England sailors and fishermen focus on the post-1700 period, and maritime records before that time are scarce. See Albion, *New England and the Sea*; Bailyn and Bailyn, *Massachusetts Shipping*; Heyrman, *Commerce and Culture*; Linebaugh and Rediker, *Many Headed Hydra*; and Vickers, *Young Men and the Sea*.
19. Shurtleff, ed., *Records of the Governor and Company of the Massachusetts Bay*, 4:2:537 (hereafter cited as MBR).
20. Shoemaker, "How Indians Got to be Red," 625–27.
21. Bragdon, *Native People*, 170; Axtell, *Invasion Within*, 168.
22. For examples of this usage see "Indian" in the indexes of Shurtleff, ed., MBR.
23. Morison, *Harvard College*, 356.

24. On the "deed game" see Jennings, *Invasion of America*, chap. 8; and Salisbury, *Manitou and Providence*, 190–202. Views of land transactions more sympathetic to the English appear in Vaughan, *New England Frontier*, xxxv, lxi–lxiii, 310–13; and Cogley, *John Eliot's Mission*, 30–35, 228–39. For a recent, balanced overview of Indian land sales in Plymouth see Bangs, *Indian Deeds*.
25. Suffolk Deeds, 8:421.
26. On Indian conceptions of land use see Bragdon, *Native People*, 137–39.
27. Clark, ed., *Eliot Tracts*, 222.
28. Mass. Archives, 30:260a.
29. Mass. Archives, 30:259a. Interestingly, even before his kin blew the whistle on Wompas, Massachusetts had begun to block sales such as his (Sainsbury, ed., *Calendar of State Papers*, 9: #1023). As early as 1634 the General Court prohibited sales of Indian land without their express consent (Shurtleff, ed., MBR, 1:112; see also 4:1:282). In 1652 the General Court acknowledged the Indians' right to lands they traditionally used (Shurtleff, ed., MBR, 4:1:102; see also MBR, 3:189).
30. Davis, *Rise of Shipping Industry*, 120.
31. Suffolk Deeds, 5:540–43.
32. Mass. Archives, 30:259a.
33. *Records of Suffolk County Court*, 1:267, 330.
34. Sainsbury, ed., *Calendar of State Papers*, 9: #1023.
35. While there had been Indian visitors to England before, most famously Pocahontas in the early 1600s, they remained an exotic rarity until the following century. See Vaughan, *Transatlantic Encounters*; and Hinderaker, "'Four Indian Kings.'"
36. Weiser, *Charles II*, 74–80; Pulsipher, *Subjects unto the Same King*, 207–8.
37. Pulsipher, *Subjects unto the Same King*, 195–96, 207–8.
38. Sainsbury, ed., *Calendar of State Papers*, 9: #1023.
39. Pulsipher, *Subjects unto the Same King*, 27–32.
40. Middlesex Folios, 93:2b.
41. Drake, *King Philip's War*, 169.
42. Pulsipher, "'Our Sages,'" 437–41. For more on the status of Indians following King Philip's War see Calloway, ed., *After King Philip's War*; O'Brien, *Dispossession by Degrees*; and Kawashima, *Puritan Justice*, chap. 8 and epilogue.
43. Suffolk Court Files, #1642.
44. For example, in 1665 the Massachusetts magistrates fined Thomas

Bredon two hundred pounds for refusing to acknowledge their supreme authority (Pulsipher, *Subjects unto the Same King*, 51).

45. Suffolk Court Files, #1642.
46. Mass. Archives, 30:259a, 260a.
47. Suffolk Court Files, #1642.
48. Maine Historical Society Archives.
49. Pulsipher, *Subjects unto the Same King*, 195–99.
50. Suffolk Court Files, #1642.
51. Suffolk Court Files, #1642.
52. Middlesex Court Records, 3:196.
53. Pulsipher, "'Our Sages,'" 446.
54. "Rev. John Eliot's Records," 297–98.
55. Pulsipher, "'Our Sages,'" 440–41.
56. For more on this process see Salisbury, ed., introduction to *Sovereignty and Goodness of God*; and Mandell, *Tribe, Race, History*.
57. Humes, "John Wampas," 31–32.
58. Bellin, *Medicine Bundle*, 81.
59. Maine Historical Society Archives.
60. For more on this incident see Pulsipher, "Massacre."
61. Pulsipher, "'Our Sages,'" 445.
62. For use of the phrases "send out of the country" or "send away" in connection with Indian slavery, see Shurtleff, ed., MBR, 5:58; Mass. Archives, 30:239a; and Church, *Diary of King Philip's War*, 92, 129. On Indian slavery see Lauber, *Indian Slavery*; Newell, "Changing Nature"; and Lepore, *Name of War*, chap. 6.
63. Wompas escaped prison in Cambridge in October 1678 (Middlesex Court Records, 3:196) but was recaptured and sent to prison in Boston. The following spring he was jailed in Connecticut after trying to secure possession of land left to his wife (Sainsbury, ed., *Calendar of State Papers*, 10: #928).
64. Middlesex County Registry of Deeds, 7:157–60; Bragdon, *Native People*, 170; Cogley, *John Eliot's Mission*, 33.
65. Mass. Archives, 30:260a.
66. *Acts and Resolves*, 8:46.
67. Brubaker and Cooper, "Beyond Identity," 28.
68. Humes, "John Wampas," 26–27.

Works Cited

The Acts and Resolves, Public and Private, of the Province of the Massachusetts Bay. Boston: Wright and Potter, 1869–1922.

Albion, Robert Greenhalgh. *New England and the Sea*. Middletown CT: Wesleyan University Press, 1972.

Appleton, William S., ed. *Boston Births, Baptisms, Marriages, and Deaths, 1630–1699*. Baltimore: Genealogical Publishing, 1978.

Axtell, James. *The Invasion Within: The Contest of Cultures in Colonial North America*. New York: Oxford University Press, 1985.

Bailyn, Bernard, and Lotte Bailyn. *Massachusetts Shipping, 1697–1714: A Statistical Study*. Cambridge MA: Belknap Press of Harvard University Press, 1959.

Bangs, Jeremy Dupertuis. *Indian Deeds: Land Transactions in Plymouth Colony, 1620–1691*. Boston: New England Historical and Genealogical Society, 2002.

Bellin, Joshua David. *Medicine Bundle: Indian Sacred Performance and American Literature, 1824–1932*. Philadelphia: University of Pennsylvania Press, 2008.

Bragdon, Kathleen J. *Native People of Southern New England, 1500–1650*. Norman: University of Oklahoma Press, 1996.

Breen, T. H., and Stephen Innes. *"Myne Owne Ground": Race and Freedom on Virginia's Eastern Shore, 1640–1676*. New York: Oxford University Press, 1980.

Brown, Jennifer S. H. "Métis, Halfbreeds, and Other Real People: Challenging Cultures and Categories." *History Teacher* 27 (1993): 19–26.

Brubaker, Rogers, and Frederick Cooper. "Beyond Identity." *Theory and Society* 29, no. 1 (2000): 1–47.

Calloway, Colin G., ed. *After King Philip's War: Presence and Persistence in Indian New England*. Hanover NH: University Press of New England, 1997.

Chaplin, Joyce E. "Race." In *The British Atlantic World, 1500–1800*, ed. David Armitage and Michael J. Braddick, 93–112. New York: Palgrave Macmillan, 2002.

Church, Benjamin. *Diary of King Philip's War, 1675–76*. Ed. Alan and Mary Simpson. Chester CT: Pequot, 1975.

Clark, Michael P., ed. *The Eliot Tracts: With Letters from John Eliot to Thomas Thorowgood and Richard Baxter*. Westport CT: Praeger, 2003.

Clifton, James A., ed. *Being and Becoming Indian: Biographical Studies of North American Frontiers*. Chicago: Dorsey, 1989.

Cogley, Richard W. *John Eliot's Mission to the Indians Before King Philip's War*. Cambridge MA: Harvard University Press, 1999.

Connole, Dennis A. *The Indians of the Nipmuck Country in Southern*

New England, 1630–1750: An Historical Geography. Jefferson NC: McFarland, 2001.

Davis, Ralph. *The Rise of the English Shipping Industry in the Seventeenth and Eighteenth Centuries.* London: Macmillan, 1962.

Deloria, Philip J. *Playing Indian.* New Haven: Yale University Press, 1998.

Drake, James D. *King Philip's War: Civil War in New England, 1675–1676.* Amherst: University of Massachusetts Press, 1999.

Garroutte, Eva Marie. *Real Indians: Identity and the Survival of Native America.* Berkeley: University of California Press, 2003.

Hannaford, Ivan. *Race: The History of an Idea in the West.* Baltimore: Johns Hopkins University Press, 1996.

Heyrman, Christine Leigh. *Commerce and Culture: The Maritime Communities of Colonial Massachusetts, 1690–1750.* New York: Norton, 1984.

Hinderaker, Eric. "The 'Four Indian Kings' and the Imaginative Construction of the First British Empire." *William and Mary Quarterly* 3rd ser. 53 (1996): 487–526.

Humes, John Fred. "John Wampas and the Beginning of Sutton." In *History of the Town of Sutton, Massachusetts*, ed. John C. Dudley, 19–40. Town of Sutton, Massachusetts, 1952.

Jennings, Francis. *The Invasion of America: Indians, Colonialism, and the Cant of Conquest.* New York: Norton, 1976.

Kawashima, Yasuhide. *Puritan Justice and the Indian: White Man's Law in Massachusetts, 1630–1763.* Middletown CT: Wesleyan University Press, 1986.

Kupperman, Karen. *Indians and English: Facing Off in Early America.* Ithaca: Cornell University Press, 2000.

Lauber, Almon W. *Indian Slavery in Colonial Times Within the Present Limits of the United States.* New York: Columbia University Press, 1913.

Lepore, Jill. *The Name of War: King Philip's War and the Origins of American Identity.* New York: Knopf, 1998.

Linebaugh, Peter, and Marcus Rediker. *The Many-Headed Hydra: Sailors, Slaves, Commoners, and the Hidden History of the Revolutionary Atlantic.* Boston: Beacon, 2000.

Maine Historical Society Archives. William S. Southgate Collection. Collection 77, Box 1/4. Portland, Maine.

Mandell, Daniel R. *Tribe, Race, History: Native Americans in Southern New England, 1780–1880.* Baltimore: Johns Hopkins University Press, 2008.

Massachusetts Archives Collection (Mass. Archives). Massachusetts State Archives. Columbia Point, Boston.

Middlesex County Registry of Deeds. Cambridge, Massachusetts.

Middlesex Court Records. David Pulsifer transcript. Massachusetts State Archives. Columbia Point, Boston.

Middlesex Folios. Massachusetts State Archives. Columbia Point, Boston.

Morgan, Edmund S. *The Puritan Family: Religion and Domestic Relations in Seventeenth Century New England*. New York: Harper and Row, 1966.

Morison, Samuel Eliot. *Harvard College in the Seventeenth Century*. Part 1. Cambridge MA: Harvard University Press, 1936.

Newell, Margaret Ellen. "The Changing Nature of Indian Slavery in New England, 1670–1720." In *Reinterpreting New England Indians and the Colonial Experience*, ed. Colin G. Calloway and Neal Salisbury, 106–36. Boston: Colonial Society of Massachusetts, 2003.

O'Brien, Jean M. *Dispossession by Degrees: Indian Land and Identity in Natick, Massachusetts, 1650–1790*. Cambridge: Cambridge University Press, 1997.

Pulsipher, Jenny Hale. "Massacre at Hurtleberry Hill: Christian Indians and English Authority in Metacom's War." *William and Mary Quarterly* 3rd ser. 53 (1996): 459–86.

———. "'Our Sages are Sageles': A Letter on Massachusetts Indian Policy after King Philip's War." *William and Mary Quarterly* 3rd ser. 58 (2001): 431–48.

———. *Subjects unto the Same King: Indians, English, and the Contest of Authority in Colonial New England*. Philadelphia: University of Pennsylvania Press, 2005.

Records of the Suffolk County Court, 1671–1680. 2 vols. Boston: Colonial Society of Massachusetts, 1933.

"Rev. John Eliot's Records of the First Church." *New England Historical and Genealogical Register* 33 (July 1879): 297–98.

Sainsbury, W. Noel, ed. *Calendar of State Papers, Colonial Series, America and West Indies, 1674–1676*. Vol. 9. 1880; Vaduz: Kraus Reprint, 1964.

———. *Calendar of State Papers, Colonial Series, America and West Indies, 1677–1680*. Vol. 10. 1880; Vaduz: Kraus Reprint, 1964.

Salisbury, Neal. *Manitou and Providence: Indians, Europeans, and the Making of New England, 1500–1643*. New York: Oxford University Press, 1982.

Salisbury, Neal, ed. *The Sovereignty and Goodness of God, by Mary Rowlandson, with Related Documents*. Boston: Bedford, 1997.

Shoemaker, Nancy. "How Indians Got to Be Red." *American Historical Review* 102 (June 1997): 625–44.

———. *A Strange Likeness: Becoming Red and White in Eighteenth-Century North America*. New York: Oxford University Press, 2004.

Shurtleff, Nathaniel B., ed. *Records of the Governor and Company of the Massachusetts Bay in New England* (MBR). 6 vols. Boston: William White, 1854.

———. *Records of Plymouth Colony*. 12 vols. Boston: William White, 1855–61.

Suffolk Court Files. Massachusetts State Archives. Columbia Point, Boston.

Suffolk Deeds. Massachusetts State Archives. Columbia Point, Boston.

Vaughan, Alden T. *New England Frontier: Puritans and Indians 1620–1675*. 3rd ed. Norman: University of Oklahoma Press, 1995.

———. *Roots of American Racism: Essays on the Colonial Experience*. New York: Oxford University Press, 1995.

———. *Transatlantic Encounters: American Indians in Britain, 1500–1776*. Cambridge: Cambridge University Press, 2006.

Vickers, Daniel, with Vince Walsh. *Young Men and the Sea: Yankee Seafarers in the Age of Sail*. New Haven: Yale University Press, 2005.

Weiser, Brian. *Charles II and the Politics of Access*. Woodbridge, Suffolk, UK: Boydell, 2003.

[8]

"This Wretched Scene of British Curiosity and Savage Debauchery"

Performing Indian Kingship in Eighteenth-Century Britain

Timothy J. Shannon

In early 1765 Virginian militia officer Henry Timberlake led a delegation of Cherokee Indians to London. The trip was cursed from the start. One of the Indians died before the party left America; another died the day of their landfall in England. Shortly after their arrival in London the person who had agreed to underwrite the visit died as well, leaving Timberlake, already in considerable debt, to pay the expenses of the three surviving Indians. His difficulties were compounded by the reluctance of government officials to arrange for the Indians to visit King George III or to assume the cost of their maintenance. Lord Halifax, representing the king's Privy Council, told Timberlake that the crown bore no responsibility for the Indians because their journey had not been authorized by royal officials in America. As far as Halifax was concerned, Timberlake had brought the Indians over, and he could take them back.

Timberlake lamented that he could not afford to entertain the Indians without the crown's support. They spent most of their time confined to their lodgings and were not able to go "so often to public diversions as they should have done." Meanwhile, newspapers reported that the Indians were not men of consequence at all but only common warriors Timberlake had brought over for public exhibition. Timberlake denied this charge, claiming that his Cherokee diplomats were being confused with an imposter who was dressing in their style and exhibiting himself for profit and a party of Mohawk Indians who were visiting London for the same reason. Such imposters and show Indians were "immediately confounded by the public with the Cherokees," leaving Timberlake "accused of making a shew all over England of Indians who never stirred out of London."[1]

It had not always been like this. In 1762 Timberlake had escorted another party of Cherokees to London, where they were graciously received by the royal court and treated with presents and tours of London landmarks. Those same Indians had been celebrated as Cherokee "kings" in print and in person, enjoyed private visits with such luminaries as Lord Chesterfield and Oliver Goldsmith, and attracted large crowds when they attended the city's theaters and pleasure gardens.

What then had gone wrong the second time around? What circumstances had changed to make Timberlake's second Cherokee embassy such a disaster? As Timberlake himself suggested, his problems arose from questions concerning the authenticity of his Indian companions as judged by government officials and "the public," London's crowds and newspapers. Were Timberlake's charges in fact Indians, and if so, were they the dignitaries he claimed they were? Closely attached to these questions were others concerning Timberlake's motive for bringing them to London. Was this a diplomatic mission undertaken by Native rulers from one of the crown's overseas dominions, or was this an entrepreneurial scheme to exhibit human curiosities before paying audiences?

Timberlake's travails in 1765 illustrate the ways in which official and public reception of Indian travelers in Britain shifted after the Seven Years' War (1756–63). That war ignited in the British public a new fascination with North America and its indigenous inhabitants. During the 1760s Britons read a burgeoning popular literature on the empire that included pamphlets, plays, and ballads about America. Veterans of the war returned home with Indian artifacts as souvenirs and exhibited such objects in cabinets of curiosities, coffeehouses, and fairs. Depictions of Native Americans in British visual culture—prints, paintings, magazines, maps, and cartoons—became commonplace and, for the first time, strove for ethnographic accuracy. As Timberlake's experience indicates, some Britons even paid to view Indians in person in theaters, taverns, and pleasure gardens. Popular interest in North America made Indians representative of the British imperial enterprise, a tangible way for Britons to imagine and experience new dominions they had reportedly conquered an ocean away.[2]

Yet such popularity, by increasing the amount of information available about Indians, raised new questions about their authenticity. Previous Indian diplomatic embassies to London had created a ritualized set of expectations whereby Indian "kings"—that is, Indians presented to the royal court as leaders of their people and allies of the crown—balanced their exposure to the curious public with the projection and preservation of their status as foreign dignitaries. In the aftermath of the Seven Years' War those guidelines collided with the new commercial interest in these Indian visitors. The exploitation of Indians as human curiosities in Britain had a sordid history all its own dating back to Elizabethan times and involving the kidnapping, enslavement, and premature deaths of its Native participants.[3] During the 1760s both the diplomatic and the commercial types of Indian performance resumed after a hiatus of nearly thirty years, but changing public attitudes about Indians and empire made it increasingly difficult to separate the performance of Indian kingship from the abuses associated with show Indians. The 1762 and 1765 Cherokee embassies to London found themselves performing for audiences increasingly skeptical about Indian kingship, making it nearly impossible to play this role as it had been rendered in the past.

Timberlake's first Cherokee embassy, in 1762, exposed the fault lines between official and public expectations for Indian kings. As a colonial military officer, Timberlake had served in several North American campaigns, including the Virginia-Cherokee War of 1761, after which he traveled among the Cherokees as a diplomatic envoy of the Virginia governor. In that capacity he escorted a party of chiefs from the Cherokee Overhill towns (modern eastern Tennessee) to Williamsburg in early 1762 for a treaty conference. While there, one of the leading Overhill chiefs, Ostenaco, dined with Timberlake at the College of William and Mary, hosted by the Reverend James Horrocks, a professor and future president of the college. When Horrocks showed his guests a portrait of King George III, Ostenaco studied it for a long time and announced, "Long have I wished to see the king my father; this is his resemblance, but I am determined to see himself; I am now near the sea, and never will depart from it till I have obtained my desires." Arrangements were made for Ostenaco and two Cherokee companions to sail for England with Timberlake, another officer named Thomas Sumter, and an interpreter named William Shorey.[4]

Neither Timberlake nor Ostenaco had visited London before,

but each had reason to be familiar with precedents established by earlier Indian embassies. A native of Hanover County, Virginia, Timberlake most likely knew of the visit John Rolfe, Pocahontas, and a dozen other Powhatan Indians had made to London in 1616. He may also have heard of the splash the "four Indian kings"—three Mohawks and one Mahican—had made when they visited London in 1710. This latter visit had left a profound impression on British perceptions of Native Americans, creating a corpus of paintings, engravings, chapbooks, and ballads that presented Indian kings as foreign in their language, dress, and habits, yet possessed of the dignity Britons associated with political leadership and elite social status. Although not one of the four carried political influence greater than that of local chief, crown and public alike regarded them as kings because their exotic appearance and personal comportment gave them an undeniably regal air.[5]

At the outset of the eighteenth century, Britons still conceived of their empire in terms of maritime trade rather than dominion over distant and racially distinct populations. The notion of Indian kingship reflected this official and popular attitude: Britons projected their own values about social and political hierarchy onto the peoples they encountered in Asia, Africa, and America, assuming that all societies ordered themselves into ranks of power and wealth and that the physical traits, manners, and habits exhibited by elites were transcultural because they were endemic to human nature. Britons believed that regardless of origin, language, or race, Indian kings would exhibit the same graceful comportment, self-control, and gravitas that elevated European nobles above the rabble of their own nations.[6] In other words, it was the performative dimension of kingship that mattered most. Any Indian could play the role, so long as he or she exhibited the right demeanor.

Two Indian embassies that visited London during the 1730s

tell us something more about how the label "king" became attached to Indian visitors. In 1734 Tomochichi, the aged leader of the Yamacraws, a small nation on the Savannah River affiliated with the Creek Confederacy, traveled to London with his wife, son, and six other Indians to meet with the trustees of the new Georgia colony. The trustees arranged for Tomochichi and his companions to tour London's sites and attend its theaters but took care to keep them at arm's length from the crowds who came out to see them. They also outfitted the visitors with new clothes and arranged for two portraits, one of the chief and his son and the other a group portrait of the Indians' meeting with their hosts. An engraving based on the former, identifying Tomochichi as "King of the Yamacraw," was also published. The popular press reported frequently and favorably on the visit and praised Tomochichi for possessing "*the most natural eloquence*" in his speeches before the king.[7]

More significant to Timberlake's 1762 embassy, a party of seven Cherokees, three of whom were identified in the British press as "kings" or "princes," visited London in 1730. Their meeting with George II initiated a diplomatic relationship with the British crown that endured through the era of the American Revolution. This party of Cherokees was sponsored by Sir Alexander Cuming, a Scottish adventurer who, like Timberlake, expected his guests to provide proof positive of his influence among the Cherokees and thereby steer valuable royal patronage his way. While that plan did not work out for Cuming (he spent most of his remaining years in debtors prison), the 1730 embassy did put the Cherokees on the imaginative map that British officials and the London press were constructing of the British empire in North America.[8]

Another legacy of the 1730 visit figured prominently in Timberlake's first embassy. One participant in that earlier trip, Attakullakulla or the Little Carpenter, was still alive in 1762 and had become a prominent leader among the Overhill Cherokees. He frequently attended treaty conferences in Virginia and South Carolina during the 1750s and 1760s, and colonial governors esteemed him as a reliable ally. At a 1756 treaty conference he reminded South Carolina's governor that "I am the only Cherokee now alive who was in England or that Saw the Great King George."[9] In 1762 Ostenaco was a rising Cherokee leader who, according to Virginia Governor Francis Fauquier, led a party opposed to the aging Attakullakulla. Thus when Ostenaco decided to go to England and see the great king for himself, he may have been hoping to acquire some of his older rival's prestige and influence.[10] Though less is known about the motives of the other two Cherokees who accompanied Ostenaco, it would appear that neither he nor Timberlake arrived in London as a naïve sightseer, and both likely had precedents in mind for their trip.

The British government, press, and public greeted Ostenaco as a Cherokee "king," the first Indian visitor to London to be received in that manner since Tomochichi almost thirty years earlier. A handful of other Indians had visited in the interim, so what did it take to convince officialdom and the public to regard an Indian visitor as a king? First, it was important to appear in London on the pretense of conducting diplomacy. As had been the case with the embassies in 1710, 1730, and 1734, this meant having a sponsor with connections to the king's ministers and the financial resources to provide the lodgings, clothing, and entertainment appropriate for a foreign dignitary. Timberlake himself was not especially wealthy or well-connected in London, but he did carry credentials from Governor Fauquier, sanctioning his trip as necessary to the colony's Indian relations. Second, it helped if the embassy appeared as allies rather than clients to the crown. Indians received as kings in the eighteenth century, such as the Iroquois and Cherokees, came from nations strategically important to British interests, whose favor had to be curried by royal officials. Even the Yamacraws, though a much smaller group, were linked to the powerful Creek Confederacy; their support was indispensable if the fledgling Georgia colony was to defend itself against Spanish Florida. During the eighteenth century several parties of New England Indians traveled to Britain to seek redress for land frauds, but their strategic insignificance and military weakness in America dictated against receiving them as kings in London.[11] An Indian king visited the royal court as an equal, not as a supplicant.

It was also important for an Indian king to travel with retainers who could provide visual testimony of his influence back home. Among the four Indian kings in 1710, one was identified in public papers and prints as the "Emperour of the Six *Nations*." Meanwhile, among the seven Cherokee visitors in 1730, two were typically identified as "kings" and the rest as their "generals" or "attendants." Tomochichi was likewise received as the leading figure among the party with whom he traveled.[12] A king could not be a king without subjects, and so even in a group as small as Timberlake's 1762 embassy, it was important that hierarchy be evident.

Indian kings also needed to dress for the part. Timberlake took care to have Ostenaco and his companions outfitted with clothing and accoutrements in "the mode of their own country" that would convey their exotic background but also their genteel status: long linen shirts, leggings and moccasins, silver gorgets and armbands, wampum beads, and scarlet mantles trimmed with gold lace.[13] Following the protocol established by previous embassies, Timberlake arranged for Ostenaco and his companions to tour Westminster Abbey, St. Paul's Cathedral, the Tower, and similar London landmarks. They dined with the lord mayor and other dignitaries, and Ostenaco and one of his companions, Cunne Shote, had their portraits painted.[14] On July 8 the Cherokees had an audience with the king at St. James's Palace, where Ostenaco made a speech professing the friendship of his people. All of these official encounters transpired smoothly, even though William Shorey, the interpreter who had accompanied the party, died "in a consumption" shortly after their arrival in Britain.[15] Timberlake served in Shorey's place as best he could, but more important, everyone involved knew what roles to follow based on the experiences of earlier embassies: the Cherokees affirmed their alliance with the crown, admired the wealth and power evident in London's landmarks, and in return received a generous present of trade goods to carry home as a mark of the king's esteem for them.

It was more difficult to stay on script, however, when Ostenaco and his companions appeared in public. The problem, according to Timberlake, was the effrontery of the crowd that pressed upon the Cherokees everywhere they went. Their party attracted gawkers even before it landed in Bristol. As sailors rowed the Cherokees ashore, Ostenaco sang "a solemn dirge with a very loud voice" that drew "a vast crowd of boats, filled with spectators." Wherever the Cherokees went, "great crowds of people of all ranks" followed them, even pressing upon them as they dressed in their private lodgings. Timberlake tried to control the situation by ordering the Indians' landlord to limit admittance to "none but people of fashion." Nevertheless, he found "the whole rabble of the town was ushered in the next day."[16]

Timberlake eventually fell out with the Indians' landlord over this issue, accusing him of charging an admittance fee to see his guests. Timberlake expressed distaste for such "money-taking works," no doubt believing that the landlord's profiteering compromised the Cherokees' status as diplomats. But Timberlake also realized that the Cherokees needed to be seen. Indians became kings not just by having audiences with government officials; they also needed to appear in public and convince the people of their regal qualities. For Timberlake's purposes, it would not do to sequester Ostenaco and his companions in their lodgings, but neither could he allow them to mix promiscuously with "the whole rabble of the town." Judging from newspaper reports and advertisements that announced when the Cherokees would be attending theaters and pleasure gardens, Timberlake knew that public appearances were necessary to fuel the Indians' celebrity, but he wanted to orchestrate these in such a manner that they would not be confused with show Indians exhibited in taverns and similar venues.[17]

Timberlake's plans unraveled during a night in late July that the Cherokees spent at Vauxhall Gardens, a London pleasure garden. According to a report in the *St. James's Chronicle*, "not less than Ten Thousand Persons" gathered that night "to obtain a Sight of these Indians," indicating that the proprietors had circulated advance word of their attendance. One of the Indians, unnamed in the newspaper report, was seen walking arm-in-arm with a female patron of the Garden. The curious crowd pressed so heavily on the Indians and their female companion that the Indians retreated "into the Orchestra," where they entertained "the gaping Multitude" by sounding the keys of an organ, scraping the bow across a violin, and clapping their hands in response to applause from their audience. The crowd plied the Indians with alcohol, and they became intoxicated.

Sometime around 3:00 a.m., as the Indians made their way through the crowd to leave, Ostenaco's cloak caught the hilt of a gentleman's sword. "The Sword by some Accident was drawn, and broke," and in the altercation, Ostenaco bloodied his hands. The aggrieved chief displayed his injuries "as if in Remonstrance and Complaint," then threw himself on the ground "in a Fit of Sullenness or Intoxication, or both," refusing to move "for a considerable Time." At last, bystanders lifted him by the "Neck and Heels" into a waiting carriage, which took the group home. Timberlake blamed the fracas on the proprietors of Vauxhall and the "ungovernable curiosity of the people."[18] The press was less forgiving of the Cherokees, calling the episode "this wretched scene of British Curiosity and Savage Debauchery."[19]

Ostenaco recovered from this night, but his reputation did not. Press coverage of the Cherokees after the misadventure at Vauxhall raised questions about their identities. For example, the *Royal Magazine* had earlier described the Cherokees as having a "mixture of majesty and moroseness in their countenances" and Ostenaco in particular as possessing "a sense of true honour, and great generosity of mind," but the issue following the Vauxhall episode carried two pieces critical of the visiting Cherokees. One informed readers that Ostenaco was not "the king of the Cherokees" but only "one of their principal warriors" and that he had come to London in hopes that a visit to the royal court would launch him into power at home. The second piece questioned the notion of Indian kingship altogether, explaining that Native Americans "have nothing like a King or supreme governor," only chiefs who gained influence by distinguishing themselves in war. The article lambasted Ostenaco for his presumed royalty by comparing him to Attakullakulla, the leader of the delegation in 1730. According to the author, "Attakullakulla, or the Little Carpenter, resided for some time among us. Yet I do not find from searching the news-papers of that period, that his Majesty was kept drunk all the while, or that public notice was given, when he should be at this or the other public place of entertainment." Unlike Timberlake's Cherokees, Attakullakulla had exhibited a gentleman's moderation in his drinking, taking only a little cider and small beer for refreshment and once even suspecting poison when a prankster had put a little brandy in his tea.[20]

An anonymous correspondent writing under the pseudonym "You Know Who" in the *St. James's Chronicle* equated Indian kingship with fraud and imposture. Referring to Ostenaco as "his Most Ignorant Majesty," the writer condemned those parties responsible for "bringing over this outlandish Monarch to be stared at" and suspected that the motive of the entire enterprise was to exploit the public's curiosity: "It is sufficient to dress up a common Grenadier with high-healed Shoes and a lofty Turband, and Numbers of Fools will walk in to see the Outlandish Giant." To illustrate further the public's gullibility when it came to exotic foreigners, "You Know Who" recounted a story about an enterprising theater owner who hired four Irishmen to impersonate the Moroccan ambassador and his attendants. After dressing the Irishmen in character and darkening their complexions with walnut juice, the proprietor sat them in a box where the rest of the audience could see them. The ruse worked well for a while: audience members mistook the impersonators' "jabbering to one another in the Irish Language" for the Moroccan tongue and their prodigious taste for porter as a natural penchant for a beverage they could not enjoy in their own country. Alas, the jig was up when the players became too intoxicated to stay in character, and their brogue and cursing in the name of St. Patrick gave them away. Realizing they had been duped, the audience tore up the stage and marched "the sham Ambassador, together with his mock Retinue" before a local magistrate, who had them jailed.[21]

Timberlake tried to defend his reputation and that of his Cherokee visitors from such aspersions by publishing his own account of events, but his words only inspired more criticism.[22] "You Know Who" again lampooned Ostenaco's supposed royalty (this time calling him "his Cherokeean Imperial Majesty") and wrote that "It is now high Time to unking, depose, or dethrone this Usurper or Pretender, whose Monarchy consists only in the Imaginations of the Ignorant."[23]

Another editorialist who signed himself "A Plebian" (possibly Sir Alexander Cuming or someone associated with Tomochichi's 1734 embassy), deflated the notion of Indian kingship by offering eyewitness evidence from America. Tomochichi, he wrote, lived in a hut on the Savannah River that was "a good deal inferior to the worst Cabin I ever saw on the Road between Cork and Dublin," and he dined, like the rest of his countrymen, squatting on his haunches around a common bowl. Yet when this supposed Indian king had visited London in 1734, English nobles fretted over whether they could sit in his presence. "A Plebeian" found such performances absurd and suggested that in the future, visiting Indians should be treated only with the same "Humanity and Hospitality" they showed visitors in their own country.[24]

The Cherokees' reported proclivity for drink and women even inspired a bawdy satire written to the tune of a popular eighteenth-century ballad about adultery and cuckolds. "A New Humorous Song, on the Cherokee Chiefs" was published as a broadside with an illustration of Ostenaco and his companions as its headpiece. Invoking the "Folks at *Vauxhall*," the ballad taunted British "*Wives, Widows* and *Matrons*, and pert little *Misses*" for so lustily pursuing "*Cherokee* Kisses." The "Females of *Britain*," who "love even Monkies," had been smitten by "The *Cherokee Indians*, and stranger *Shimpanzeys*." To meet this threat to British manhood, the ballad proposed castrating the Cherokees with their own scalping knives: "A soft Female Hand, the best Weapon I wean is / To strip down the Bark of a *Cherokee P—s*."[25] The four kings' visit in 1710 had inspired an outpouring of prints, broadsides, and even a popular ballad about love between an Indian king and an English maiden, but nothing in 1710 came close to impugning so aggressively the Indian kings' humanity and manhood as this piece.

After that fateful night at Vauxhall, public and official opinion turned decisively against Ostenaco and his companions. The Cherokees' drunkenness, belligerence, and promiscuity had revealed them to be frauds—not as Indians but as gentlemen and kings. Timberlake's party stayed in London another month but received no more favors from the crown. When the Earl of Egremont, who had served as Timberlake's patron, arranged for their return home via a ship heading to Charlestown, Ostenaco insisted on going directly to Williamsburg. Timberlake refused to accompany the Indians from Charlestown to Williamsburg unless the crown paid his expenses. Egremont, having had his fill of everyone involved, resolved the situation by sending the Indians back without Timberlake and by telling Ostenaco the ship was headed for Williamsburg, even though the captain's orders remained unchanged. In a classic bit of British understatement, Egremont sent a letter along with the ship to the South Carolina governor, indicating that the Indians might arrive discontented and instructing him to make amends before they proceeded home.[26]

The fallout from Timberlake's first Cherokee embassy helps explain the cold reception his second delegation received in 1765. In the eyes of the royal court and popular press, Ostenaco had been exposed as a fraud for his drunken loss of composure at Vauxhall, Timberlake's reputation had been tarred with the same brush, and the entire notion of Indian kingship had been called into question. But other circumstances beyond Timberlake's control had also converged to make his situation difficult. In 1762 he had tried to follow an old script that held Indian kings at arm's length from the crowd and preserved their aura of nobility by admitting "none but people of fashion" to their company. His efforts collided with a marketplace for public entertainments in London that was eager to capitalize on interest in America sparked by the Seven Years' War. This impulse to commodify Indians, to regard them as human curiosities and the spoils of war, made Timberlake's diplomatic embassies suspect and raised additional questions of imposture.

As the official and public reaction to the Cherokees' fateful night at Vauxhall demonstrates, the growing hunger for Indian curiosities had made it difficult for Indians to perform kingship without raising concerns about their impersonation of status. Newspaper writers compared Ostenaco's raucous and drunken behavior to the sober, dignified Attakullakulla, who had visited London thirty-two years earlier. No one doubted that Ostenaco was an Indian, but his behavior that night at Vauxhall led many to conclude that he could not possibly be a king. That kingly status was eroded further by the association of Timberlake's embassy with the commercial exploitation of the Indians. In such venues as taverns, theaters, and pleasure gardens, the Indians lost their diplomatic significance and became mere exhibits on display, the strange and savage natives of a newly conquered American empire.

This thin line between an Indian king and a domesticated savage confounded Timberlake in 1762 and 1765. On both occasions he tried to present his Indian companions as diplomats conducting official business of state, but each time he was thwarted by their association with public exhibitions and curious crowds. To be taken seriously by the crown and its ministers, Timberlake's Cherokees needed to perform as Indian kings. The people and the press had to be convinced of their regal status, but each time they appeared in public, they ran the risk of being regarded as mere curiosities, as credible as a museum waxwork.

The presence in London of other Indians and Britons impersonating Indians for profit also damaged the credibility of Timberlake's Cherokees. As Timberlake noted in his account of the second trip, it was his party's misfortune to be confused with some Mohawks who were at the same time advertised as being "made a shew of in the Strand."[27] Timberlake was referring to two Mohawks from New York who visited Europe in early 1765 as part of a business venture launched by Lorentz Blessius, a German colonist in the Mohawk Valley, working in partnership with New York City merchant Hyam Myers. The two Indians, named Sychnecta and Trosoghroga, appear to have entered into this enterprise willingly, expecting compensation for their services. Sometime after they landed in Bristol, Blessius absconded with Sychnecta, taking him to Amsterdam for exhibition in a tavern there. Myers caught up with his erstwhile partner, sued him to recover Sychnecta, and brought the two Mohawks back to London, where in early March 1765 they were advertised at the Sun Tavern in the Strand for an admission fee of one shilling. The House of Lords intervened, summoning Myers and the tavern keeper to appear before them and ordering that the exhibition cease because "making a publick shew of Indians, ignorant of such proceedings is unbecoming and inhuman."[28]

The Mohawk affair associated Indian exhibition with the same sort of deceit "You Know Who" had condemned three years earlier when he compared Ostenaco to the Irish impersonators of the Moroccan ambassador. Nonetheless, the market for such ventures was obvious. During both of his sojourns in London, Timberlake had to contend with reports of individuals dressing up as Indians and exhibiting themselves as Cherokees. During the 1762 visit the *St. James's Chronicle* reported that three men "in Imitation of the Cherokee Kings, and having their Faces painted like them, have been shewn at many of the

Places of public Entertainment for the real Indians."[29] During Timberlake's 1765 visit an English imposter calling himself "Chucatah," after one of the Indians in Timberlake's party, took to displaying himself in public.[30]

The most famous Indian impersonator in Britain during the 1760s was Peter Williamson, a Scot who claimed he had been kidnapped from Aberdeen as a child, sold into servitude in Pennsylvania, and held as an Indian captive before returning to Britain in 1757. Williamson published a lurid narrative of his American adventures titled *French and Indian Cruelty; Exemplified in the Life and Various Vicissitudes of Fortune of Peter Williamson*. Filled with scenes of scalping, torture, and similar frontier atrocities, the book went through six editions within nine years and was published in York, Edinburgh, Glasgow, London, and Dublin. Williamson also ran a coffeehouse in Edinburgh called "Indian Peter's," where he became well known for exhibiting himself in Indian costume and telling his tales.[31] He occasionally took this show on the road. The frontispiece of *French and Indian Cruelty* depicted him "In the Dress of a Delaware Indian" but not as an Indian king. Instead of being draped in a scarlet mantle and holding a wampum belt (a tool of diplomacy), he wore war paint, smoked a pipe tomahawk, and held an unsheathed scalping knife. In June 1759 this same image was reproduced in Dublin in *The Gentleman's and London Magazine*. The accompanying article introduced Williamson as a former Indian captive who had come to London and "exhibits himself in the Indian dress, displaying and explaining their method of fighting."[32]

The success of impersonators such as Williamson and the unnamed opportunists who passed themselves off as Timberlake's Cherokees is indicative of how the Seven Years' War changed British perceptions of Indianness. The vague exoticism invoked by turbans and scarlet mantles gave way to war paint, tomahawks, and scalping knives. The savage warrior was supplanting the Indian diplomat in the British imagination. It is noteworthy that the image of Williamson in his Indian dress, which appeared in several editions of his narrative, eventually gained a second life as a supposed ethnographic reality. A Dublin publisher reprinting Pierre Charlevoix's *A Voyage to North-America* in 1766 used it as the frontispiece to the second volume, only with a new caption that removed all references to Williamson and instead identified the figure as "A Delaware Indian with his Tomohawk [and] Scalping Knife."[33] The imposter, playing Indian for coffeehouse audiences, could now be taken for the genuine article.

Neither the crown nor Parliament made any attempt to interfere with the business of Indian impersonators such as Williamson. Instead, the king's ministers and the House of Lords stepped in when they suspected that genuine Indians were being exhibited for fraudulent purposes. The entertaining of Cherokee "kings" who were not in fact men of influence could drain the royal treasury and upset genuine Native rulers in America. Likewise, Mohawks kidnapped and defrauded for private purposes could damage an important Anglo-Indian alliance. Put another way, the state was concerned not with impersonators of race but with imposters of rank. Within the expanding postwar market for Indian exhibitions, the crown wished to prevent the commercial exploitation of common Indians from interfering with the mediation of relations with Indian leaders in America.

The paying public, on the other hand, became less interested in Indians as representatives of distant kingdoms and more concerned with their display of artifacts such as tomahawks and scalping knives that popular literature like Williamson's narrative ascribed to Native Americans.[34] By dramatizing the American war, these Indians (or their British imposters) presented to domestic audiences the bloody nature of building empire among savage peoples abroad.[35] The editorialists who criticized Timberlake's Cherokees made evident the Indians' inferiority by comparing them to the Irish, long the poster children in English letters for cultural degeneracy. Derogatory comparisons of Indian kings to Irishmen impersonating Moroccan ambassadors cast Indians in a way that London readers would instantly recognize, as the brute natives of an imperial marchland, best suited for subjection, not alliance.

In sum, it was not simply individual misbehavior but the redefinition of Britain's connection to North America that sank Timberlake's Cherokee embassies. The Seven Years' War brought a continental dominion under British rule and shifted notions of empire away from their seventeenth-century mercantilist roots to a new emphasis on dominion over foreign lands and their native peoples.[36] That conflict also exposed many Britons for the first time to the brutality of American warfare, and the stories and artifacts they brought home altered the public's perception of Indians. The hopes for peaceful alliance and conversion that had been embodied in Pocahontas and Queen Anne's four Indian kings gave way to new impressions shaped by stories of torture and captivity and images of scalping knives and tomahawks. At the same time a resurgence in show Indians and their impersonators reduced Native travelers to the level of other human and natural curiosities displayed for London's crowds. The European tours of Buffalo Bill's Wild West Show were still more than a century away, but that enterprise differed from the Indian exhibitions of Timberlake's era only in scale. In both cases, entrepreneurs hoped to profit by satisfying the public's desire to see imperial conquests abroad packaged and displayed for consumption at home.[37]

The fate of Timberlake's Cherokee embassies suggests that the performance of Indian kingship passed irrevocably into burlesque after the Seven Years' War. Indeed, parody was evident in representations of Indian kingship on both sides of the Atlantic during the 1790s. In Edinburgh, Peter Williamson opened his coffeehouse, continued to perform his tale of captivity in Native garb, and took to calling himself "King of the Indians."[38] American author Hugh Henry Brackenridge lampooned the notion of Indian kingship and diplomacy in his frontier picaresque *Modern Chivalry* (1792–97), which featured an unscrupulous "treaty maker" who defrauds government agents by hiring Irish servants to impersonate Indian kings at treaty conferences.[39]

It is also worth noting, however, the celebrity of two individuals who successfully presented themselves as Indian kings during visits to London in the closing decades of the eighteenth century. At the outset of the American Revolution, loyalist Mohawk chief Joseph Brant traveled to London with royal Indian superintendent Guy Johnson and a Mohawk warrior named Ohrante. No one, including Johnson, called Brant an Indian king, but his treatment by the royal court, public, and press indicate he was received as such. Along with Ohrante (whom royal officials and the press seemed to regard as Brant's attendant), he toured London's sites, dined with ministers of state, and received presents. He also had his portrait painted by George Romney.[40] James Boswell met with Brant and, in a laudatory profile published in the *London Magazine*, commended his civility. But one thing bothered Boswell. Brant was so thoroughly anglicized in his religion, manners, and dress that he seemed like an Indian only when he donned "the dress of his nation." When Boswell commissioned an artist to draw Brant's likeness, he made sure the subject posed in a feathered headdress with a scalping knife clasped to his chest, so as to bring out his savage demeanor.[41]

Fifteen years later another figure appeared in London exhibiting all the airs of an Indian king. William Augustus Bowles was an Anglo-American born in Maryland, who enlisted in the British cause during the American Revolution and ended up living among the Creek Indians on the Florida frontier. In 1790 he brought a delegation of Indians to London, published a narrative of his life, and gained notoriety as the self-proclaimed "Director-General of the Creek Nation."[42] While Bowles was in London he had an audience with the king and posed for his portrait, wearing Native dress, beads, and gorget.

Brant and Bowles seemed to restore the respectability of Indian kingship that had been damaged so severely by Timberlake's Cherokee embassies. Both presented themselves as powerful, independent allies of the crown, and both appear to have avoided the sort of public appearances that would have reduced them to coffeehouse sideshows. In dress and comportment they balanced exoticism and gentility (Bowles even wore a turban in his portrait), and each traveled with a retinue that testified to his status. Boswell had been struck by how much Brant resembled a genteel Englishman; Bowles represented the opposite phenomenon of an Englishman who had gone Native. These final "Indian kings" of the eighteenth century were not inscrutable, exotic foreigners but cultural chameleons, adept at ethnic impersonation and straddling cultural divides. Their performative power derived not from their cultural and physical distance from their audience but from the ease with which they negotiated that distance, reconciling in their person the twin acts of separation and amalgamation that constituted the British imperial enterprise. In them, the culturally and physically distant figure of the Indian king was replaced by the adroit negotiator of imperial subjecthood.

Notes

1. Williams, ed., *Timberlake's Memoirs*, 170–73. Timberlake intended to publish his memoir as a defense for his conduct in this affair; he died shortly before it came off the presses in London in late 1765.

2. On America's place in the empire and British notions of national identity, see Colley, *Britons*, 132–45; Landsman, "Provinces and the Empire"; Wilson, *Sense of the People*, 178–202; and Gould, *Persistence of Empire*, 53–69. On literary and visual images of Indians as emblems of America and empire, see Fulford, *Romantic Indians*, 49–59; Bickham, *Savages within the Empire*, 21–109; Pratt, *American Indians in British Art*, 30–69; Tobin, *Picturing Imperial Power*, 81–109; and Olson, *Emblems of American Community*, 79–102. On the collecting of Indian artifacts, see Feest, "Collecting Indian Artifacts," and King, "Woodland Artifacts." On the British taste for and public display of curiosities, see Brewer, *Pleasures of the Imagination*, 56–122, and Altick, *Shows of London*, 22–33.
3. For a comprehensive history of Indian visitors to Britain during the colonial era, see Vaughan, *Transatlantic Encounters*. Vaughan's meticulous research supplants the more episodic and descriptive analysis provided in Foreman, *Indians Abroad*.
4. Williams, *Timberlake's Memoirs*, 129–31.
5. On the visit of the four Indian kings to London, see Hinderaker, "'Indian Kings'"; and Bond, *Queen Anne's American Kings*.
6. See Shoemaker, *Strange Likeness*, 35–60; Kupperman, *Indians and English*, 92–103; and Cannadine, *Ornamentalism*, 101–20.
7. On Tomochichi's visit, see Vaughan, *Transatlantic Encounters*, 150–62, and Shoemaker, *Strange Likeness*, 35–39. The quote concerning Tomochichi's eloquence is from the *Grub-Street Journal* (London), August 8, 1734.
8. See Vaughan, *Transatlantic Encounters*, 137–49.
9. Cited in Vaughan, *Transatlantic Encounters*, 150.
10. For a discussion of Ostenaco's motives for the 1762 trip, see Oliphant, "Cherokee Embassy."
11. New England Indians who traveled to Britain included Mohegans in 1736, Mashpees in 1760, Stockbridge Indians in 1766, and Narragansetts in 1768. See Vaughan, *Transatlantic Encounters*, 162–63, 176–81.
12. See Vaughan, *Transatlantic Encounters*, 117–18, 140–41, 153.
13. Williams, *Timberlake's Memoirs*, 135.
14. Pratt, "Reynolds' 'King of the Cherokees,'" 142–47.
15. Pratt, "Reynolds' 'King of the Cherokees,'" 132, 143–44.
16. Pratt, "Reynolds' 'King of the Cherokees,'" 133, 139, 141.
17. Pratt, "Reynolds' 'King of the Cherokees,'" 138. For newspaper

advertisements concerning the Cherokees' appearances, see *Public Advertiser* (London), July 24, 28, 30 and 31, 1762.

18. Williams, *Timberlake's Memoirs*, 137; *St. James's Chronicle*, July 29–31, 1762: 4.
19. *St. James's Chronicle*, July 29–31, 1762: 4.
20. *Royal Magazine* 7 (July 1762): 16–17; *Royal Magazine* 7 (August 1762): 71–72, 83–84.
21. *St. James's Chronicle*, August 5–7, 1762: 5.
22. Timberlake published a letter in the *Public Advertiser* on August 4 claiming that Ostenaco had not even been in attendance at Vauxhall that night, and that the commotion had been caused by unscrupulous revelers taking advantage of the other two Cherokees. See *St. James's Chronicle*, August 7–10, 1762: 4.
23. *St. James's Chronicle*, August 7–10, 1762: 4.
24. *St. James's Chronicle*, August 10–12, 1762: 3. Cuming, sponsor of the 1730 Cherokee embassy, was still living in a London debtors prison in 1762.
25. Howard, *New Humorous Song*. This broadside is reproduced in Pratt, *American Indians in British Art*, 55.
26. Williams, *Timberlake's Memoirs*, 145–46.
27. Williams, *Timberlake's Memoirs*, 171.
28. The most complete account of this affair is Hamell, "Mohawks Abroad." Eight years later, another colonial operator ran afoul of crown officials when he brought a Mohawk Indian to London to advance his private fortunes. See Preston, "George Klock."
29. "You Know Who" makes reference to such impersonators in *St. James's Chronicle*, August 5–7, 1762: 5.
30. Williams, *Timberlake's Memoirs*, 171.
31. On Williamson's career and dubious claims to having been an Indian captive, see Shannon, "King of the Indians."
32. See Williamson, *French and Indian Cruelty*. This modern edition is a reprint of the fifth edition, originally published in Edinburgh in 1762. The engraving depicting Williamson in Indian dress first appeared in the fourth edition, published in London in 1759. Also see "Peter Williamson" and Williamson, "Short Account."
33. See Charlevoix, *Voyage to North-America*, vol. 2: frontispiece.
34. During and after the Seven Years' War visual images of Indians produced in Britain prominently featured Native American weaponry, particularly tomahawks and knives. Besides the images of Williamson described, see also *brave old Hendrick*; and McArdell, *Cunne Shote*.

Political cartoons published during the Revolutionary Era made use of the same motif. See Olson, *Emblems of American Community*, 79–102.

35. For the impact the Seven Years' War had on British perceptions of Indians, see Colley, *Captives*, 168–202, and Way, "Cutting Edge."
36. On the changing meaning of empire, see Bayly, "British and Indigenous Peoples"; Baugh, "Maritime Strength"; and Marshall, "Empire and Authority."
37. See Kasson, *Buffalo Bill's Wild West*, 65–91.
38. See Shannon, "King of the Indians," 37–42.
39. Brackenridge, *Modern Chivalry*, 72–80.
40. See Kelsay, *Joseph Brant*, 161–74.
41. *London Magazine*, July 1776: 339. An engraving of the portrait of Brant commissioned by Boswell also appeared in this issue.
42. See Bowles, *Authentic Memoirs*. For biography see Wright, *William Augustus Bowles*.

Works Cited

Altick, Richard D. *The Shows of London*. Cambridge MA: Harvard University Press, 1978.

Baugh, Daniel A. "Maritime Strength and Atlantic Commerce: The Uses of 'a grand marine empire.'" In *An Imperial State at War: Britain from 1689–1815*, ed. Lawrence Stone, 185–223. London: Routledge, 1994.

Bayly, C. A. "British and Indigenous Peoples, 1760–1860." In *Empire and Others: British Encounters with Indigenous Peoples, 1600–1850*, ed. Martin Daunton and Rick Halpern, 119–41. Philadelphia: University of Pennsylvania Press, 1999.

Bickham, Troy. *Savages within the Empire: Representations of American Indians in Eighteenth-Century Britain*. New York: Oxford University Press, 2005.

Bond, Richmond P. *Queen Anne's American Kings*. Oxford: Clarendon Press, 1952.

Bowles, William Augustus. *Authentic Memoirs of William Augustus Bowles*. 1791; New York: Arno, 1971.

Brackenridge, Hugh Henry. *Modern Chivalry: Containing the Adventures of Captain John Farrago and Teague O'Reagan, His Servant*. 1792–97; Lanham MD: Rowman and Littlefield, 2003.

The brave old Hendrick, the great Sachem or Chief of the Mohawk Indians. London, 1755.

Brewer, John. *The Pleasures of the Imagination: English Culture in the Eighteenth Century*. New York: Farrar, 1997.

Cannadine, David. *Ornamentalism: How the British Saw Their Empire*. New York: Oxford University Press, 2001.

Charlevoix, Pierre F. X. *A Voyage to North-America: Undertaken by Command of the Present King of France. Containing the Geographical Description and Natural History of Canada and Louisiana*. 2 vols. Dublin: John Exshaw and James Potts, 1766.

Colley, Linda. *Britons: Forging the Nation, 1707–1837*. New Haven: Yale University Press, 1992.

———. *Captives: Britain, Empire, and the World, 1600–1850*. New York: Random House, 2002.

Feest, Christian F. "The Collecting of American Indian Artifacts in Europe, 1493–1750." In *America in European Consciousness, 1493–1750*, ed. Karen Ordahl Kupperman, 324–60. Chapel Hill: University of North Carolina Press, 1995.

Foreman, Carolyn Thomas. *Indians Abroad, 1493–1938*. Norman: University of Oklahoma Press, 1943.

Fulford, Tim. *Romantic Indians: Native Americans, British Literature, and Transatlantic Culture, 1756–1830*. New York: Oxford University Press, 2006.

Gould, Eliga H. *The Persistence of Empire: British Political Culture in the Age of the American Revolution*. Chapel Hill: University of North Carolina Press, 2000.

Hamell, George R. "Mohawks Abroad: The 1764 Amsterdam Etching of Sychnecta." In *Indians and Europe: An Interdisciplinary Collection of Essays*, ed. Christian F. Feest, 175–93. Lincoln: University of Nebraska Press, 1999.

Hinderaker, Eric. "The 'Four Indian Kings' and the Imaginative Construction of the First British Empire." *William and Mary Quarterly* 3rd ser. 53 (1996): 487–526.

Howard, H. *A New Humorous Song, on the Cherokee Chiefs: Inscribed to the Ladies of Great Britain*. London, n.d.

Kasson, Joy S. *Buffalo Bill's Wild West: Celebrity, Memory, and Popular History*. New York: Hill and Wang, 2000.

Kelsay, Isabel Thompson. *Joseph Brant*. Syracuse: Syracuse University Press, 1984.

King, J. C. H. "Woodland Artifacts from the Studio of Benjamin West, 1738–1820." *American Indian Art Magazine* (1991): 35–47.

Kupperman, Karen Ordahl. *Indians and English: Facing Off in Early America*. Ithaca: Cornell University Press, 2000.

Landsman, Ned. "The Provinces and the Empire: Scotland, the American Colonies, and the Development of British Provincial Identity." In *An Imperial State at War: Britain from 1689–1815*, ed. Lawrence Stone, 258–87. London: Routledge, 1994.

Marshall, P. J. "Empire and Authority in the Later Eighteenth Century." *Journal of Imperial and Commonwealth History* 15 (1987): 105–22.

McArdell, James. *Cunne Shote*. London, 1763.

Oliphant, John. "The Cherokee Embassy to London, 1762." *Journal of Imperial and Commonwealth History* 27 (1999): 1–26.

Olson, Lester C. *Emblems of American Community in the Revolutionary Era: A Study in Rhetorical Iconology*. Washington DC: Smithsonian Institution, 1991.

"Peter Williamson (1730–1799)." *Dictionary of National Biography*. 63 vols. London: Smith, Elder, and Company, 1885–1997. 21: 487–78.

Pratt, Stephanie. *American Indians in British Art, 1700–1840*. Norman: University of Oklahoma Press, 2005.

———. "Reynolds' 'King of the Cherokees' and Other Mistaken Identities in the Portraiture of Native American Delegations, 1710–1762." *Oxford Art Journal* 21 (1998): 135–50.

Preston, David L. "George Klock, the Canajoharie Mohawks, and the Good Ship *Sir William Johnson*." *New York History* 86 (2005): 473–99.

Shannon, Timothy J. "King of the Indians: The Hard Fate and Curious Career of Peter Williamson." *William and Mary Quarterly* 3rd ser. 66 (2009): 3–44.

Shoemaker, Nancy. *A Strange Likeness: Becoming Red and White in Eighteenth-Century America*. New York: Oxford University Press, 2004.

Tobin, Beth Fowkes. *Picturing Imperial Power: Colonial Subjects in Eighteenth-Century British Painting*. Durham NC: Duke University Press, 1999.

Vaughan, Alden T. *Transatlantic Encounters: American Indians in Britain, 1500–1776*. Cambridge: Cambridge University Press, 2006.

Way, Peter. "The Cutting Edge of Culture: British Soldiers Encounter Native Americans in the French and Indian War." In *Empire and Others: British Encounters with Indigenous Peoples, 1600–1850*, ed. Martin Daunton and Rick Halpern, 123–48. Philadelphia: University of Pennsylvania Press, 1999.

Williams, Samuel Cole, ed. *Lieut. Henry Timberlake's Memoirs 1756–1765*. 1927; Marietta GA: Continental, 1948.

Williamson, Peter. *French and Indian Cruelty: Exemplified in the Life and Various Vicissitudes of Fortune of Peter Williamson*. Introduction by Michael Fry. Bristol: Thoemmes Press, 1996.

———. "A Short Account of the Indians of North America." *Bulletin of the Archaeological Society of New Jersey* 31 (1974): 14–16.

Wilson, Kathleen. *The Sense of the People: Politics, Culture, and Imperialism in England, 1715–1785*. Cambridge: Cambridge University Press, 1995.

Wright, J. Leitch Jr. *William Augustus Bowles: Director General of the Creek Nation*. Athens: University of Georgia Press, 1967.

[9]

Performing Indian Publics

Two Native Views of Diplomacy to the Western Nations in 1792

Phillip H. Round

Native peoples in the Americas have been engaged in diplomatic exchanges with Europeans since contact. In early America indigenous diplomats presented their political positions with a highly elaborated sense of the "public" with whom they were communicating, whether using their own or European languages. Europeans, meanwhile, from the beginning of intercultural diplomacy in the New World, made a concerted effort to portray Native understanding of the emerging colonial public sphere as naïve, inferior, and Other. Columbus famously reported that he used Native captives to proclaim to indigenous peoples "in a loud voice 'Come, come, and you will see the celestial people.'"[1] He thus became the first in a long line of Europeans to claim that the public sphere of diplomatic discourse provided European peoples an opportunity to confound and awe their Native interlocutors. In the early contact period, Indian discourse in the public sphere was thus situated on a very uneven playing field, pictured by Europeans as ineffective when not wholly nonexistent.[2]

By the dawn of the eighteenth century, however, this situation had changed dramatically. Over the course of the next hundred years, especially in North America, Native negotiators would shift the terms of diplomatic engagement, forcing Europeans to accommodate or even adopt traditional tribal practices and protocols. Intercultural discursive performances between Natives and non-Natives, mixing European and indigenous practices, provided the materials Richard White would later identify as characteristic of the middle ground in the *pays d'en haut*.[3] Such performances are likewise the basis for James Merrell's analysis of the "cacophonous" and "kaleidoscopic" intermixing of materials, practices, and performances in the eighteenth-century Pennsylvania backcountry.[4] Amid such intercultural protocols, borrowed performative practices like alphabetic literacy began to emerge. Such literacy then allowed tribal communities to evolve a nascent set of American Indian "publics" through which they could negotiate with each other, argue with colonial adversaries, and preserve for posterity their motives and deliberations during diplomatic struggles. In 1761 the Cherokees enlisted the services of English Virginian Henry Timberlake, who served as a sort of scribe/hostage during tense treaty negotiations with the British that year. Timberlake was taken to the Chota "townhouse," the centerpiece of frontier Cherokee life, where he acted as a secretary for the Native "Senate," who employed him in "reading and writing letters." From about 1750 on, Cherokee leader Atakullakulla and his successors would maintain what has come to be known as the "Cherokee Archive," a body of diplomatic materials written on paper, but treated like ceremonial ritual paraphernalia, to supplement tribal oral negotiations and recitations.[5]

The emergence of American Indian publics accelerated in the 1790s, after the Constitution established an officially American political economy and institutions of Indian policy.[6] The new United States began to make intensive diplomatic efforts to appease the Native "Western Nations" in the lands of the Ohio River Valley, where Anglo-American settlers were beginning to venture. In this charged atmosphere the federal government turned to Native negotiators, some of whom were alphabetically literate, to plead their case before "hostile" tribes. To explore how this process unfolded, I examine here two texts from the canon of early Native alphabetic manuscript literature, Hendrick Aupaumut's "Journal of a Mission to the Western Tribes of Indians" (1791) and Benjamin Williams's "Life of Governour Blacksnake" (c. 1854). Through a close reading of their scribal practices, I investigate the repercussions of this U.S. diplomatic effort on Native identity formation. Works like Aupaumut's and Williams's represent some of the first halting efforts of indigenous nations in the East to construct and perform a public, political *Indianness*. They thus model an emerging indigenous speaking subject in American political discourse. They also mark the beginning of a process of constructing an imagined mixed audience of Native and non-Native auditors in the public sphere of the early Republic.

By the 1790s Native diplomacy in the Northeast was already deeply imbricated with Euro-American public writing, of which treaties and land grants are perhaps the best known examples.[7] But in a broader sense, the public writing that Native peoples began increasingly to engage in during this period embraces any form of communication designed to address the emerging concept of "the public." During the eighteenth century European intellectuals envisioned a communicative space for the circulation of manuscript and print productions that was relatively free of and unencumbered by church and state. Some called this space a "republic of letters," and to them it signaled the serendipitous convergence of individual liberty, civic humanism, and communicative practice that epitomized an era Immanuel Kant called "The Enlightenment." Frankfurt School sociologist Jurgen Habermas, who coined the term *public sphere* to describe this eighteenth-century space of communicative interchange, argued that civil society itself—"private people coming together as a public"—was born as a result of this revolution in communication. As this new public began to engage in open debates about political governance, social relations, and labor rights, it produced a body of texts that came to be known as "public opinion." For later scholars of early American public culture like Michael Warner, print was the "decisive mark" (to use Habermas's phrase) of this emergent public sphere and the public opinion it engendered.[8]

Subsequent critics (Sandra Gustafson in particular) have critiqued Warner for "overemphasiz[ing] the role that print plays in defining public discourse . . . [by] assuming a sharp divide between printed texts and oral performances."[9] Nevertheless, Warner's description of the early American public sphere remains a powerful explanatory model for understanding how writers positioned their work for public consumption in the first century of full-scale printing and distribution in America. Warner's most recent work is especially salient in this regard, seeking to introduce the notion of "counterpublic" discourse into scholarship on the public sphere. A counterpublic, according to Warner, "is usually related to a subculture, but there are important differences between these concepts. A counterpublic, against the background of the public sphere, enables a horizon of opinion and exchange; its exchanges remain distinct from authority and can have a critical relation to power; its extent is in principle indefinite, because it is not based on a precise demography but mediated by print, theater, diffuse networks of talk, commerce, and the like."[10]

There is no question that the many tribal communities that made up nineteenth-century Indian country constituted subcultures within the dominant Euro-American political/structural framework supported by federal Indian policy and print culture. Yet my argument regarding Indian publics does not rest in merely calling them "subcultures," thus implying a simplistic and subservient relation to a "dominant culture." As Warner makes clear, a true counterpublic must reflect "a critical relation to power." Nineteenth-century Indian publics, although profoundly mediated by the material culture of the print and manuscript media they were wielding with increasing sophistication, sought to perform these mediations within special tribal cultural practices and languages. Their "critical relation to power," as Robert Warrior has defined it, was one of *intellectual* sovereignty. This form of sovereignty (as opposed to purely political or land-tenure usages), Warrior writes, constitutes "a praxis." Native diplomacy took the form of a discursive praxis that was performed within a communicative space where Native speakers, writers, and readers availed themselves of "the wide array of pain, joy, oppression, celebration, and spiritual power of . . . American Indian community existence."[11]

Most descriptions of early America's public sphere—whether they involve counterpublics or not—barely mention Indian peoples.[12] Yet there is ample evidence to show that Native peoples, as surely as their Euro-American contemporaries, were grappling with the new communicative and affiliative phenomena that scholars such as Warner and Gustafson have described. Native peoples conceptualized and utilized these phenomena differently from Europeans, however. While the story of the Native conception of the public sphere often parallels that of Euro-American writers and intellectuals, there are many cases in which the tribal context inflects a sense of "public" that diverges significantly from that of the United States.[13]

The kind of modification that Indian peoples introduced into the public sphere can be glimpsed in the preface to one of the most famous of early Native American texts, Samson Occom's *Sermon Preached at the Execution of Moses Paul* (1772). Here Occom reflects on the nature of the "public" for which his work must perform: "The world is already full of books; and the people of God are abundantly furnished with excellent books upon divine subjects . . . and the people indeed have had precept upon precept, line upon line, . . . and so in the whole, they have had, yea, very much. . . . And when I come to consider these things, I am ready to say with myself, what folly and madness is it in me to suffer anything of mine to appear in print, to expose my ignorance to the world."[14] Critics commonly interpret Occom's opening lines as the self-deprecating abasement necessary to his public position as an Indian. Yet in so doing they may overlook a more obvious point: the force of Occom's comments seems directed toward the overabundance of theological niceties in most printed religious tracts of the period. Reading his comments about his sermon's position in light of the way he imagines his public, we can understand his performance semiotic as part of the New Light's disparagement of learning for the sake of learning and of books for books' sake. A world full of books does not need more books unless those books are somehow different.

And indeed, Occom's next paragraph suggests how his book *will* be different. Its "service to the world," he writes, will come from its "plain, everyday talk" issuing from "an uncommon quarter."[15] In other words, its distinction lies in its *Indianness*. Internal evidence in the sermon suggests that Occom did indeed conceive of an "Indian public" and of himself as an "Indian" speaker (he often addresses his readers/listeners as "brethren" when speaking of specifically Native concerns). The famous discussion in a 1765 letter to his missionary sponsor, Eleazar Wheelock, of how others questioned his Indianness prior to his departure for a fund-raising tour of England ("Some say,

I cant talk Indian") provides further background for Occom's statements about the sermon's origination in an "uncommon quarter" of the public sphere.[16] Similarly, when read against the twenty other manuscript sermons that Joanna Brooks has collated in her *Collected Writings of Samson Occom*, it becomes clear that Occom's "everyday talk" included phrases and metaphors meant to appeal not only to Euro-Americans but to non-whites, including African slaves and Native tribal members.[17] In light of this background it becomes clear that Occom's reflections on the public sphere have far less to do with appeasing a Euro-American audience than with challenging that audience to accept the possibility of an Indian addressing them *in* the public sphere.

Occom's insistence on the Indianness of his public performance became a foundation for Native self-representation throughout the eighteenth and nineteenth centuries. As late as 1858, long after several Native authors had copyrighted their printed works, the Narragansett writer and hymnodist Thomas Commuck wrote that he was "fully aware of the difficulties attendant upon an attempt to appear successfully as an author before a scrutinizing and discerning public, especially . . . being descended from that unfortunate and proscribed people, the Indians." He confesses to "appear[ing] at the bar of public opinion" with "great diffidence."[18] Commuck was merely underscoring what most Native intellectuals already knew: sedimented in their engagement with America's new and supposedly democratic public sphere was a long and torturous history of discursive interaction with Europeans that sharply attenuated Native agency and fundamentally miscast Native public personhood. That oppressive history was rooted in the centuries-old intercultural discourse of diplomacy, and it was thus within this discursive field that the construction of Indian counterpublics first began.

Mohawk theorist Taiaiake Alfred helps non-Native readers understand more fully the depth of Native discursive difference that both Thomas Commuck and Samson Occom were attempting to tap into as a new colonial public sphere took hold across North America. First, he points out that Native "people's reality is communal" and remained so throughout the period. Unlike the anonymous print format that Warner sees as essential to the eighteenth-century public sphere, this communal discursive space is profoundly grounded in, "known" by, specific Native communities. Later Alfred expands this definition of difference to suggest that the ultimate goal of indigenous diplomacy is to challenge "mainstream society to question its own structure . . . to convince others of the wisdom of the indigenous perspective." With "no separation between society and state" in traditional indigenous social systems, the ideal public sphere is "a non-coercive, participatory, transparent, consensus-based system." As fundamental challenges to liberalism, these positions thus represent "counterpublics" in the sense Warner has articulated.[19]

With these definitions of Native publics in mind, I now turn to the Aupaumut and Williams texts. "A Journal of a Mission to the Western Tribes of Indians" (1791) was written by Hendrick Aupaumut (1757–1830), grand sachem of the Mahican Nation and an important leader of the Stockbridge people. Aupaumut was educated by the Moravians at Stockbridge in the 1760s and enlisted in the Continental Army at the start of the Revolutionary War. When the Stockbridge settlement removed to Oneida country after the war, Aupaumut became an emissary between Indian interests and the U.S. government, traveling at the request of Secretary of War Henry Knox for eleven months in 1790–91 among the Delawares, Miamis, Shawnees, and others in the Ohio River Valley. It was after this journey that he penned the "Journal."

A different account of these negotiations appears in the as-told-to autobiography collaboratively produced by grand sachem and Seneca elder Chainbreaker and Benjamin Williams, an alphabetically literate Seneca man from Cold Spring on the Allegheny Reservation. Chainbreaker, known to whites as Governor Blacksnake, was an important leader of the Six Nations, his two maternal uncles being Cornplanter and Handsome Lake. He too fought in the Revolutionary War, on the British side, and was involved in complex negotiations with the Americans after the conflict. While Aupaumut was traveling in the Ohio Valley on behalf of the U.S. government, Chainbreaker was making a similar journey on behalf of the Six Nations. Sometime during the 1840s Chainbreaker narrated his life story in Seneca to Williams, who transcribed it into English. At the urging of Chainbreaker's son, Williams attempted to sell the manuscript for publication to Wisconsin antiquarian Lyman C. Draper, in whose voluminous collection of manuscripts it remains today.[20]

Both of these texts offer historians a wealth of information about the events that transpired in the Ohio Valley in the 1790s. Both also detail the indigenous diplomatic protocols that framed negotiations between Indian communities in the postwar period. Perhaps most significant, both texts narrate these events and performances from Native points of view, focusing largely on Native-to-Native interactions. In the process, they articulate varying indigenous perspectives on the 1790s diplomatic mission, allowing us to appreciate the array of American Indian interests at play across the Northeast and the Ohio Valley. They also help us broaden the ground for our conceptualization of Native public performance in the period, offering us a sense of the diversity of opinion and complexity of motive that informed Indian diplomacy.

Both Aupaumut and Chainbreaker emphasize the performative intricacy of their negotiations by highlighting the Native protocols involved. Their meetings with the Western Nations took place in preestablished, ceremonially prepared forest clearings or creekside villages. Aupaumut relates how negotiators ritually cleansed each other so that all might "hear plain." One Native diplomat embraces Aupaumut, saying, "I put my hand to take away the dust from your ears." The night before such meetings, Chainbreaker tells us, his party would gather in council to "talk on the subject . . . for to see clear with the Naked eyes and open . . . ears," not wishing to "hold their heads down and see nothing." These rituals, the sachem Tautpuhqtheet explains to Aupaumut, are those "our good ancestors did hand down to us [as] a rule or path where we may walk."[21]

Both men also dramatize scenes of political division within their respective negotiating parties. When traveling with his cohort of warriors and diplomats, Aupaumut had a chance encounter with the Mohawk sachem Joseph Brant and gave him an overview of his planned arguments. In an ominous sign of dissentions to come, Brant "gave him no answer." Later, in the Ohio Valley, Brant would call Aupaumut "a deceiver and a roag [*sic*]." Nor is Aupaumut's careful description of his run-in with the famous Six Nations leader the only time he represents political dissent among Indians. His repeated reflections on political dissent suggest that such matters are not merely personal, or even bilaterally intertribal (that is, between Mohawks in Canada and Mahicans in the new United States), but rather part of the confusing new discursive matrix within which negotiations were now taking place. Aupaumut is careful to delineate the complex political divisions that have affected several tribes among the Western Nations and that are the result of imperial pressures from British and American forces as well as of internal social unrest within the tribes themselves. The Wyandots, for example, are "divided" over whether to go to war with the Americans (as the dominant Shawnees insist upon) and "only one part of them held the opinion of the Delaware" that war was the right thing. In addition, Aupaumut differentiates the main players among the Western Nations (Shawnees, Delawares, Miamis) from those of the "Back Nations" (Wyandots, Ottawas, Chippewas, and Pottawattamies), all of whose decision-making processes seem to have been much more grounded in self-interest than in consideration of Euro-Native imperial alliances. While the Munsees are so happy to see Aupaumut's party that "they did a dance" for the group, the Shawnees repeatedly refuse him audience.[22]

Chainbreaker's narrative is likewise rife with descriptions of dissent, particularly between Brant and Cornplanter, Red Jacket, and nearly everybody else. Chainbreaker recalls that warriors in intertribal councils "had great dail of controversy created amongst themselves Some for Brant and some for Cornplanter [this] appeared to create it in two party."[23] Because both authors spend so much time explicating these "controvers[ies]," it seems clear that they wished to add political texture to negotiations that Europeans might otherwise have dismissed as merely ceremonial, largely untrustworthy, and (to use a word common to the European descriptions of the period) little more than "harangues." In this respect, it is precisely these political differences that create the "critical relations to power" that in turn make Chainbreaker and Aupaumut's manuscripts much more than autobiographies or histories of the period—that make them, that is, such significant records and representations of the emerging Indian public sphere.

This process of emergence becomes particularly evident when one notes that the diplomatic negotiations that gave rise to so much rhetorical "controversy" were conducted via the agency of a range of ritual objects—printed texts, treaties written on a "pease of skin," tin boxes stuffed with legal papers, medicine bags filled with ancient wampum, land plats, and even commemorative oil portrait paintings—most of which were not yet fully integrated into Native ceremonial and rhetorical practices. Indeed, this lack of integration could itself become a source of controversy. Chainbreaker describes Joseph Brant's histrionics in 1784 at being handed a sheaf of "receipts," a "written contract, and a letter" in support of an American alliance during a tribal council: "Brand took it in his hand and read a few lines and begun to sweare and stamp down and turn right faces round [toward] us."[24] This incident and others like it scattered in journals describing similar negotiations during the period suggest that it was not only the content of the message but its medium that drew Brant's ire. For Brant and others, printed and written paper documents sometimes disrupted oral protocols, driving a material wedge between negotiators.

Nevertheless, as James Merrell so capably documents for the comparable Pennsylvania context, such hybrid negotiating practices and materials were becoming increasingly common in the backcountry during this period.[25] The presence of hybrid performative techniques described in Aupaumut's and Chainbreaker's texts, then, suggests that the formal properties of these two manuscript reports may themselves represent extensions of actual woodland diplomatic performances. That is, the documents may reflect the new materials being integrated, sometimes ceremonially, into the fabric of traditional autobiographical recollection and historical commemoration. And as such, these textual performances offer unique insight into the late eighteenth-century processes by which Native political figures constructed an Indian public sphere, while demonstrating how the written word came to play a major part in that process.

The original manuscript of Aupaumut's "Short Narration," housed in the Pennsylvania Historical Society, is bound as a book. Its hand-lettered and framed title page states: "Journal of a Mission to the Western Tribe of Indians by Hendrick Aupaumut, 1791." The chronicle is written both as a journal—a personal reminiscence, and therefore constructive of self or identity—and as a report, a political document in the public sphere. This dual purpose may be seen in the ways Aupaumut marked his manuscript to make it easier to "read" as a public document: hand-drawn rules separate the days of the week, tribal groups, and speakers; occasional marginal brackets and other markings denote asides and interjections. The rules also stand out as signs of Native scribal difference when compared with the small bracketed inserts apparently introduced by the editors of the 1827 *Memoirs of the Historical Society of Pennsylvania* edition of Aupaumut's manuscript. These inserts are clearly derived from print culture practice (a typical entry reads: [Sig.14—fol. 101]). While Aupaumut's hand is quite good, and he is very careful to indent for paragraph divisions in his narrative, he is just as likely to use extended dashes and great swaths of white space and brackets to set off ceremonial practices that exceed the conventions of scribal practice. On page 22 of the manuscript, for example, Aupaumut finishes a paragraph of narration by drawing a vertical line underneath, down the center of the page, and writing on the left side, "Then they rose and shake our hands," while on the right side of the division he comments, "This all I have to say—four strings of wampum of three feet long delivered." Centered below this line and division is a single sentence: "Few minutes after this." The regular narration then resumes with conventional paragraphing, including, however, a hand-drawn marginal bracket that extends over the following two pages of the narrative, indicating the rest of the meeting that day.

While these textual markers indicate how Aupaumut's "book" engaged the Anglo-American public sphere with a critical performance of scribal difference, the first sentence of his report specifically invests the journal with a uniquely indigenous agency. It works to position its speaker in a public space somewhat outside the sphere of influence of the United States. Aupaumut begins by asserting that he has "agreed with the Great Men of the United States to take a tour with their Message of peace to the hostile nations." Calling himself both an "Indian, and a true friend," Aupaumut continues this textual shuttle diplomacy, framing his contemporary colonial activities within an ancestral tribal tradition of peacemaking and peacekeeping. Protocol and family, clan obligations and civility, as essential in the 1790s Ohio Valley as they are in Indian country today, are fundamental to Aupaumut's textual performance. He makes it clear that his performance is intended to "reflect in the path of [his] ancestors": "Before I proceed in the business I am upon," he writes, "I think it would be necessary to give a Short Sketch of the friendship and connections our forefathers and we have had with the western tribes."[26] The "connections" Aupaumut describes are familial: the Shawnees, Miamis, Munsees, Wyandots, Ottawas, Pottawattamies, Ojibwas, and Kickapoos all stand in relation to the speaker and his journal as so many uncles, cousins, fathers, and younger brothers in a family tree.

Such familial relations are themselves time-honored, and accordingly they allow Aupaumut to link his written narrative to the "time-immemorial" space of oral tradition. "It was the business of our forefathers to go around the towns of these nations to renew the agreements between them," he states, just as it is his duty to engage in his current diplomatic mission. His ancestors were required to tell the Western Nations "many things which they discover is among the white people in the east." So too it is Aupaumut's lot to write such details down on paper in the form of a report. The medium is modern, but the message is rooted in tradition, and the text itself is committed to forging continuity between new and old, between written words and pictographic records on wood, shell, and stone. Aupaumut's allegiance to tribal tradition is especially evident at one crucial moment in the negotiations when it appears that an English officer (a Colonel McKee) is attempting to lure him away from the bargaining table with a spurious "urgent" message requesting that Aupaumut meet him at Fort Jefferson. Aupaumut's indignant response marshals all the performative intercultural practices at his disposal: "But I said, I have not seen any token or Message, in strings of wampum, or writing, nor Tobacco, I will not go—I am not to regard emty messages, &c."[27]

Benjamin Williams's biography of Chainbreaker initiates similar claims of continuity with Seneca history in its opening page, anchoring these in narrative and scribal practices similar to those found in Aupaumut's manuscript. Williams positions Chainbreaker's narration within a tradition "handed down from Generation to generation—we cannot tell the number of years ago, for we have no written account, only what we get from the oldest and good man statements."[28] Williams's text is especially interesting in this regard: the text not only introduces Chainbreaker's memoir by placing it in relation to the Seneca origin story, but later provides his detailed recitation of Handsome Lake's prophecy and code, thus locating both him and his story within an emergent, modern Seneca nativism. After explaining and explicating Chainbreaker's name (this is his "real" name, Williams states, although the whites call him Governor Blacksnake), the manuscript defends its interpretations by arguing that it "can be ascertained fect of the Said Life of governour Blacksnake and others connected with it and the traditions of ancient history—the creation of the world and late prophet [Handsome Lake]." Williams goes on to claim even that some blanks in the old warrior's memory have been filled in by referring to details found "on the head of an ancient pipe."[29]

Williams's text, though less formally marked than Aupaumut's, also opens with a carefully lettered title "Life of Blacksnake" and is similarly punctuated by marginal asides and glosses. While Williams sometimes uses these corrections and marginalia to set off speeches from the main narrative, at other times they are self-conscious corrections of factual detail pitched, like Aupaumut's defensive comments, to a Euro-American audience that demands a culturally specific kind of historical accuracy. Still other asides in the Williams text are written in syllabic Seneca and appear to be directed at maintaining communal and cultural integrity for an indigenous audience. Such asides often involve words that cannot readily be translated or show how the typical Euro-American phrase is inadequate to explain or perform what really happened. The process begins almost immediately in the text with Williams's ritual recitation of Chainbreaker's name and ancestry, a paragraph directed at both non-Seneca audiences unfamiliar with the linguistic complexities of the old man's formal title and at the Seneca oral tradition's customary way of locating a speaking subject within family and clan lineages. Interestingly, it was this very cross-cultural performance that Williams's contemporary editor, Thomas Abler, an accomplished ethnologist with close ties to the Senecas, relegated to an appendix, calling it "a lengthy, confused introduction, not closely related to the story that follows and possibly more difficult to read than any other section of the text."[30] Yet it is precisely its impenetrability to the modern reader that suggests its relevance to another, alternative set of scribal practices. These practices echo those found in Aupaumut and are a further illustration of how writing in manuscript and print during the first decades of U.S.-Native diplomacy was (however uncomfortably) being woven into the fabric of Native protocols.

Williams introduces Chainbreaker's narrative with this "cacophonous" and "kaleidoscopic" set of sentences:

> The birth of governour Blacksnake or more correctly of Ten wr, nyrs—for Such was his Real name—interpretation is Chainbreaker his las name give to him at the time he became a chief warrior . . . but when in Boyhood was then called—Daghgr, yan, Doh—until he became a young man . . . following to according to their custome of their Rules and Traditions . . . this can be asurtained fect of the Said Life of governour Blacksnake, and others connected with it and traditions of their ancient history, account of creation of the world and late prophet, and Sanctuary three times a year.[31]

Williams also feels obligated to supplement conventional Euro-American writing practice in his method of marking time in the old warrior's narrative. When recounting deeds that occurred in 1749, Williams inscribes a broad-stroked number "1749" in the left-hand margin, followed by a bracketed gloss: "what called by the Seneca Language gau, Dr, ă."[32] This self-conscious marking of time in both the traditional Seneca way and the European continues throughout the manuscript. In other passages it seems clear that Williams is thinking in Seneca even as he writes the elder's story in English. Given to writing vertical marginal glosses during crucial points in Chainbreaker's story, Williams narrates the Senecas' fight at Fort Stanwix by marking it twice with the marginal gloss "Fort Stanwix." On the third page, however, he writes, "fort Ga, doh, ga, Battle." Like Aupaumut, Williams follows what seems to have become a scribal convention of setting off traditional Native oratory from the main body of the narrative by employing white space, indentation, dashes, and ceremonial salutations (e.g., "Brothers—"). On page 113 of the manuscript he follows Aupaumut's practice exactly when he centers the phrase "Red Jackett given answer," followed by a separate paragraph of oratory: "Brothers we are suppose you are ready to hear . . ."[33]

Neither of these manuscript performances of Indian publics is without its own tension and irony. Thus, for example, when transferred to the page to be performed by the speaking subjects of these written texts, the embodied performances carry with them the marks of "intersubjectivity," the term Greg Sarris has used to describe "the specific social contingencies of the exchange" between Natives and non-Natives. For instance, whenever Aupaumut cites a Native negotiator's speech, he either brackets or indents it and takes care to mention the wampum exchange. At one point he even pauses to explicate the meaning of an especially important belt. It was a "large belt . . . which contains 15 rows and in the middle there is 15 square marks which denotes 15 united sachems and path of peace goes through these marks." In this manner he performs his expertise in the Native semiotic system, thereby bridging the gap between the political selves he described earlier as alternately "Indian" and "friend." In a later aside he bristles that if his Euro-American readers need proof of his loyalty, he can "show the wampum of their speech."[34] Here Aupaumut's Indian subjectivity is in danger of being eclipsed by a colonial relation of inequality and a discursive field that immediately marks Indian utterance as suspect.

Yet in a particularly vivid and assertive moment in the text, Aupaumut suggests a way out of this dilemma. It occurs during his description of Delaware ally Big Cat's diplomatic performances. In trying to help Aupaumut steer the Western

Nations away from war, Big Cat articulates his support of some European politics and practices while rejecting others on Native grounds. Questioned by Captain Eliot of the British command about the precise membership of his negotiating committee and their recent comings and goings, Big Cat responds with a furious argument for sovereignty: "Did you ever see me at Detroit or Niagara, in your councils, and there to ask you where such and such white man come from? Or what is their Business? Can you watch, and look all over the earth to see who come to us? Or is what their business? Do you not know that we are upon our own Business? And we have longed to see these our friend." At this, Aupaumut reports, Eliot's "mouth was stopd immediately." In moments such as these, and in his final rousing defense of his own character (one he thinks has been "darkened" by rumor and innuendo), Aupaumut represents his diplomacy and that of his Indian allies as a product of specifically Native publics, never of subaltern obeisance to colonial authority.[35]

The "social contingencies of exchange" are somewhat different in the case of the Chainbreaker manuscript, divided as they are between Chainbreaker's own goals in narrating his life to a fellow Seneca tribal member and Williams's efforts to communicate Chainbreaker's story to a sometimes-skeptical Draper. Chainbreaker expresses his intersubjective stance when he explains that he is narrating his story as part of his duty to the "welfare" of his people and when he apologizes to an imagined non-Indian readership: "the Readers must Excuse me for I do not Regelect on what month or what Day of the month for I have no larn or to understand English Either I only what I hear from the enterpreter."[36] Williams performs his own intersubjectivity when he inserts vertical marginal glosses that simultaneously explain Seneca things to non-Seneca readers and that, perhaps self-consciously, model nineteenth-century print conventions. (Marginal glosses were routinely used during this period to mark narrative movement, directing reader attention to the high points of a story.)[37] Yet Williams's marginal asides go beyond even these important functions. At several key points in the narrative Williams acidly pens ironic marginal critiques of the perfidy surrounding the 1777 negotiations between the Six Nations and the British ("the time the Indians was bribe by the British"), all the while accurately recording Chainbreaker's own recollections of the meeting.[38]

In thus foregrounding the social contingencies of exchange that lay behind their narratives, both authors push toward something Native literary theorist Scott Richard Lyons has termed *rhetorical sovereignty*. This kind of sovereignty, related as it is to the political and economic sovereignty that men like Chainbreaker and Aupaumut were seeking to negotiate with the United States in the 1790s, lies in the rhetorical gestures Indian writers make in their texts. Rhetorical sovereignty, Lyons argues, "is the inherent right and ability of *peoples* to determine their own communicative needs and desires . . . to decide for themselves the goals, modes, styles, and languages of public discourse."[39] Toward the end of his journal Aupaumut pointedly asserts his rhetorical sovereignty when he reports what he *did not* say to the Western Nations: "I . . . were oblige to say nothing with regard to the Yorkers. How they cheat my fathers. How they taken our Lands Unjustly—and how my fathers were groaning as it were to their graves In losing their Lands for nothing—although they were faithful friends to the Whites . . . had I mention these things to the Indians—it would aggravate their Prejudices against all white people."[40] This is, of course, a comment aimed directly at his Euro-American sponsors. But it is also a further example of

Aupaumut's complex performance of Native political identity. He is simultaneously someone who "agreed" to be sent West, someone who views himself as both "Indian and friend," and someone whose political power in both Native and non-Native circles derives from the self-conscious (and sometimes ironic) manipulation of what he knows to be true as well as what he deems it prudent to say. Yet, as with most of his narrative, this comment is directed toward reinforcing the sovereignty of his own tribe's position, letting his white sponsors know that he sees them for what they are, often untruthful manipulators of Indian public opinion. Throughout the manuscript the speaking subject of the narrative remains a man who refers to himself as "I, the Muhheuconneew," refusing translation and asserting linguistic and tribal sovereignty.[41]

Chainbreaker, meanwhile, tells us that as a young man, he was "nothing but passengers among the warriors . . . to hear all the business going on." He did, however, listen carefully, committing "the business" to memory. He would eventually decide to recite it to Benjamin Williams because "it seem . . . very in Deed important business to be understood on the most important part, and put myself to feel interest in our welfare."[42] The phrase "interest in our welfare" provides a good gloss on the guiding principles of these two texts, firmly locating their production in the space of an emerging Indian public, which both authors perform simultaneously as voice in their text and audience for their words. That is, both narratives manifest their authors' rhetorical sovereignty by placing Native speakers and Native auditors at the center of their manuscript performances. That the "welfare" they seek is *Indian* welfare, and that these political publics are *Indian* publics, is made quite clear in Aupaumut's manuscript, where both pro- and anti-American factions repeat a constitutive rhetorical formula to their Native auditors when they ask for support of their respective positions: "That you may contemplate the welfare of our own colar [color]."[43]

Although print has become the most highlighted aspect of the early republic's public sphere, it is clear from these examples, and other non-Native cases Gustafson has explicated in her recent critique of Warner's thesis, that scribal and performative practices shared the stage with print. It is also clear that "these emerging media cannot be mapped neatly onto a binary social geography divided between publics and counterpublics any more than 'print culture' can be meaningfully distinguished from 'oral culture.'" Both Aupaumut's and Williams's scribal practices confirm Gustafson's assertion that focusing "on the semiotic properties of speech and writing and of material artifacts such as maps, baskets, and wampum offers alternative frameworks for understanding that avoid rigid distinctions between media." Certainly both of the Native manuscripts under consideration exhibit efforts to highlight "voice" over script in coming to terms with the new diplomatic discourse of the 1790s. At the conclusion of his failed effort to convince the Shawnees not to enter war with the United States, Aupaumut writes of the other peaceful Nations, "they will send their voice to the US that the US may know what were the obstacles to the path of peace." The emphasis here is on voice, not treaty document or even journal report, and it is perhaps for this reason that Aupaumut concludes his narrative on a profoundly personal note, vigorously defending his own character and the "occasion of my speaking this sort."[44] The primacy of voice in early Indian publics is found even in the work of Williams, a writer who definitely had print in mind when he penned Chainbreaker's oral narrative. What comes through clearly in the tortured letters that trace the negotiations for his work's publication is that it may have been the profound orality of Williams's writing style (what Six Nations ethnographer Anthony F. C. Wallace termed "very bad reservation English") that most influenced Draper's decision not to print the Chainbreaker narrative.[45]

The manuscript practices Hendrick Aupaumut and Chainbreaker employed in their respective responses to diplomatic events in the Ohio Valley during the 1790s reflect emerging, often intertribal, conceptions of Indian publics that supplement our present understanding of eighteenth-century Indian country. They suggest, as well, the increasingly important role alphabetic writing would play in the formation of newly reconstituted Native nations, communities whose understanding of their own "welfare" (as Chainbreaker put it) would importantly include intercultural performances in manuscript and print. Like Aupaumut and Chainbreaker, later Native writers and speakers would seek to render traditional indigenous performative practices in new ways within the medium of the written word. Whether, as Chainbreaker did, they employed a literate Native or mixed-blood writer to transcribe their words and deeds, or took up the pen themselves to recount their actions, they clearly considered their performances to be extensions of, not substitutions for, tribal sovereignty.

By the first decades of the nineteenth century many indigenous peoples in North America had begun the routine use of innovative literacies they had developed as a result of their interactions with Europeans and the social transformations in their communities exacerbated by European colonial expansion. During the Removal crisis of the 1830s, printed memorials and constitutions, genres derived from the Euro-American print public sphere, would become especially salient venues for Native expression among those tribal communities most directly affected by the Indian Removal Act. While Euro-Americans doggedly repeated the mantra that Native Americans were "an unlettered people," in reality several

Indian Nations of the period were represented in the Congress, courts, and press by alphabetically literate tribal members such as the Cherokee writer Elias Boudinot (1804–39), Stockbridge leader John Quinney (1797–1855), and Seneca activist Maris Pierce (1811–74).[46]

Some indigenous intellectuals, like Pablo Tac, a member of the Quechnajuichom (Luiseño) nation in California, responded to European colonization with autoethnographic manuscripts that subtly perform their resistance against the imperialist powers even as they seemingly praise the invaders' spiritual project. Tac's Spanish-language manuscript "Conversion de los Luiseños de Alta California" (c. 1840), although intended for a European audience, exhibits the sentiments of a seventeen-year-old whose pride in his tribal community equals his sense of duty to his new patrons. After describing how his nation converted to Catholicism out of a desire for Spanish protection from their local indigenous enemies, Tac relates how his tribal leader on first meeting the Spaniards challenged them, "What is it you seek? Get out of our Country," thus destabilizing the manuscript's otherwise triumphant tale of conversion.[47]

Other Native writers ventured into the realm of historiography and worked to rewrite the dominant Euro-American scripts surrounding important events in their tribal histories. George Stiggins, a man born at Talladega in 1788 to a European father and a Natchez mother, rose to the position of Indian agent to the Creek Nation in 1830 and soon thereafter penned an eighty-eight-page manuscript history of the Muskogee Red Stick War, "A Historical Narration of the Genealogy Traditions and Downfall of the Ispocaga or Creek Tribe." In his text Stiggins speaks with nationalistic pride of his "woe-worn and pitiable country" (the Muskogee nation). The manuscript's title promises a "history of the genealogy traditions of the . . . Creek tribe and its downfall, by a member of the tribe," underscoring its author's tribal membership and the narrative's grounding in clan relations. Part of a large body of work written during the period to "explain" the Red Stick War and Tecumseh's rebellion, Stiggins's work differs from its Euro-American counterparts in its rootedness in Muskogee orature and storytelling practice, in its insistence that even in rebellion the Muskogee had a civil polity, and in its anxiety over whether written narrative is even capable of conveying the events it recounts.[48]

In still other cases Native communities put forward written and printed works that retained their traditional languages, rendering their political needs and desires in new Roman type orthographies that approximated the sound and sense of their spoken words. The "Statement Made by the Indians," a bilingual petition to the U.S. commissioner of Indian affairs created by the elders of the Chippewa Nation of Lake Superior in 1864, for example, featured bilingual, facing-column translations of Ojibwa and English that detailed the Chippewas' concern over the government's continued payment of its debts in inflated paper currency. As John D. Nichols, the modern-day editor of this text, observes, both the physical properties of the manuscript and the collaborative performative practices detectable in its mode of transcription, orthography, and translation demonstrate "the control of writing practiced by some speakers of Ojibwe in the past."[49]

The manuscript practices of Pablo Tac, George Stiggins, and the Chippewa Nation of Lake Superior reflect a sustained use of the written word across time and space in Indian country in the years after Aupaumut and Chainbreaker's early forays into the new medium, practices that perhaps trace the contours of a heretofore unexplored "tradition" of nonfiction writing and performance by American Indians in the nineteenth century. Though many tribal members who employed such alphabetic performances were accused of writing "in the character of a white man," most were actually engaged in the complex intercultural practice of performing Indian publics, a praxis that reached from the council fires of traditional meeting places to the print shops of New Echota, Washington, Buffalo, and New York City.[50]

Notes

1. Columbus, "Letter of Columbus on the Discovery of America" (1493), in Castillo and Schweitzer, *Literatures of Colonial America*, 25.
2. Elsewhere I have traced the complex negotiations indigenous peoples engaged in with metropolitan colonial authorities through transatlantic letters (Round, "Neither Here Nor There," 436–38).
3. See White, *Middle Ground*, xiv, where he calls this performative space a "joint Indian-white creation."
4. Merrell, *Into the American Woods*, 51.
5. Timberlake, *Memoirs of Lt. Henry Timberlake*, 41. See also Alden, "Cherokee Archive," 240. For an exhaustive list of the appearance of such papers in eighteenth-century reports from Indian country, see Shoemaker, *Strange Likeness*, 160 n. 32.
6. See Schweitzer's discussion of the federal government's implementation of the distribution of peace medals in 1790 as an index to its mobilization of a rhetoric of "friendship" with tribal communities that supported its national policies. Schweitzer reads these newly implemented material symbols of U.S.-Indian diplomacy as "ritual objects in a complex performance of power and allegiance [that] . . . underscore[s] the close relationship of international diplomacy and friendship discourse" (*Perfecting Friendship*, 18).
7. O'Brien's study of Natick, Massachusetts, *Dispossession by Degrees*, discusses the many kinds of texts and literacy practices that informed Native subject formation in that Praying Town during the first half of the eighteenth century (68, 75, 91–96). See the essays and documents in Bross and Wyss's *Early Native Literacies* for more examples of intertwined literacy practices.
8. Habermas, *Structural Transformation*, 19, 16. For further discussion of the role of print in the development of the U.S. public sphere, see Warner, *Letters of the Republic*, esp. 38–39.
9. Gustafson, "American Literature and the Public Sphere," 465.

10. Warner, *Publics and Counterpublics*, 56–57.

11. Warrior, *Tribal Secrets*, 114. In a more recent work Warrior sharpens this definition of praxis to include "a process that highlights the production of meaning through the critical interaction that occurs between a text as a writer has written it and a text as a reader understands it" in Indian country (*People and the Word*, xiv).

12. Loughran's *Republic in Print*, for example—although purportedly describing "the nation (and nation state) in the most materialist way possible" (xix), emphasizing the actual rather than theorized institutions through which information, argument, and identity flowed in the early republic—totally disregards the Indian Removal Act of 1830, a federal law that simultaneously (and forcibly) cleared the geographic national space of its indigenous inhabitants, produced a print culture explosion in books like *The Life of Black Hawk* (1833), and set in motion a suite of deeply significant Supreme Court rulings with states' rights implications, *Cherokee Nation v. Georgia* (1831) and *Worcester v. Georgia* (1832).

13. In recent studies of the emerging public culture of the early republic, both Schweitzer and Dillon have offered new models for understanding how memberships in a diverse group of "publics" were being constituted in relation to dominant ideological formations like "liberalism" and "friendship." Dillon, for example, has observed that the Euro-American public sphere was based on a political liberalism that was a "structuring force" behind publication in America. She specifically describes how "gender is one of the categories through which liberalism scripts the interrelated public and private lives of citizens" (Dillon, *Gender of Freedom*, 2). Following Dillon, I would argue that liberalism treated Native peoples in a way parallel to its treatment of women: while "liberalism does not exclude" Native peoples entirely, it "reserves a discrete position" for them in society (3)—a position both rhetorical and material, with Indian Territory and reservations serving as very real spaces for the sequestration of the indigenous presence in America. In a similar way, Schweitzer has argued that the emerging public sphere engendered discourses of affiliation and friendship that knit together not only Euro-American social groups but also "non-elites, people of color, and women" (Schweitzer, *Perfecting Friendship*, 13). Of course, the term *friend* would be a much contested one in the construction of Native voices and political actions in the public sphere.

14. Occom, *Collected Writings*, 177.

15. Occom, *Collected Writings*, 177.

16. Occom, *Collected Writings*, 74.

17. See Bouwman's account of Occom's "Temperance and Morality Sermon" (c. 1768), in which she argues that "the Temperance and Morality Sermon, like the Moses Paul sermon, shows that Occom used his position as an Indian preacher to address various constituencies in his mixed audiences" and that "this was part of a larger pattern—evident throughout his sermons—of playing to multiple audiences and addressing white constituents as well as Indian constituents in complex and multilayered ways" (Bouwman, "Samson Occom," 68).

18. These comments appear in the unpaginated preface to Commuck, *Indian Melodies*.

19. Alfred, *Peace, Power, and Righteousness*, xvi, 21, 25, 28.

20. In the following discussion I rely on the manuscript version (in Aupaumut's hand) of the "Journal of a Mission" preserved at the Pennsylvania Historical Society, and a manuscript version of Chainbreaker's oral history housed in the Draper Papers at the Wisconsin Historical Society. All quotations concerning Aupaumut's scribal practices refer to this manuscript, which has hand-written pagination in parentheses in the upper corner of each page (Aupaumut, "Journal"). For quotations and discussions of thematic elements of the text, I use the only full printed version of the manuscript, the 1827 edition published in the *Memoirs of the Pennsylvania Historical Society*: "A Narrative of an Embassy to the Western Indians from the Original Manuscript, with prefatory remarks by Dr. B. H. Coates" (Aupaumut, "Narrative"). All quotations from Chainbreaker are from Abler's modern edition (Abler, *Chainbreaker*), except those in which manuscript practice are at issue. These manuscript examples are taken from Williams, "Life of Governour Blacksnake" (Draper Mss. 16-F-107-219). The page numbers I use to describe Williams's scribal practice thus refer to the hand-lettered pagination Draper provides for the narrative. Draper does not begin his pagination of the "Life" on page 1 but rather numbers it cumulatively, as part of the larger collection he titles "The Brant Papers."

21. Aupaumut, "Narrative," 87; Abler, *Chainbreaker*, 52.

22. Aupaumut, "Narrative," 78, 129, 86.

23. Abler, *Chainbreaker*, 75.

24. Abler, *Chainbreaker*, 170, 163.

25. See Merrell, *Into the American Woods*, 215–19. Merrell finds "contention between the . . . media" of these Indian country discourses

and "the weight each side accorded" the various communication technologies. For other descriptions of hybrid Native/Euro-American diplomatic discourses and materials, see Shoemaker, *Strange Likeness*, 65–68; and Saunt, *New Order of Things*, 190.

26. Aupaumut, "Narrative," 76.
27. Aupaumut, "Narrative," 106.
28. Abler, *Chainbreaker*, 228. This comment appears at the head of the manuscript, but Abler has chosen to publish it as an appendix to the main body of the work. On the process of editing such texts see Round, "Reprinting the Literature."
29. Williams, "Life of Governour Blacksnake," 227–28.
30. Abler, *Chainbreaker*, 17.
31. Williams, "Life of Governour Blacksnake," 227.
32. Williams, "Life of Governour Blacksnake," 108.
33. Williams, "Life of Governour Blacksnake," 116, 113. The third page of the manuscript is otherwise numbered because, as already indicated, Draper numbers the pages of Williams's narrative consecutively within a larger collection of manuscripts titled "The Brant Papers."
34. Sarris, *Keeping Slug Woman Alive*, 85; Aupaumut, "Narrative," 95, 54.
35. Aupaumut, "Narrative," 103, 130.
36. Williams, "Life of Governour Blacksnake," 123.
37. Abler notes that Williams, in another manuscript he sent to Draper, "put the Seneca creation myth into a format resembling the English Bible, including chapter and verse" (Abler, *Chainbreaker*, 11).
38. Williams, "Life of Governour Blacksnake," 129.
39. Lyons, "Rhetorical Sovereignty," 450–51.
40. Aupaumut, "Narrative," 95–96.
41. Aupaumut, "Narrative," 91.
42. Abler, *Chainbreaker*, 54.
43. Aupaumut, "Narrative," 91, 93, 112.
44. Gustafson, "American Literature and the Public Sphere," 473, 475; Aupaumut, "Narrative," 122, 131.
45. Wallace, quoted in Abler, *Chainbreaker*, 12. Abler takes a more judicious stance toward Williams's non-standard style, commenting, "readers must be forewarned that Blacksnake's narrative is not elegant or lucid prose," but he too echoes Wallace in saying that "in some respects it is even worse than 'reservation English,' . . . since one must add confusion about spelling and punctuation to the other

non-standard aspects of English as spoken by Indians for whom it was neither a first language nor even one used in everyday communication" (Abler, *Chainbreaker*, 12).

46. The phrase "an unlettered people" was used by Supreme Court Justice John McLean in his concurring opinion for *Worcester v. Georgia* 31 U.S. 515 (1832). Although that finding supported Cherokee tribal sovereignty, McLean's language continued the Marshall court's policy of characterizing the Cherokees as uncivilized and in a state of "pupilage" (Chief Justice John Marshall's words). In "Indian Literacy," Konkle notes the persistence during the Removal era of calling Native Americans "unlettered."
47. Tac, "Conversion of the San Luiseños," 94.
48. Stiggins, "Historical Narration," 17.
49. Nichols, "Statement Made by the Indians," 1.
50. The quote is from Snelling, "Life of Black Hawk," 70.

Works Cited

Abler, Thomas S. *Chainbreaker: The Revolutionary War Memoirs of Governor Blacksnake as told to Benjamin Williams*. Lincoln: University of Nebraska Press, 2005.

Alden, John. "The Cherokee Archive." *American Archivist* 5 (1942): 240–44.

Alfred, Taiaiake. *Peace, Power, Righteousness: An Indigenous Manifesto*. New York: Oxford University Press, 1999.

Aupaumut, Hendrick. "Journal of a Mission to the Western Tribes of Indians by Hendrick Aupaumut, 1791." Indian Papers, MS 310. Historical Society of Pennsylvania, Philadelphia.

———. "A Narrative of an Embassy to the Western Nations, from the Original Manuscript, with prefatory remarks by Dr. B. H. Coates." *Memoirs of the Historical Society of Pennsylvania* 2, no.1 (1827): 61–131.

Bouwman, Heather. "Samson Occom and the Sermonic Tradition." In *Early Native Literacies in New England: A Documentary and Critical Anthology*, ed. Kristina Bross and Hilary E. Wyss, 63–71. Amherst: University of Massachusetts Press, 2008.

Bross, Kristina, and Hilary Wyss, eds. *Early Native Literacies in New England: A Documentary and Critical Anthology*. Amherst: University of Massachusetts Press, 2008.

Castillo, Susan, and Ivy Schweitzer, eds. *The Literatures of Colonial America: An Anthology*. Malden MA: Blackwell, 2001.

Commuck, Thomas. *Indian Melodies. By Thomas Commuck, a Narragansett Indian. Harmonized by Thomas Hastings, Esq.* New York: G. Lane & C. B. Tippett, 1845.

Dillon, Elizabeth Maddock. *The Gender of Freedom: Fictions of Liberalism and the Literary Public Sphere.* Stanford: Stanford University Press, 2004.

Gustafson, Sandra M. "American Literature and the Public Sphere." *American Literary History* 20 (2008): 465–78.

Habermas, Jurgen. *The Structural Transformation of the Public Sphere: An Inquiry into a Category of Bourgeois Society.* Cambridge MA: MIT Press, 1989.

Konkle, Maureen. "Indian Literacy, U.S. Colonialism, and Literary Criticism." *American Literature* 69 (1997): 458–86.

Loughran, Trish. *The Republic in Print: Print Culture in the Age of U.S. Nation Building, 1770–1870.* New York: Columbia University Press, 2007.

Lyons, Scott Richard. "Rhetorical Sovereignty: What Do American Indians Want from Writing?" *College Composition and Communication* 51 (2000): 447–68.

MacLean, John. Concurring Opinion. *Worcester v. Georgia* 31 U.S. 515 (1832).

Merrell, James. *Into the American Woods: Negotiators on the Pennsylvania Frontier.* New York: Norton, 1999.

Nichols, John D. *"Statement Made by the Indians": A Bilingual Petition of the Chippewas of Lake Superior, 1864.* Studies in the Interpretation of Canadian Languages and Cultures. London, Ontario: University of Western Ontario, 1988.

Occom, Samson. *The Collected Writings of Samson Occom, Mohegan: Leadership and Literature in Eighteenth-Century Native America.* Ed. Joanna Brooks. Oxford: Oxford University Press, 2006.

O'Brien, Jean M. *Dispossession by Degrees: Indian Land and Identity in Natick, Massachusetts, 1650–1790.* New York: Cambridge University Press, 1997.

Round, Phillip H. "Neither Here Nor There: Transatlantic Epistolarity in Early America." In *A Companion to the Literatures of Colonial America*, ed. Susan Castillo and Ivy Schweitzer, 426–45. Malden MA: Blackwell, 2005.

———. "Reprinting the Literature of the Middle Ground." *Early American Literature* 43 (2008): 487–96.

Sarris, Greg. *Keeping Slug Woman Alive: A Holistic Approach to American Indian Texts*. Berkeley: University of California Press, 1993.

Saunt, Claudio. *A New Order of Things: Property, Power, and the Transformation of the Creek Indians, 1733–1816*. Cambridge: Cambridge University Press, 1999.

Schweitzer, Ivy. *Perfecting Friendship: Politics and Affiliation in Early American Literature*. Chapel Hill: University of North Carolina Press, 2006.

Shoemaker, Nancy. *A Strange Likeness: Becoming Red and White in Eighteenth-Century North America*. New York: Oxford University Press, 2004.

Snelling, William Joseph. "Life of Black Hawk." *North American Review* 40 (1835): 68–87.

Stiggins, George. "A Historical Narration of the Genealogy, Traditions and Downfall of the Ispocaga or Creek Tribe." In "Creek Nativism and the Creek War of 1813–1814," part 1, ed. Theron A. Nunez Jr. *Ethnohistory* 5 (1958): 1–47.

Tac, Pablo. "Conversion of the San Luiseños to Christianity." In "Indian Life and Customs at Mission San Luis Rey." Ed. and trans. Mina Hewes and Gordon Hewes. *Americas* 9, no. 1 (July 1952): 87–106.

Timberlake, Henry. *The Memoirs of Lt. Henry Timberlake: The Story of a Soldier, Adventurer, and Emissary to the Cherokees, 1756–1765*. Ed. Duane H. King. Cherokee NC: Museum of the Cherokee Indian Press, 2007.

Warner, Michael. *The Letters of the Republic: Publication and the Public Sphere in Eighteenth-Century America*. Cambridge MA: Harvard University Press, 1990.

———. *Publics and Counterpublics*. New York: Zone, 2002.

Warrior, Robert Allen. *The People and the Word: Reading Native Nonfiction*. Minneapolis: University of Minnesota Press, 2005.

———. *Tribal Secrets: Recovering American Indian Intellectual Traditions*. Minneapolis: University of Minnesota Press, 1994.

White, Richard. *The Middle Ground: Indians, Empires, and Republics in the Great Lakes Region, 1650–1815*. New York: Cambridge University Press, 1991.

Williams, Benjamin. "Life of Governour Blacksnake." Draper MSS, 16-F-107-219. State Historical Society of Wisconsin, University of Wisconsin, Madison.

[10]

Editing as Indian Performance

Elias Boudinot, Poetry, and the *Cherokee Phoenix*

Theresa Strouth Gaul

Elias Boudinot (Cherokee) appeared before New England audiences on numerous occasions over the course of his career as a spokesman for Cherokee rights. He first undertook a speaking tour of New England in 1826, gathering funds for the proposed publication of the *Cherokee Phoenix*, a newspaper he would edit from 1828 to 1832.[1] He returned to the New England lecture circuit in 1832, delivering speeches representing the Cherokee Nation's position in its conflict with the U.S. government over removal, a crisis that reached a peak in that year with the Supreme Court's decision in favor of the Cherokees in *Worcester v. Georgia*.[2]

Little is known of Boudinot's public performances on these occasions, but a letter penned by author Louisa Jane Park offers a tantalizing insight into his manner of presentation and its reception. In April 1832, Park, accompanied by several younger girls and a servant, attended an event at the Federal Street Church in Boston which featured a number of orations on Cherokee rights. Speakers included Congressman Edward Everett, minister Lyman Beecher, activist and author William Apess (Pequot), and Boudinot. As she described in a letter to her mother, Park's young companions found Boudinot a particularly disappointing performer:

> [The previous speaker] was followed by Mr Elias Boudinot—a swarthy, independent-looking gentleman, drest like *other people*, to the great astonishment and disappointment of Caroline Knowles and her companions; I could scarcely persuade them that this [was] one of the Indians they came to see; little Charlotte Coolidge seemed to think she had been imposed upon, and declared she "would not have stirred a step if she had known"; mighty was her wrath at not beholding a "real wild Indian with his hair streaming down his back, a tomahawk in his hand, and a wampum belt, making a speech to us in Cherokee." What especial edification they thought of deriving from such an harangue, I know not. Mr Boudinot was educated at Yale College, is the Editor of the Cherokee Phoenix, and talked like a man of sense and education. He has a fine command of language, but there was nothing figurative in his style; and his address was very long, sometimes dry and uninteresting.[3]

Boudinot's perceived failure to represent Indianness on a Boston stage takes on added complexity when one considers his performance in relation to an earlier spectacle involving Boudinot: the burning of his effigy in a New England town seven years earlier. In 1825, his fiancée Harriett Gold, a member of a prominent white family of Cornwall, Connecticut, announced her engagement to her relations and townspeople, who knew Boudinot from his residence as a student at a local mission school. In a wave of anti-amalgamation furor, a gang of youths gathered on the village green and set fire to what Gold described in a letter as a "painting of a beautiful young lady and an *Indian*."[4] Given dominant modes for visually representing American Indians in the early nineteenth century and Gold's underlining of the word "Indian," one can safely assume that the Indian depicted on the painting displayed all the stereotypical qualities of Indianness—"hair streaming down his back, a tomahawk in his hand, and a wampum belt"—that Boudinot refused to perform on the stage in Boston.

These two moments in Boudinot's history underline the potential and perils of Indian performance in the 1820s, a decade characterized by mounting controversy over the question of Indian removal and public fascination with "Indian dramas" on the stage.[5] For at least some members of his Boston audience, Boudinot's failure to meet Anglo-American criteria for Indianness undercut the credibility and power of his performance. In Cornwall, stereotyped notions of Indian identity trumped even the facts of his distinguished record as a scholar at a local academy, his conversion to Christianity, and contemporaries' acknowledgment of his polished appearance.[6] When representing himself, Boudinot refused to "play Indian."[7] When depicted by whites, he was reduced to the stereotypical savage of captivity narratives, who imperiled white civilization via his sexual threat to white womanhood and whose body must be purged from the nation's borders.

These diametrically opposed responses to his public presentations and representations must have rendered Boudinot acutely aware of the nuances, power, and pitfalls of the performance of Indianness and in so doing prepared him for another kind of performance, arguably the most important of his career. Though not occurring on a physical stage, Boudinot's work as editor of the *Cherokee Phoenix* can usefully be read as an example of what Peggy Phelan calls the "discursive performative." Absent "the living, performing body" that centers most analysis of performance, theorists of the discursive performative attend to "the acts of signifying systems themselves (language and the codes of textuality)."[8] As editor of the first American Indian newspaper published in the United States—and thus as the individual who brought into being one iteration of a "signifying system" conveying an array of potential meanings to its readers—Boudinot influentially intervened in print discourses of Indianness. Through its alternating columns of Cherokee and English typeface, the bilingual *Cherokee Phoenix* enacted a textualized version of the linguistic exchanges between Cherokees and European colonists and, later, U.S. citizens that had been occurring for more than a century.

Just as importantly, the newspaper functioned as a sophisticated locus of cultural exchange through its incorporation of content first appearing in other publications. Like most early American newspapers, the *Cherokee Phoenix* was filled with items originating in other periodicals that were reprinted, sometimes without attribution. Editors of this era commonly "exchanged" newspapers with other editors through the mail, aided by postal laws designed to facilitate the development of the press by eliminating postage on newspapers; they then simply scissored items from other papers to fill their own columns.[9] Boudinot exchanged with as many as one hundred other editors, and the pages of his newspaper show that he extensively borrowed from these sources for the *Cherokee Phoenix*.[10] The *Phoenix*'s content was thus highly diverse and eclectic, like most papers of the day comprised of "miscellany, unattributed borrowings, fragmentary sketches, correspondences, transcripts, and opinions on everything from the French revolution to the ethics of snuff." Only a fraction of it pertained directly to the Cherokee conflict with the U.S. government, and an even smaller fraction was original. One of Boudinot's most important functions as editor was thus to "orchestrate a complex nexus of voices and sources."[11]

The response of most scholars who have examined the newspaper is to dismiss this material as filler and to focus on the overtly politicized content of the paper, especially Boudinot's editorials.[12] It is my intent instead to attend carefully to the selection and placement of reprinted materials in the *Cherokee Phoenix* as a means of illuminating new ways of understanding American Indians' adroit engagement with and performance of print culture. With Meredith McGill, I recognize reprinting as "a form of textual production" that stands as "an independently signifying act."[13] Boudinot himself considered the selection of reprinted materials an important component of his editorial work, writing, "I have to select pieces for publication, & this requires some time in order to be Judicious."[14] By placing the paper's construction and constructedness at the center of the analysis, thereby reversing the traditional scholarly mining of newspapers solely for their content, my approach grants Boudinot a larger sphere of agency in the *Cherokee Phoenix* than the mere space of his editorials and acknowledges his editorial choices as constituting a meaningful discursive performance. Reprinted pieces appeared throughout all of the pages of the *Cherokee Phoenix*, but the section completely composed of reprinted material and labeled "Miscellaneous" often began on page four. A poem was usually the first item printed under the heading. It is on the selection of these poems that I will dwell in this essay, as I argue that Boudinot enacts a complex "cultural reappropriation"[15] in his strategic inclusion of poems originating in periodicals directed toward white, middle-class readers.

The *Cherokee Phoenix* began its run in 1828, with Boudinot editing the paper through 1832. The paper's inception illustrates two trends characteristic of the 1820s: the rapid growth in the number of U.S. newspapers (from 863 in 1828 to around 1200 in 1833), and the increasingly partisan nature of newspapers during this period, a result of the presidential election of 1828 and the growing visibility of reformist, activist, and political groups that utilized the press to support their causes.[16] Boudinot explained in the newspaper's prospectus in 1827 that the *Cherokee Phoenix* had as its "great and sole motive" the "benefit of the Cherokees." Printed on a press purchased by the Cherokee Nation with funds Boudinot gathered while on his 1826 speaking tour of the North, the paper was wholly under Cherokee control, directed by the Cherokee Legislature, and edited by a Cherokee. Boudinot emphasized that the newspaper would function as a "*free paper*," a space for debating the issues of the day, and would follow such rules as would be "most conducive to the interests of the people, for whose benefit, this paper has been established."[17] In order to encourage readership among the approximately 43% of Cherokee households whose members were literate in Cherokee, subscription rates were less expensive for Cherokee readers than for English-language subscribers.[18]

As the author of one of the largest bodies of writing by an American Indian in the nineteenth century—an oeuvre that displays the incision of a keen intellect, confident rhetorical and stylistic flourishes, and a determined sense of purpose—Boudinot might be expected to have received the kind of sustained critical attention directed at his contemporary, William Apess. Yet this has distinctly not been the case. It seems likely that Boudinot's later politics have impeded his critical reception. Indeed, most considerations of Boudinot have dwelt on the motivations, implications, and consequences of his co-signing of the 1835 Treaty of New Echota, which relinquished Cherokee lands in the Southeast to the U.S. government for $5 million dollars and set the Cherokees' forced emigration to Oklahoma in motion.[19]

But there is another compelling explanation for Boudinot's exclusion from canons of American and, even, Native American literature, an explanation that highlights the failure of literary criticism to account for forms of cultural production that reside outside of the single-author paradigm. Boudinot writes in the genres of the newspaper editorial, the letter, or the political essay, all forms for which literary criticism lacks ready analytic frameworks. Moreover, his career path suggests that the literary activities that were most central to his life's work—on a par with writing, if not exceeding it in importance—were those of editing and translation. It is almost needless to point out that if traditions of literary criticism have failed to yield critical tools for making sense of the editorial or the letter, they offer even less explanatory usefulness for the latter intermediary textual acts.[20] While there remains much important work to be done on Boudinot's translations of hymns and the Bible into Cherokee, as well as on the Cherokee content of the *Cherokee Phoenix*, it was in his role as editor that Boudinot wielded his greatest influence, unprecedented for an American Indian, as he reshaped representations of Native peoples in the national news media. As such, it is in this role that one can most fully recognize Boudinot's performative engagement with the dominant culture and its forms of print production.

Once viewed largely as "filler," periodical poetry seems to recent scholars to be integrally important to nineteenth-century periodicals.[21] Critics have particularly emphasized periodical poetry's social engagement. In her study of women's poetry, Paula Bernat Bennett places "newspaper and periodical poetry within the tradition of social dialogue and debate from which it sprang and to which it belongs," while Mary Loeffelholz similarly argues that "particular social contexts or sites of poetry's production and consumption" afforded poets "possibilities already endowed with social significance."[22] Working within this tradition of the social significance and potential for dialogue embedded in poetry, Boudinot strategically chose poems from other periodicals and redeployed them for political ends. In consequence, the meanings generated by these poems for white, middle-class readers in their periodicals of origin were profoundly destabilized by the context provided by the *Cherokee Phoenix*.

Boudinot's purpose in including poetry in the newspaper begins to be revealed as early as 1827 in the paper's Prospectus, which stated the paper's goals and its four main content areas. Literary writings, a category that implicitly includes poetry, would contribute to the paper's effort to document the Cherokees' "progress in Education, Religion, and the *arts* of civilized life" and simultaneously to the paper's goal to "promote Literature, Civilization, and Religion among the Cherokees."[23] In the prospectus Boudinot thus suggests that literary writings would be included both as proof that Cherokees were attaining a "civilized" status and as tools for promoting civilization among the Cherokees. This dual purpose might at first seem to map handily onto the paper's dual audience: while writings providing proof of the Cherokees' "progress" would seem directed at non-Indian readers, whom Boudinot called in one editorial "distant readers," material intended to promote civilization would appear to be directed at Cherokee readers within the Nation, whom Boudinot called "home readers."[24]

An understanding of the *Cherokee Phoenix*'s audience unsettles these conclusions, however. The fact that only 18 percent of Cherokee households included a member who was literate in English suggests that the primary audience of all of the literary material, which was generally *not* translated into Cherokee, was non-Indian.[25] The literary content cannot, then, be read as primarily didactic, intended to improve Cherokees by exposing them to the Anglo-American values the materials espouse. And if the literary content was *not* primarily directed at Cherokee readers, then the paper's purpose of documenting the Cherokees' "progress" for "distant readers" rises to the foreground: to English-language readers, the presence of the literary material—especially poetry, which was associated with the highest level of literary distinction—would suggest a civilized identity in the process of being achieved and substantiated by that very content. As Linda K. Hughes notes, poetry's inclusion in a periodical "could enhance the cultural value and prestige of the periodical itself" as well as, I would add, the cultural prestige of its producers.[26] The *Cherokee Phoenix* thus serves *as* and *as the site for* a performative rendering of Cherokee identity acutely attuned to its audience, one through which Boudinot positions Cherokees within the community to which white readers of the paper belonged and from whose periodicals the reprinted poems originated. For the remainder of this essay, I will explore this performative process by training my attention on two categories of poetic inclusions in the *Cherokee Phoenix*: poems that do not treat explicitly Indian themes yet covertly level a political critique when read in relation to other contents of the paper, and poems that overtly take Indian themes as their subjects.

Recent scholarship has persuasively demonstrated the interpretive value of reading items printed in newspapers in relation to other items surrounding them. Hughes synthesizes the conclusions of such scholarship on poetry and periodicals: "poetry like other material in periodicals is context-dependent, inflected by topicality, marketplace competition, available contributors, and the shifting editorial policies and class register of specific titles, as well as by pressures exerted from within poetic tradition and aesthetic innovation."[27] When such an approach is applied to the *Cherokee Phoenix*, poems that seem upon first glance to be disengaged from Cherokee politics assume another resonance. Take, for example, the poem appearing on 15 April 1829, "Who Is Thy Neighbor?":

Thy neighbor? It is he whom thou
Hast power to aid and bless;
Whose aching heart or burning brow,
Thy soothing hand may press.

Thy neighbor? 'tis the fainting poor
Whose eye with want is dim,
Whom hunger sends from door to door,—
Go thou and succor him.

The poem continues in this vein for several stanzas, citing as neighbors the old, sick, widowed, and orphaned—as well as the "toiling slave"—before concluding:

Whene'er thou meet'st a human form
Less favored than thy own,
Remember 'tis thy neighbor worm,
Thy brother, or thy son.
Oh, pass not, pass not heedless by;
Perhaps thou canst redeem
The breaking heart from misery,—
Go share thy lot with him.

Read as an example of the religious sentiment characteristic of much nineteenth-century poetry, the stanzas seem a simplistic reiteration of the biblical sentiment: "You shall love your neighbor as yourself" (Mark 12.31). Read as printed in the *Cherokee Phoenix*, however, the poem takes on additional varied and unstable meanings. This particular issue of the newspaper was situated in the midst of the Cherokees' burgeoning controversy over their right to retain their land; the poem appears alongside letters written by Thomas McKenney, superintendent of Indian affairs, regarding the dispersal to eager whites of lands vacated by Cherokees, a letter from the residents of one part of the Cherokee Nation stating their reasons for rejecting removal as an option, and several pieces originally printed in other newspapers espousing sentiments sympathetic to the Cherokees. A poem on Christian neighborliness looks suspiciously ironic when placed in the same issue with writings that reveal the greed and rapaciousness of the Cherokees' white "neighbors." Indeed, the word "neighbor" even appears in one of the articles: a piece entitled "Red Jacket" reprinted from the *Massachusetts Journal* describes Anglo-Americans' claiming of Indian lands with the metaphor, "We might as well seize upon our neighbor's wealth, upon the plea that we could spend it more judiciously than he." In the United States of 1829, the Cherokees' white "neighbors" were engaged in stealing and other depredations, acts frequently catalogued in the *Cherokee Phoenix*. These actions by Anglo-Americans against American Indians clearly violate the sentiments espoused in the poem, according to which wealth is shared and the poor are succored. Read in this way, the poem becomes a political commentary.

When considered in relation to Boudinot's characteristic editorial strategy of ironic use of Christian rhetoric in defense of Cherokee rights, such commentary becomes even clearer. In an editorial published on 16 April 1831, Boudinot addresses the fears of a white editor that the Cherokees will rise against the citizens of the United States after the Supreme Court's 1831 ruling against the Cherokees in *Cherokee Nation vs. the State of Georgia*:

> The Cherokees are for peace—they have been in amity with the United States for the last forty years—they have been her faithful allies in time of war—they have buried the hatchet long since, and given their word that the blood of the white man shall not stain their hands. . . . It is more blessed to suffer than to be the oppressors.—It is more blessed than to gain by unrighteous means

> [*sic*]. If the white man must oppress us—if he must have the lead, and throw us penniless upon the wild world, and if our cries and expostulations will avail nothing at the door of those who have promised to be our guardians and protectors, *let it be so*. We are in the path of duty, and the Judge of all the earth will vindicate our cause in his own way and in his own good time.[28]

Here Boudinot begins with parodic use of the clichéd language used by white writers to represent the speech patterns and rhetorical flourishes of American Indian oratory: "bury the hatchet," "the blood of the white man," "stain their hands." After engaging in this textualized version of "playing Indian," Boudinot follows with a veritable pastiche of Biblical allusions.[29] The sophisticated interweaving of Biblical language, following upon the trite representation of stereotypical Indian discourse, showcases Boudinot's ability to shape Anglo-American discourse to his own purposes. As with the poetry he reprints, Boudinot's indictment of whites as embodying the opposite of the Christian values they claim to espouse employs to new effect two kinds of discourse familiar to his readers.

The poems included in the paper tend to cluster around certain topics, such as death, intemperance, nature, and interpretations of Biblical verses. The reprinting of many of these poems seems too politically pointed to be coincidental. "Who Is Thy Neighbor?," for example, appeared a few issues after poems entitled "Nature's Farewell" (17 September 1828) and "A Parting Song" (1 October 1828), both by British poet Felicia Hemans, a favorite for inclusion in the *Phoenix*. "Nature's Farewell" follows "a youth" who "rode forth from his childhood's home" and is warned by the leaves, trees, fountains and streams that he will be forever haunted by memories of the place where he spent his early days. The stream, for example, pleads,

We have been thy playmates through many a day,
Wherefore thus leave us?—Oh! Yet delay!

Listen but once to the sound of our mirth;
For thee 'tis a melody passing from earth!
Never again will thou find in its flow
The peace it could once on thy heart bestow.

The last stanza concludes with the dark image:

And a something of gloom on his spirit weigh'd,
As he caught the last sounds of his native shade;
But he knew not, till many a bright spell broke,
How deep were the oracles nature spoke!

Context transforms the romantic quest motif of the poem into a presentiment of what the Cherokees would experience should they bow to the government's demands. In a similar vein, "A Parting Song" poses a question of remembrance: "When will ye think of me, my friends? / When will ye think of me?—" Though the poem ostensibly discusses death, surely the shadow of looming removal changes the poem to subtle protest: if the Cherokees are forced to remove, this is the very plea they might make of Anglo-Americans.

The threat of removal similarly hangs over a poem from 5 August 1829, "They Are Not There!," which mourns the absence of those who had once inhabited a romantic landscape: "They are not there! by the lone fount, / That once they loved by eve to haunt." While again the poem ends with a reflection on death, the similarity to the conditions produced by removal is striking. The issue of 19 August 1829 contains two poems, "The Farmer" and "Norwegian War Song." "The Farmer" contains praise of western agricultural pursuits, central to U.S. government civilization programs among American Indians, ending with the stanzas:

All hail, ye farmers, young and old;
Push on your plough with courage bold;
Your wealth arises from your clod,
Your independence from your God.

If then the plough supports the nation,
And men of rank in every station,
Let kings to farmers make a bow,
And every man procure a plough.

Interestingly, this poem reaffirming for white readers the Cherokees' commitment to the values of Euro-American civilization is followed immediately by the "Norwegian War Song." Voicing an injunction to fight off the invading Swedes, the poem urges besieged individuals to "drive the invader far, far from [their] door[s]":

Then down from the mountain, and up from the lake!
And out from the forest! Norwegians, awake!
And rush like the storm on the thick coming foe—
With hearts for old Norway, and death in your blow.

Read within the paper's context, the poem envisions what might have happened if American Indians had resisted European invasion more aggressively. Or perhaps more immediately, Boudinot's inclusion of the poem allows him to voice an endorsement of violent resistance, which he otherwise eschewed in his editorials.

In the 1830s, as the Cherokee crisis gained urgency, more of the reprinted poems overtly addressed Indian themes or the politics of the period. The paper printed poems by well known poets, such as "An Indian at the Burying Place of His Fathers" by William Cullen Bryant, and "Indian Eloquence and Grief" from Lydia Sigourney's *Traits of the Aborigines*, along with other poems carrying titles like "The Indian with his

Dead Child," "The Indian Boy," "The Indians," "The Indians' Farewell," "Indian's Lament," "The Exile of the Indians," and "Dirge of the Indian Widow."[30] As the titles convey, these poems resonate with themes of loss, grief, and exile. Indian removal is portrayed as having already been accomplished with Native Americans as (if not willing) at least passive victims. While some of the poems do offer a critique of Anglo-American actions, that criticism is undercut by images of thriving and prospering Euro-American settlements on formerly Indian lands. Though there is nothing surprising about these poems and any search of U.S. literature during the early national period turns up dozens like them, their placement in the pages of the *Cherokee Phoenix* complicates their manifest content. Why would a paper with the purpose of benefiting the Cherokees include poems conveying images most readers today would agree were damaging to Native American interests? And why would Boudinot, adept at identifying and fighting race-based prejudice and inequity, select them?

The most obvious, and for me least satisfying, answer has been proposed frequently in regard to Boudinot and others like him: that his high degree of assimilation led him to internalize the dominant culture's stereotypes, to distance himself from and turn upon his own people. Historian Theda Perdue, for example, makes this sort of argument when she states, "so completely did [Boudinot] embrace the tenets of Western culture that he seems to have accepted the dominant white attitudes toward Indians." I have made the argument elsewhere that this view of Boudinot is too simple. Instead, he reveals the delicate and fraught maneuvers—the Indian performances—necessary to position oneself as both civilized and Native in a world that insisted upon the opposition of the two identities.[31]

Once again, Boudinot's editorial strategies offer a starting point for understanding the inclusion of stereotyped poetic images of the Indian in the *Phoenix*. Just as Boudinot employs vocabularies familiar to his white readers, such as Biblical language, within the context of Cherokee politics to a resistant end, he uses images of the stock Indian in a purposeful manner and with multiple goals. A careful analysis of the contents in the issue printed on 12 November 1831 will illuminate some of Boudinot's purposes. The first page of the issue is comprised of reprinted materials from a range of newspapers covering the recent imprisonment of missionaries Elizur Butler and Samuel Worcester for refusing to take an oath of allegiance to the state of Georgia. Through these reprints, Boudinot monitored the Cherokees' broader media coverage for his readers. The second page of the issue contains most of the original material emanating from the Cherokee Nation, including Boudinot's editorial. The third and fourth pages contain reprinted articles on a variety of topics ranging from food poisoning to dispatches from Russia.

Most strikingly for the purposes of this argument, this miscellany section begins with "The Indian's Exile" by G. W. P. Custis. Critical of the actions of the U.S. government toward Indians, the poem nonetheless is full of demeaning images:

The Indian's degen'rate—no longer the bold.
The proud Forest chief, who before his sad fall,
Had a world for his empire—and he uncontroll'd,
The lordly possessor, and monarch of all.

He has fall'n, indeed, from his once high estate,
The gleam of his glory forever has faded,
And will no gen'rous spirits now pity his fate,
A Noble of Nature thus lowly degraded?

The poem regrets the fate of the "poor worms" who lost their "dreary domains" to the invading colonists and is critical of the "lust of dominion and gain" driving the United States in its Indian policy. There is no questioning, however, of the metaphor that closes the poem, which imagines Indians as "the poor native songsters, that will soon sing no more."[32]

What is Boudinot's purpose in including this poem, which seems almost offensive in the crudeness of its stereotypes? He may have had a number of intersecting goals, I would argue. Boudinot's choice to include such poems may have, for example, been intended to soothe his Anglo-American readers. If while reading the first pages of the paper, the reader found him/herself disturbed by any contentiousness of tone or any threatening sense of transgression of the racial hierarchies to which even supporters of the Cherokees might have adhered, in the poem the same reader encounters the familiar and safe image of the Indian popularized in the pages of many a romantic text of the 1820s. Stoking the complacency of the reader has an important function in the larger goal of the newspaper: Boudinot in effect manipulates the sympathetic identification of that reader with the romantic and vanishing Indian encountered in the poems in order to urge the reader to action. Susan Ryan has argued that benevolence depends upon "distancing rhetorics" rather than the acts of identification prioritized by sentimentalism. In benevolent exchanges, a "recognition of difference, something that made one social actor the helper and the other a proper recipient of that help," was necessary. Any abridging of difference could thus effect "a degree of social leveling that most donors would have resisted." Ryan concludes, "The simultaneous erasure and persistence of difference facilitates both the sentimental bond that creates the desire to give and the maintenance of hierarchy that suggests that such giving is safe, that it does not threaten the identity or status of the giver, that it does not, ultimately, make helper and helped the same."[33] So while the content of the Indian poems worked to garner sympathy for the Cherokees' plight, the *Phoenix*'s images of stereotyped Indians simultaneously worked to maintain the benevolent white reader's sense of superiority over Native Americans and thus to create the conditions that might lead the reader to "give"—in this context, to give his/her support to the Cherokee position by taking action. For Boudinot, such action always remained central to his vision: as he wrote in a personal letter, he believed that much could be accomplished if only "the good people of the U. States can be induced to *arouse*, to *feel* and to ACT on this momentous subject."[34]

Another possible goal is distinct from the ones I've just described, and, in less skillful hands, might have worked at cross-purposes with them. It is most readily discerned in a cluster of pieces on page two in the 12 November 1831 issue that call into question the conventional images of "The Indian's Exile" and perform another version of Indian identity altogether. Leading off is Boudinot's editorial. Refuting the commonplace notion that "An Indian will still be an Indian," Boudinot claims that Cherokees are not prevented from becoming "civilized" by their "nature" nor their "degraded and ignorant" status but by the fact that "they have to contend with obstacles as numerous as they are peculiar." He then goes on to give a brief history of the United States' dealings with the Cherokees from Washington's era through their present crisis. The first half of the editorial seems to work on a system of values which accepts Anglo-American civilization's superiority and bemoans the Cherokees' lack of civilization, although Boudinot assigns historical rather than biological reasons for this state. The editorial, however, executes a clever turn midway through. When Boudinot reaches the era of Cherokee history involving the Jackson administration, he employs italicization—as when he writes, "The *guardian* has deprived his *wards* of their rights"—to underscore the failures of the U.S. government to live up to the promises of its rhetoric. Thus when the reader next encounters the word "civilization," Boudinot's irony rings clearly: the Cherokees' "own laws, intended to regulate their society, to encourage virtue and to suppress vice, must now be abolished, and civilized acts, passed for the purpose of expelling them, must be substituted."[35] Boudinot thus redefines the Cherokees as behaving in a more civilized manner than the U.S. government.

Several pieces immediately following upon Boudinot's editorial also resist the stereotyped notion of Indianness the poem promotes and instead construct an identity for the Cherokees founded on their own agency. First, the printing of an 1821 petition presented by Cherokee women to the National Council states their steadfast resistance to removal and faith in the Council's power to avert such a result. Next, excerpts from a letter to "a friend in this Nation" by an "intelligent Gentleman" disseminate information, gleaned from travels through Texas and Arkansas, about the quality of the land and the status of Chickasaws and Choctaws who had removed to the proposed Indian territories. The writer offers the information for the Cherokees' use in their autonomous deliberations regarding removal. Following, resolutions resulting from a meeting in one of the Cherokee districts reveals the Cherokees' intent to "solemnly protest" the U.S. government's actions and to "pledge ourselves, individually and collectively, to use our best endeavors" to support the Nation's leadership. One of the resolutions states that the Cherokees "sympathize with them [the imprisoned missionaries and their families] in all their sufferings." In all of these resolutions, the Cherokees position themselves as agents, taking action and lending sympathy, rather than requiring it. Immediately after, a paragraph submitted by Ann Worcester, wife of imprisoned missionary Samuel Worcester, relays her gratitude for the support and monetary assistance she received from Cherokees during her husband's imprisonment. An Anglo-American woman thus presents herself as the subject of Cherokee sympathy, a reversal of the dynamics put forward by "The Indian's Exile." Next, a Cherokee author identified only as A.R.E. offers a satirical depiction of the false promises and reasoning conveyed to Cherokees of the Hickory Log District by an agent of the government in his conversations with them. After criticizing the agent, A.R.E. concludes his letter with a strong anthem: "The land is ours, we must and will contend for it." The tone and message of this piece could not contrast more starkly with the image of the Indians presented in the poem. Finally, the Cherokee language pieces, which conclude page two, testify to the Cherokees' dynamic and living culture.

This grouping of pieces, nestled at the center of the newspaper, presents an active Cherokee community engaged in a deliberative and unflinching battle with the U.S. government. By setting the dynamic Cherokee identity that pieces like the ones on page two of this issue produce in relation to the stock images of "The Indian's Exile," Boudinot undercuts the validity of the latter representations. In the pages of the *Cherokee Phoenix*, the Cherokees are not vanishing, are not mournful emblems of a dying race, seemingly occupied day and night in proclaiming death dirges at the graves of their forebears, melting like dew drops before the morning sun, falling like leaves from an autumnal tree, or gliding off silently into a western sunset. They are a vibrant people whose national newspaper demonstrates the complexity of their culture, the richness of their language, the concerns of their daily lives, the importance of their political battles, and the acuity of their ability to manage and fight those battles. If the Anglo-American writers who penned these poems and the readers who typically consumed them tended to accept removal and the vanishing of the Indian as necessary and inevitable, the poems' effects were destabilized in the pages of the *Phoenix*, placed as they were in a paper unflinchingly opposed to removal.

In a personal letter, Boudinot noted, "Perhaps few will properly know the extent of my duties, by merely seeing the Phoenix, which carries but little evidence of much labour." In the lengthy list of his duties that follows this statement, he minimizes his editorial writing, upon which recent critics have dwelt, commenting only briefly, "then I have to prepare what little editorial may be seen in the Phoenix."[36] This essay has attempted to make visible one facet of the editorial labor of constructing a newspaper that, as Boudinot recognized, is too easily overlooked. More broadly, this essay models one approach to recovering the range of American Indians' active engagements with print culture during the early national period. Significant room remains for exploration of the ways Indian authors claimed agency by adapting, revising, manipulating, and redeploying print conventions to serve Native ends. Seen in this way, print culture, one nexus of cultural exchange increasingly engaged by Native peoples in the course of the nineteenth century, becomes a crucially important stage upon which an array of Indian performances can be dramatized and textualized.

Notes

My thanks go to Karen Steele and Mona Narain for comments on an earlier draft of this essay and to TCU*'s Research and Creative Activities Fund for grant support in completing the research for this essay.*

1. The text of a speech from this lecture tour, entitled "An Address to the Whites, Delivered in the First Presbyterian Church, on the 26th of May, 1826," was Boudinot's first publication, aside from some of his schoolboy letters published in periodicals. For its text see Perdue, *Cherokee Editor*, 68–83.
2. For a general introduction to events surrounding Cherokee removal,

see Perdue and Green, *Cherokee Removal* and *Cherokee Nation and the Trail of Tears*.

3. Louisa Jane Park to Agnes Major Park, April 29, 1832. Konkle discusses this letter in *Writing Indian Nations*, 99. Park is incorrect in one detail: Boudinot did not attend Yale University.
4. Gaul, *To Marry an Indian*, 84.
5. For considerations of "Indian dramas," see Gaul, "'Genuine Indian'"; Mielke, *Moving Encounters*, chap. 8; and Richards, *Drama, Theatre, and Identity*, chap. 8.
6. Perdue, *Cherokee Editor*, 8. The comment comes from an observer of a school examination: "Elias Boudinot, in a declamation, confuted the idea more completely by his appearance than by his arguments, that savages are not capable of being civilized and polished."
7. In *Playing Indian* Philip Deloria discusses examples of "native people [who] turned to playing Indian—miming Indianness back at Americans in order to redefine it" (125). Deloria notes the danger of this move: "Although they might alter Indian stereotypes, native people playing Indian might also reaffirm them for a stubborn white audience" (127). I am arguing here that Boudinot eschewed such a chancy performance.
8. Phelan, "Reciting the Citations," 15.
9. For a description of this aspect of an editor's work, see Garvey, "Scissorizing and Scrapbooks," 213. Garvey plumbs the nuances of the word *exchange* in her discussion of the editorial practice of exchanging newspapers: "*Exchange* might suggest a simple one-for-one passing back and forth of papers, but as we might guess from some of its other uses, such as the telephone exchange and the stock exchange, the term also comprises circuits of connection and diffusion" (212). The concept of exchange has similarly been a powerful motif in studies of contacts between Native peoples and Europeans and the texts that emerged from that contact; see Bellin's *Demon of the Continent* for an approach to American literature that considers texts "in light of their position within a network of cultural conflict, negotiation, and interchange encompassing diverse material and ideological points of encounter" (3).
10. Perdue, *Cherokee Editor*, 145 n. 4. In turn, a range of newspapers, particularly those that were anti-Jacksonian in their political tendencies, widely reprinted materials from the *Cherokee Phoenix*. I thank John Nerone for his conversations on this topic at the American Antiquarian Society's Summer Seminar on the History of the Book in

2008. Though outside the scope of this essay, charting the reprintings of the *Cherokee Phoenix*'s articles in other papers and compiling editors' comments on the *Cherokee Phoenix* would be one route to reconstructing Anglo-American reader responses to the newspaper.

11. Gardner, "Literary Museum," 744–45, 750. Typically only Boudinot's editorials, the Cherokee language materials, and the correspondence section were original in content.
12. Perdue's *Cherokee Editor* remains the most substantive study of Boudinot and the *Cherokee Phoenix*. Though Perdue describes other aspects of Boudinot's editorial activities, his editorial writing remains her central focus. See also Hudson, "'Forked Justice.'"
13. McGill, *American Literature and the Culture of Reprinting*, 5. McGill's emphasis on "culture as iteration not origination" (4) informs my view of Boudinot's editing as a creative activity worthy of study.
14. Gaul, *To Marry an Indian*, 161.
15. Lehuu, *Carnival on the Page*, 42.
16. Humphrey, *Press of the Young Republic*, 113. For discussions of the development of the newspaper during this era, see Barnhorst and Nerone, *Form of the News*; Lehuu, *Carnival on the Page*; and Loughran, *Republic in Print*. Bacon discusses the first African-American newspaper, which also began its run in 1828, in *Freedom's Journal*.
17. Perdue, *Cherokee Editor*, 90, 92.
18. Perdue, *Cherokee Editor*, 63 n. 38, 146 n. 14.
19. For considerations of Boudinot's signing of the Treaty of New Echota, see Bellin, *Medicine Bundle*, 87–100; Gabriel, *Elias Boudinot*, chaps. 19 and 20; Gaul, *To Marry an Indian*, 60–62; Justice, *Our Fire Survives the Storm*, chap. 2; Konkle, *Writing Indians*, chap. 1; Perdue, *Cherokee Editor*, 25–33; Schneider, "Boudinot's Change"; and Weaver, *That the People Might Live*, 69–75.
20. It is tempting to consider how different the trajectory of Boudinot's critical reception might have been had he written one autobiographical narrative.
21. Within a U.S. context Bennett persuasively argues against seeing periodical poetry as filler in "Not Just Filler," while in a British context Hughes argues that "poetry and periodicals . . . were interrelated in highly complex terms" and that poetry can reveal dimensions of "periodicals' cultural politics, editorial principles, authorship, formal dynamics, and visuality" (Hughes, "Wellesley Index," 115). I owe special thanks to Bennett for suggesting to me, many years ago in a

chance encounter, the poetry in the *Cherokee Phoenix* as a topic of investigation.

22. Bennett, *Poets in the Public Sphere*, 5; Loeffelholz, *From School to Salon*, 3.
23. Perdue, *Cherokee Editor*, 90, my emphasis. The remaining two content areas are "The laws and public documents of the Nation" and "The principal interesting news of the day."
24. Perdue, *Cherokee Editor*, 109.
25. Perdue, *Cherokee Editor*, 63 n. 38.
26. Hughes, "Wellesley Index," 94.
27. Hughes, "Wellesley Index," 91.
28. Perdue, *Cherokee Editor*, 127.
29. The repetition of "more blessed" evokes Acts 20:35: "It is more blessed to give than to receive." The King James Bible includes 64 usages of the word "unrighteous" and 23 usages of "oppressor," language usage to which a translator of the Bible such as Boudinot would be especially sensitive. "Let it be so" echoes common translations of "amen": "let it be" or "so be it." And the final reference to "the Judge of all the earth" comes from Genesis 18:25: "Shall not the Judge of all the earth do right?"
30. The poems named were printed on the following dates, respectively: July 29, 1829; September 30, 1830; July 9, 1829; June 10, 1829; November 4, 1829; March 31, 1830; April 30, 1831; November 12, 1831; December 17, 1831.
31. Perdue, *Cherokee Editor*, 10; Gaul, *To Marry an Indian*, 19–23. On the dilemma of the "civilized" Indian, see also Wyss, *Writing Indians*, 6.
32. Most of the reprinted items on the missionaries' imprisonment on the first page of this issue are generally congruent with the image of Indians projected in the poem—passive recipients of benevolent Americans' sympathy or heroism—as exemplified by Butler and Worcester. A piece reprinted from the *Northampton Courier*, for example, calls Indians "wretched objects of ignorance and debasement," who provoke "strong feelings of sympathy."
33. Ryan, *Grammar of Good Intentions*, 19.
34. Gaul, *To Marry an Indian*, 175. In the manuscript Boudinot underscored "arouse" with one line, "feel" with two lines, and "act" with three lines.
35. Perdue, *Cherokee Editor*, 140–43.
36. Gaul, *To Marry an Indian*, 161. The tasks he describes himself as ac-

complishing each publication cycle include selecting pieces to reprint, translating and composing Cherokee-language materials, proofreading, corresponding with subscribers, and keeping financial records.

Works Cited

Bacon, Jacqueline. *Freedom's Journal: The First African-American Newspaper*. Lanham MD: Lexington, 2007.

Barnhorst, Kevin G., and John C. Nerone. *The Form of the News: A History*. New York: Guilford, 2000.

Bellin, Joshua. *The Demon of the Continent: Indians and the Shaping of American Literature*. Philadelphia: University of Pennsylvania Press, 2001.

———. *Medicine Bundle: Indian Sacred Performance and American Literature, 1824–1932*. Philadelphia: University of Pennsylvania Press, 2007.

Bennett, Paula Bernat. "Not Just Filler and Not Just Sentimental: Women's Poetry in American Victorian Periodicals, 1860–1900." In *Periodical Literature in Nineteenth-Century America*, ed. Kenneth M. Price and Susan Belasco Smith, 202–19. Charlottesville: University of Virginia Press, 1995.

———. *Poets in the Public Sphere: The Emancipatory Project of American Women's Poetry, 1800–1900*. Princeton: Princeton University Press, 2003.

Deloria, Philip. *Playing Indian*. New Haven: Yale University Press, 1999.

Gabriel, Ralph Henry. *Elias Boudinot, Cherokee and His America*. Norman: University of Oklahoma Press, 1941.

Gardner, Jared. "The Literary Museum and the Unsettling of the Early American Novel." *ELH* 67 (2000): 743–77.

Garvey, Ellen Gruber. "Scissorizing and Scrapbooks: Nineteenth-Century Reading, Remaking, and Recirculating." In *New Media: 1740–1915*, ed. Lisa Gitelman, 207–27. Cambridge MA: MIT Press, 2003.

Gaul, Theresa Strouth. "'The Genuine Indian Who Was Brought upon the Stage': Edwin Forrest's *Metamora* and White Audiences." *Arizona Quarterly* 56, no. 1 (2000): 1–27.

Gaul, Theresa Strouth, ed. *To Marry an Indian: The Marriage of Elias Boudinot and Harriett Gold in Letters, 1823–1839*. Chapel Hill: University of North Carolina Press, 2005.

Hudson, Angela Pulley. "'Forked Justice': Elias Boudinot, the U.S. Constitution, and Cherokee Removal." In *American Indian Rhetorics of Survivance: Word Medicine, Word Magic*, ed. Ernest Stromberg, 50–65. Pittsburgh: University of Pittsburgh Press, 2006.

Hughes, Linda K. "What the Wellesley Index Left Out: Why Poetry Matters to Periodical Studies." *Victorian Periodicals Review* 40, no. 2 (Summer 2007): 91–125.

Humphrey, Carol Sue. *The Press of the Young Republic, 1776–1833*. Westport CT: Greenwood, 1996.

Justice, Daniel Heath. *Our Fire Survives the Storm: A Cherokee Literary History*. Minneapolis: University of Minnesota Press, 2006.

Konkle, Maureen. *Writing Indian Nations: Native Intellectuals and the Politics of Historiography, 1827–1863*. Chapel Hill: University of North Carolina Press, 2006.

Lehuu, Isabelle. *Carnival on the Page: Popular Print Media in Antebellum America*. Chapel Hill: University of North Carolina Press, 2000.

Loeffelholz, Mary. *From School to Salon: Reading Nineteenth-Century American Women's Poetry*. Princeton: Princeton University Press, 2004.

Loughran, Trish. *The Republic in Print: Print Culture in the Age of U.S. Nation Building, 1770–1870*. New York: Columbia University Press, 2007.

McGill, Meredith L. *American Literature and the Culture of Reprinting, 1834–1853*. Philadelphia: University of Pennsylvania Press, 2003.

Mielke, Laura L. *Moving Encounters: Sympathy and the Indian Question in Antebellum Literature*. Amherst: University of Massachusetts Press, 2008.

Park, Louisa Jane. Letter to Agnes Major Park. April 29, 1832. Park Family Papers (1800–1890), American Antiquarian Society, Worcester MA.

Perdue, Theda, ed. *Cherokee Editor: The Writings of Elias Boudinot*. 1983; Athens: University of Georgia Press, 1996.

Perdue, Theda, and Michael D. Green. *The Cherokee Nation and the Trail of Tears*. New York: Viking, 2007.

Perdue, Theda, and Michael D. Green, eds. *The Cherokee Removal: A Brief History with Documents*. Boston: Bedford, 1995.

Phelan, Peggy. "Reciting the Citation of Others; or, A Second Introduction." In *Acting Out: Feminist Performances*, ed. Lynda Hart and Peggy Phelan, 13–31. Ann Arbor: University of Michigan Press, 1993.

Richards, Jeffrey H. *Drama, Theater, and Identity in the American New Republic*. Cambridge: Cambridge University Press, 2005.

Ryan, Susan. *The Grammar of Good Intentions: Race and the Antebellum Culture of Benevolence*. Ithaca: Cornell University Press, 2003.

Schneider, Bethany. "Boudinot's Change: Boudinot, Emerson, and Ross on Cherokee Removal." *ELH* 75 (2008): 151–77.

Weaver, Jace. *That the People Might Live: Native American Literatures and Native American Community*. New York: Oxford University Press, 1997.

Wyss, Hilary. *Writing Indians: Literacy, Christianity, and Native Community in Early America*. Amherst: University of Massachusetts Press, 2000.

Afterword

Philip J. Deloria

My dad rued the day his bad back got the better of him and he had to give up wearing his cowboy boots. "Justins," he said, "are what you wear when you really need to put on the Indian." My grandfather, a Dakota clergyman, used to perform his Indianness in football stadiums and baseball diamonds, and his Christianity in Indian churches across South Dakota. My great-grandfather is supposed to have converted to the Episcopal Church upon hearing a transcendent performance of the hymn, "Guide Me, O Thou Great Jehovah." He witnessed the large church convocation performances of the early twentieth century—the camp circles, the parades, the ceremonies, the cottonwood shade bower—all of which looked a whole lot like the (banned) Sun Dance rituals. My great-great-grandfather took a Santee man's life in a performance—understood and agreed upon by (almost) all parties—that confirmed for American soldiers that the Yanktons were "friendlies." My great-great-great grandfather, a Frenchman who showed up on the Missouri River in the late eighteenth century, must have been party to numerous intercultural performances, expressed in trade, marriage, religion, and the many small acts that make up everyday life. And of course, I have just performed—through this very paragraph—some small claim on a genealogy of cross-cultural performance, a genealogy that stretches back through time, perhaps growing more interesting as one turns to the moments of early contacts and colonial power struggles.

Native Acts brings such a "perhaps" to life, demonstrating that the earliest moments of intercultural performance are indeed among the most interesting and compelling. The pieces in this volume—framed by a brilliant opening essay by Laura Mielke—open powerful new possibilities for scholars of early America, American Indians, performance and cultural contact, and race, identity and colonial power relations, among others. They deal both in the materialities of embodied performances and on the written and spoken recountings (as in my little paragraph) that perform—and thus produce—stakes and claims, identities and subjectivities, "truths" and "authenticities," new intercultural possibilities, and in the end, power relations themselves.

Historiography, like history itself, avoids origins and proliferates beginnings. One of the great virtues to be found in *Native Acts* emerges from that proliferation, as the essays take their beginnings in history, Performance Studies, literary and theater studies, and anthropology, to name only a few possibilities. My own particular beginning point for thinking about the work contained in *Native Acts* is Richard White's *The Middle Ground*—and more particularly, the ways in which it challenged readers to think about rituals, performances, metaphors, and power. White framed a number of definitions of this thing he called "the middle ground." They boiled down to a few key concepts: when power relations between peoples were more or less equivalent—that is, when no group could alter another's behavior through force or domination—those peoples were likely to develop new social and cultural forms through a process involving creative misperception, misunderstanding, and miscommunication—and a mutual tolerance for all those misses and near misses. Such new forms were the products of familiar cultural and social content from each group, but they were also built upon creative improvisations—and upon performances. These improvised performances took place in bartering sessions, diplomatic meetings, mission ceremonies, captivities and adoptions, and in violence itself. With time and repetition, many of them ceased to be improvisations and became instead new standard operating procedures. Thus, for example, the use of a term such as *Onontio* (Father) came to represent not simply an application of indigenous kinship understandings to a diplomatic and economic relationship but also an expression of French patriarchal and civilizational ideology. Though both Indians and French understood their own senses of the term—and, more important, the active *practices* that accompanied it—each also understood that the term and the practices had been altered and that what now mattered—on the middle ground, as it were—were the new meanings. And so *Onontio* became a shared word, rich with overdetermined meanings that required careful and sustained performance from all parties. Each time it was used, it quite literally called something new into being.

The concept of the middle ground pointed readers in a number of thoughtful directions. White emphasized, first of all, ways through which one might systematically understand cross-social and cultural creativity, particularly in contexts that demanded a rethinking of the familiar ideologies of Indian/non-Indian difference (civilized: savage; empire: tribe; market: subsistence; and the like). Rather than rigid oppositions, the middle ground suggested the possibilities for intelligibility, if not outright commensurability. In considering those possibilities, readers were led to think about on-the-ground practices, many of which were explicitly performative—French and English juridical rituals as much so as Algonquian diplomatic conventions. The book asked readers to consider the relation between power and social and cultural practice. It demanded that we think yet again about how one was to read European sources for knowledge about Native people. And it raised, for many readers, the question of how historical arguments are made.

The "middle ground" was both a descriptive, analytical category *and* a metaphor, and in that overlap, it reminded readers that history is at once a methodical craft and an aesthetic enterprise. As evocative metaphor, the middle ground carried a richness of meaning and possibility that perhaps proved a little *too* evocative. Almost immediately, the concept began drifting from its historical moorings in the *pays d'en haut*, becoming an all-purpose term for cross-cultural innovation of all sorts. In an effort to reclaim it as an analytical category, White and others insisted upon both the specificity of the historical context (maybe the middle ground was not so portable after all?) and the importance of balanced power relations in *forcing* both sides to open up to the possibilities of social and cultural innovation.

The metaphorical dreamscape that the middle ground had *also* suggested—a multiplicity of peoples, perceptions, and performances—receded into a more dualistic figuration. In other words, the "middle" became less an evocative mishmash of possibilities and more of a delineated zone that enveloped a sharper borderline between two peoples. Perhaps one can even see this trajectory in the book itself, as the incomprehensibilities of the earliest French and Indian performances give way in later chapters to a more focused set of political relationships between Indians and the English, and later Americans.

Or at least, that is how it all happened for me.

I found *The Middle Ground* an inspired—and inspiring—book, and I read it as I was working on my own book, *Playing Indian*. As important as White's book was, however, the middle ground was *not* my primary point of entry for that project.

Rather, I was taking aim at—and seeking conversation with—a different set of beginnings: Robert F. Berkhofer Jr.'s *The White Man's Indian*, Brian Dippie's *The Vanishing American*, and Richard Slotkin's *Regeneration through Violence* trilogy. These books had brought cultural analysis into an American Indian Studies historiography that had often been centrally concerned with federal Indian policy. These books asked American Studies questions: what did white American ideologies concerning Indians look like? How did those ideologies take shape? And how were they then manifested in political, legal, economic and social realms? I loved these books, but it also seemed to me that their cause-and-effect structure jumped a little too quickly from cultural mythologies and beliefs to oppressive policies and behaviors. I found myself interested in the ways those ideologies were made material—not simply in policy but in the performance of everyday life. It seemed to me that one could get a different purchase on those ideologies by looking at the ways individuals and groups took literary and mythological tropes and played them out in rituals and performances that went beyond literary and popular expressions.

It mattered that Indian people participated in these materializations—the Creeks and the Tammany Society; Ely S. Parker's engagement with Lewis Henry Morgan's literary fraternity; the cross-fertilization of Indian and hobbyist powwow circuits in the post–World War II United States. But my core questions were not about middle grounds so much as they were about the material practices of American ideologies and identities. Indeed, when friends suggested that a final chapter of that book should deal with Indians playing Indian, I balked. Such a treatment would only call attention to the lack of examples in earlier chapters and would push the book away from American Studies—its natural home (at least as I conceived it)—and toward ethnohistory, where it fit only awkwardly.

Though I still think that was the correct decision, a number of gaps and problems with the book soon became apparent. Was this "Indian" that white people so often appropriated a racially essentialized figure, not only in Euro-American consciousness but in my own analysis? Didn't changing material circumstances produce different racial formations across time and space? And might that not require more attention to on-the-ground interactions and questions of racial formation? Wouldn't these things complicate that essentialization, particularly across the huge span of time covered by the book? Was *Playing Indian*'s argument too closely knit to an old American Studies tradition, such that it carried more than a whiff of American exceptionalism? Was "identity" really the best way to think about these performances? What about "subjectivity"? And what about the relation between the two?

What of the dualisms that so insistently structured the argument (British: American; American: Indian; modern: primitive)? I had invoked those dualisms in order to make a big argument that had three dimensions: first, that Americans had produced a national aesthetic of "simultaneity," in which performance allowed them to be *both* civilized Europeans and authentically indigenous Americans; second, that the practices had produced a kind of negative dialectic that destroyed its oppositions and left in its wake only a national indeterminacy and uncertainty; and finally, that these first two meta-claims, framed in dialectical terms, also required a *dialogic*, historical engagement that considered the complicated particularities of change over time.

Richard White's "middle ground" sought just that—an escape from the familiar oppositional categories so often built into the meetings of (many different) Indians and (many different) Europeans. Curiously (for me at least), those same dualisms were often reenergized by the metaphoric charms of his very productive analytical category. Threatened with becoming a genial synonym for "negotiation" or "accommodation" or "hybridity," the middle ground was maintained as a concept by framing power relations primarily in political terms.

White's capacious concept was pulled reluctantly back into oppositional categories; those same categories were my starting point. Indeed, I had been profoundly interested in and dependent upon dualisms, oppositions, and dialectical relations from the very beginning. They led me to think, not about cultural blurring and creative misunderstanding but about the simultaneous expression of unresolved contradictions. I did not see American identities in terms of cross-cultural creation (though this was undeniably the case) so much as in an irresolvable claim to being both aboriginally indigenous *and* civilized European. If the middle ground grew out of a complex transformation of acculturation theories, playing Indian owed its theoretical debt to Walter Benjamin and the concept of the dialectical image. At the end of the day, however, both ended up functioning in dualistic terms, though differently. And because of these particular (undeniably productive) analytical choices, both ended up missing other possibilities.

Which is why I find *Native Acts* so revelatory, productive, and important. These essays do their work using new paradigms that shift the focus to more intimate—and thus differently complicated—settings. Despite our best readerly intentions, the almost unavoidable categories "European-Indian" have always had a perverse way of mapping seemingly coherent political identities onto complex and contradictory social relations and cultural productions. Those categories—and *The Middle Ground* and *Playing Indian* both stand as evidence—do this work even as we set out to deconstruct them, pointedly to drain them of their power. By emphasizing performance, *Native Acts* seeks to explode such categories, honing in close on moments when the play—or rather, the *act*—was the thing, moments when cultural forms were up for grabs, when power was itself contested and shaped.

The essays in *Native Acts* do not simply explore the possibilities of Indian performance and Indian power to shape non-Native performances (though they do so quite wonderfully). They also remind us again that even in the face of coherent (or at least cohering) political divisions and dominating power relations, the possibilities for new and creative social relations are many—and that the possibilities for cultural exchange and innovation are perhaps even greater. An ethnohistorical treatment of Indian and intercultural performances—the venues, the props, the costumes, the practices—forces us from any temptation to allow a simplified political mapping to overlay the craziness of culture. Such a treatment points instead back to multiplicities, contingencies, commensurabilities, and creations. It forces us to conceptualize power relations through the fluidities, flows, and contradictions that become visible when we look at particular performances. Rather than beginning with the largest social divisions and populating their given categories, then, we are asked to begin with profusions of individuals and their actions—and then work our way back up the scale. Perhaps most important, the analytical strategies implicit and explicit in *Native Acts* ask us to focus squarely on Indian people, and to consider their longstanding role, not simply as curators of Native practice but also as critical generative forces, shaping and constantly questioning the creation of new cultures in North America.

Contributors

Joshua David Bellin is a professor of English at La Roche College. He has authored three books and numerous essays on cultural encounter and performance in American literature and film.

Olivia Bloechl is an associate professor in the Department of Musicology at UCLA. She is the author of *Native American Song at the Frontiers of Early Modern Music* (2008) and has published elsewhere on music in early colonialism and on French baroque music. Her current book project, *The Politics of Memory in French Baroque Opera*, is supported by an ACLS Charles A. Ryskamp Research Fellowship.

Matt Cohen is an associate professor in the Department of English at the University of Texas at Austin. He is the author of *The Networked Wilderness: Communicating in Early New England* (2009).

Philip J. Deloria is the Carroll Smith-Rosenberg collegiate professor of history and American Studies and the associate dean for Undergraduate Education in the College of Literature, Science, and the Arts at the University of Michigan. A former president of the American Studies Association, he is the author of *Playing Indian* (1998), *Indians in Unexpected Places* (2004), and numerous articles and other writings.

Stephanie Fitzgerald is an assistant professor of English and affiliated faculty member of Indigenous Studies at the University of Kansas. She is co-editor of *Keepers of the Morning Star: An*

Anthology of Native Women's Theater (2003) and the author of numerous articles on American Indian literature and culture.

Theresa Strouth Gaul is an associate professor of English at Texas Christian University. She is editor of *To Marry an Indian: The Marriage of Harriett Gold and Elias Boudinot in Letters, 1823–1839* (2005) and *Letters and Cultural Transformations in the United States, 1760–1860* (with Sharon M. Harris, 2009). She has published a number of articles on Indian-white contacts, early Native writers, and women writers, and she is co-editor of *Legacy: A Journal of American Women Writers.*

Nan Goodman is an associate professor in the English department of the University of Colorado at Boulder and a visiting professor of law and humanities at Georgetown University Law Center in spring 2011. She is the author of *Shifting the Blame: Literature, Law, and the Theory of Accidents in Nineteenth-Century America* (1998, rpt. 2000) and the book-length manuscript "Banish'd: The Law and Language of Social Exclusion in Seventeenth-Century New England." She is co-editor of *The Turnaround Religion in American Literature* (forthcoming), is editor of *Juris-dictions*, a special issue of *English Language Notes* (2010), and has written many articles on issues related to law and the humanities.

Laura L. Mielke is an associate professor and a Conger-Gabel teaching professor (2010–13) in the English department of the University of Kansas. She is the author of *Moving Encounters: Sympathy and the Indian Question in Antebellum Literature* (2008) and articles on U.S. and American Indian literature.

John H. Pollack is a public services specialist at the University of Pennsylvania's Rare Book and Manuscript Library. He is the editor of *"The Good Education of Youth": Worlds of Learning in the Age of Franklin* (2009) and is working on a study of the early history of the French in Canada.

Jenny Hale Pulsipher is an associate professor of history at Brigham Young University. She has published articles on Native American history in the *William and Mary Quarterly*, the *New England Quarterly*, and the *Massachusetts Historical Review* and is the author of *Subjects unto the Same King: Indians, English, and the Contest for Authority in Colonial New England* (2005).

Phillip H. Round is a professor of English and American Indian and Native Studies at the University of Iowa. He is the author of *By Nature and by Custom Cursed: Transatlantic Civil Discourse and New England Cultural Production, 1620–1660* (1999), *The Impossible Land: Story and Place in California's Imperial Valley* (2008), and *Removable Type: Histories of the Book in Indian Country, 1663–1880* (2010).

Timothy J. Shannon is a professor of history at Gettysburg College in Gettysburg, Pennsylvania. He is the author of *Iroquois Diplomacy on the Early American Frontier* (2008) and *Indians and Colonists at the Crossroads of Empire: The Albany Congress of 1754* (2000).

Caroline Wigginton is an ACLS New Faculty Fellow with a joint appointment in the Departments of American Studies and Women's and Gender Studies at Rutgers, the State University of New Jersey. She has published articles about early American literatures written by Native and women authors. She is also the co-editor of *Transatlantic Feminisms in the Age of Revolutions* (2011).

Index